Rites of marrying

Rites of marrying

The wedding industry in Scotland

Simon R. Charsley

Manchester University Press

Manchester and New York

Distributed exclusively in the USA and Canada by St. Martin's Press

Published by Manchester University Press
Oxford Road, Manchester M13 9PL, UK
and Room 400, 175 Fifth Avenue,
New York, NY 10010, USA

Distributed exclusively in the USA and Canada
by St. Martin's Press, Inc.,
175 Fifth Avenue, New York, NY 10010, USA

British Library cataloguing in publication data
    Charsley, S. R. (Simon Robert) *1939–*
Rites of marrying.
1. Scotland. Marriage, Social aspects
I. Title
306.8109411

Library of Congress cataloging in publication data applied for

ISBN 0 7190 2873 6 *hardback*

Phototypeset in Great Britain
by Northern Phototypesetting Co Ltd, Bolton

Printed in Great Britain
by Billings Limited, Worcester

Contents

		page
Preface		vii
Introduction: Anthropology at home		1
Ritual	5	
1 **Contexts of Scottish marrying**		7
The legal framework	7	
The Churches in Scotland	13	
Christian marriage and Scottish liturgy	19	
2 **Engagement**		27
Getting married	27	
The engagement: *rings, announcements*		
and parties, presents	29	
Being engaged	39	
3 **Learning the lore: planning and the wedding industry**		43
The reception: *dates and times, 'the hall',*		
food, drink, the cake, music	47	
The ceremony	56	
And all the rest	62	
Conclusion	65	
4 **Casting, dressing and participation**		66
The bride and her dress	66	
The bridal party	73	
The bridegroom and the males of the company	76	
The mother of the bride and the female company	78	
The guest list	80	
Seating for the meal	86	
The experience	88	

5   **Festivities before the Day**   90
    The presents   90
    The show of presents   96
    Taking out   101
    Stags and hens   108

6   **Wedding Day 1: the ceremony**   115
    Services in the Church of Scotland   115
    The Catholic Nuptial Mass   124
    Services for mixed marriages   132
    Music   133
    Innovation   135

7   **Wedding Day 2: framing the ceremony**   139
    The pattern   139
    Photography   142
    In, through and out   145
    Scrambles   147
    Interpretation   148

8   **Wedding Day 3: the reception**   154
    The line-up   155
    The cake and toasts   156
    The meal   157
    Speeches   159
    The dancing   166
    Singing   168
    Variation   170
    Favours and the bride's responsibilities   172
    Going away   173
    Afterwards   177

9   **Familiar rites and anthropological interpretation**   179
    Marrying in the social and cultural
    context of Glasgow: *kinship and families, social class,
    religion*   181
    Cross-cultural perspectives   189
    Symbols and interpretation   195

    Notes   200
    Appendix   212
    References   217
    Index   223

Preface

This book ought to have been the joint work of 'Margaret', 'James' and myself. Indeed there are still the broken remains of the book we wrote together inside this one. This is explained in the Appendix and its lines revealed in the Index. It is to their enthusiasm and to the many hours they put into it, now so incompletely rewarded, that the book owes its existence and much of its form. It is to them therefore that first thanks are due, and to their families also. Like the many others who allowed the researchers to come into their lives at a busy and important moment, they displayed all the friendly helpfulness for which the people of Glasgow are renowned. The many wedding professionals who also provided their assistance in the original research, regardless of the valuable time it certainly consumed, went far beyond the call of duty too. It is a pity only that they cannot be named in thanking them. The ministers and priests who, in two cases particularly, contributed their own words so extensively and so willingly to the work are even more deserving of better than the anonymity which other considerations dictate. The best I can do is to offer the book itself as a token of my thanks to all these and others who contributed to it. Since they displayed so much helpful interest in the research, I trust that they will find some of that interest still alive in the final text.

There are names, however, which require no disguise. Diane McGoldrick was my collaborator in the original research. Direct signs of her contributions appear at numerous points through the book; she contributed in many more basic ways too. Sadly, she was unable to continue her collaboration beyond the original period of fieldwork. She therefore bears no responsibility for what I have made here even of her own work. Mrs Grace Campbell provided invaluable secretarial assistance in days before we caught up with the word-processing revolution. She played a role in our research team which went well beyond fingers on a keyboard. To Professor Tony Cohen the publication of the book itself is owed, though in the event he also bears no responsibility for it. He was to have been its editor, and the book would certainly have benefited had he been able to perform this role. It was not to be, but he did nevertheless provide encouragement and advice which were of great value in getting the version offered here completed.

In addition I have the ESRC to thank for their financial support for the original fieldwork, and my department and university for their support in the succeeding years. Colleagues in my own and in several other departments have provided help and encouragement on numerous occasions and I am pleased to be able to record my thanks to them too. The editorial staff of Manchester University Press are to be thanked for giving me remarkably free rein and for putting the book through the press with friendly efficiency.

The ways in which my wife and children have supported the enterprise are too numerous and various to be disentangled. They have certainly been crucial. It is my great pleasure to be able to use on the cover a photograph by the daughter who has grown up as this project has been creeping slowly towards fulfilment. Whether she will ever give me the chance to hold my own Scottish wedding remains to be seen.

Simon Charsley
Glasgow, October 1990

Introduction: Anthropology at home

'Nothing is so ill recorded as what everyone knows and takes for granted; it is the fundamental customs which are the most difficult to trace.'
(Christopher Brooke, *The Medieval Idea of Marriage*, 1989: 251.)

Historians have with ever more laborious enthusiasm been constructing accounts of favoured regions of the past. Anthropologists have been doing the same for an ever-widening range of exotic settings in the present. In the meantime the present, which is the base from which these same anthropologists and historians most often work, seems to slip away. There have been oddly few serious studies of the way life is conducted in contemporary metropolitan settings.

The feeling that there is nothing not already known is partly responsible. Could it be that, with video added to film added to print, and survey upon survey, everything about the present of western societies is already documented to excess?

Such a sense is in part well justified, yet much which is most basic to the conduct of ordinary lives escapes altogether or is registered only in indirect ways which future historians will eventually find themselves deciphering. It escapes because it is taken for granted. It is the common background which those who act and those who record share. It is the set of assumptions and values which define for most people what is worth recording at all.

But this common background is the equivalent at home of the cultural patterns which have always been the basic concern of anthropologists abroad. In the setting of someone else's life such patterns are, in their unexpectedness, often perceived relatively easily; at home they form merely the backdrop against which the newsworthy is picked out. Such values and assumptions may be almost invisible to those whose daily lives they inform, and the practices which make up that life are often too familiar to provoke interest. The object of this book is to draw into the scope of comparative discussion an area of life important for understanding the nature of contemporary British culture. When serious attention is given to it, much which is far from obvious and has great intrinsic interest is revealed. It also has, as will appear, a special comparative and theoretical importance for cultural studies generally.

This, then, is anthropology performed 'at home'. 'Home' in this case was Glasgow, a city of three-quarters of a million inhabitants which overflows its official boundaries and merges into a heavily populated and mainly urban area around the River Clyde in the West of Scotland. Rapid industrial and commercial expansion in the nineteenth century left it, in the twentieth, with a vast stock of declining industries and outdated and deteriorating housing. Efforts to deal with the resulting human problems in the period after the Second World War had at best mixed success. Glasgow has, however, always been a city with several strings to its bow. It is the commercial as well as the industrial capital of Scotland, and it has strong traditions in the arts, both fine and performing, and in education. The latter tradition reaches back as far as the medieval period when its university was founded. In the early 1980s, at the time of this study, the city was moving strongly to capitalise on this broader tradition. It was casting off a long-standing reputation for poverty, slums and violence in favour of an altogether new image as a lively and advancing centre of enterprise, with a special emphasis on the cultural and artistic spheres. It was becoming a place to visit and to enjoy. Its successful slogan of the period, 'Glasgow's Miles Better', caught the mood and, with a substantial advertising budget behind it and a succession of attention-catching events, contributed to creating its own truth (Charsley 1986).

In this lively but variegated context an attempt was made to record from the inside one of the most spectacular and commercially important manifestations of popular culture, 'the wedding industry'.[1] Marriage is therefore at the centre of this study, but the focus here is not on that popular topic of the period, the ills of contemporary marriages, but on the nature of marrying. In particular it is on the part played by ritual in the making of marriages.[2]

On the daily realities and problems of marital relationships the study therefore throws no more than an oblique light – on the contemporary family it is more direct – but something more basic, the culturally developed conception of marriage, has to be a main starting point. If an understanding is to be gained of rites of marrying anywhere in the world, this has to be done in relation to the particular local conception of marriage. Such conceptions are very various. The fact that, as a term in English, 'marriage' can be applied fairly readily to some set of ideas and practices in most societies does not mean that there is any uniformity between such sets, that there is a single thing which corresponds everywhere to the English term. In a social sense the kind of marriage with which we shall be dealing here is simpler than anything to which it may partly correspond in most other parts of the world. It is simpler in being relatively free from the functional demands of enduring social groups like lineages, houses or extended families; where these exist it creates essential links between them and provides the new members required to keep them alive. But if it lacks much of the significance to be found elsewhere, it carries with it something equally striking, a complex and unusual charge of concepts and values deriving from its importance in the religious and legal thinking of literate Christian Europe.

This conceptual context will be examined briefly in Chapter 1. Both its legal and its religious and liturgical manifestations, as these form part of the contemporary local context, will be outlined. Other more directly practical contexts are considered there too, as they arise from demography, the law and the churches. The central seven chapters of the book then take the reader through from the engagement or the decision to marry, through the detailed planning, learning and organising which this normally turns out to entail, to the beginnings of celebration and their culmination on the wedding day itself. In these chapters, as in all anthropology, ethnography blends with the discussion of issues, each informing and giving value to the other. The final chapter discusses patterns found, reflects further on the comparative perspective in the light of this study, and sums up its implications for the study and interpretation of ritual more widely.

The central chapters give scope for the participation of many of the people who took part in the study and on whose assistance its progress depended. These participants are of two kinds, each necessarily treated slightly differently.

Foremost here are the lay participants. These are people interested in marriage procedures and happy to talk about them, either because they were currently involved in the process of getting themselves or someone close to them married, or sometimes simply because they expected to be so involved in the future or had been in the past. Such a category potentially includes almost the whole population. Its leading representatives in this study are Margaret and James Maclaren, a couple whose own process of marrying was closely followed and who were themselves lively commentators on an unusually wide range of events and topics. They and their families appear repeatedly in these chapters and it is often their discussion of issues which provides the starting point for further discussion offered. Others are quoted less frequently, but the principle of selection is the same throughout: within the constraints of space it is those who have particularly enlightening comments to make who are quoted. The conversations from which quotations are taken were the basis of the original study.[3] It is they which put the reader most directly in touch with the reality which is being presented and examined here. All such research has to be a collaboration between those who seek to learn and those who are willing – and here frequently keen – to teach. The ones who are helped to learn have the additional responsibility of analysing and presenting. The book attempts by its form to provide a true representation of the relationships and roles involved in its production. Quoted conversations are therefore in no sense merely decoration or secondary to parts of the book expressed in the author's words: both are crucial to the whole.[4]

The second set of participants are experts on particular aspects of marrying and the wedding industry by virtue of their professional or commercial involvement. Enthusiasm and a willingness to teach were strongly marked here too. Often these people were tied in with the lay participants as fellow-contributors to particular weddings and they are quoted on the same principles of relevance. They are, however, given names only where they feature unavoidably in the others' conversations and performances. Preserving a degree of anonymity for them is more difficult and they are not further referenced.

With this necessary exception, the emphasis throughout is on recording the way things were rather than some version of how the author or anyone else would have liked them to be. The book is neither a cultural travelogue nor a manual of wedding etiquette, though it is intended to communicate the interest, excitement and sheer fun which those taking part in the events extract from them. A key implication of the need to take seriously a serious topic – though far from a humourless one – is the need to report accurately the speech as much as any of the other kinds of action of those involved. This means refraining from tidying it up. The forms of verbal punctuation which people adopt, their attention to and departures from orthodox grammar, the variable degrees of coherence and incoherence as they talk, these are features recorded here, not only as a significant part of the social reality, but in order to catch the subtler distinctions in the ways matters are presented.

Few things are so misleading as to assume, even if only perhaps merely for the sake of simplicity in presentation, that everything that people say is of the same kind, has the same value and the same intention. The difference between statements of well-known 'fact' and matters on which ideas have to be searched out in the course of attempting to talk about them is particularly important. The kinds of discussion on which this or other social scientific research is based are rarely simple reports of established and neutral opinion. To suggest otherwise is to misrepresent the flexibility and the marginal uncertainties which are implicit in most customary practice and are an essential basis for cultural creativity. Even when it is only with a researcher and even if only marginally, discussion is indeed a prime process by which people's views are determined. Through it people evaluate their own and others' experience and such evaluations form part of their own basis for subsequent action. It is a dynamic view of culture as something formed and reformed as it is expressed that the mode of presentation here hopes to catch.

Ritual

The 'rites of marrying' of the title are no predefined and technical category but an ample net for fishing in a cultural sea which is in some ways unfamiliar, to anthropology at least. It is intended to catch all the practices and procedures connected with getting married, apart from those arrangements which leap over the event itself directly to married life. As such, housing, though it looms large in the pre-wedding period, is not considered here. What is found in the net, even with such a limitation, is a variety of specimens which may or may not be termed 'rites' in any more technical meaning of that term. There are practices which are religious services and parts of them. In the liturgies of the Catholic Church these may be explicitly called 'rites', but the Reformed tradition shies away from the term. Contrasting with these are the profusion of popular practices of the wedding day and before. Some of these are often recognised as rites, 'rites of passage' in the term if not quite the theory invented in the early part of the century by Arnold van Gennep (1909), the great pioneer of French folklore studies.

The basic task here is twofold. It is first to reduce the conceptual isolation in which activities labelled 'religious' often languish as though they were, whatever their importance or lack of it in individual eyes, in any case quite separate. The other side of the task is then to take seriously the mass of other events. Here the problem is not one for the society at large. For the bulk of ordinary people the excitements of marrying may, as has already been commented upon, often be fun but are certainly not frivolous. A vast expenditure on wedding presents and on the wedding itself, increasing from year to year through the 1980s, bear clear witness to this. But to the intelligentsia who make studies and write books and who were at the period often deciding against marriage for themselves, such matters might be silly, even embarrassing if one were, against one's better judgement, forced by circumstances to become involved in them. In the extensive contemporary literature on marriage and its problems, the wedding day itself is at best seriously underplayed. It and the extent of the social effort which surrounds such events are often indeed conspicuous only in their absence. The effect has been to misrepresent marriage – common in the media almost to the extent of a campaign against it – as something of far more exclusively individual relevance than a study of current practice reveals.

Breaking through the preconceptions and prejudices which often distort our own view of the ritual dimension of our own lives has, therefore, to be the most basic achievement here. It is in any case necessary if the practices of this society are to be brought within the comparative frame of reference discussed above.

Beyond this, the central and abiding interest here is in the nature and significance of interpretation. Human action may be meaningful in a variety of ways both to those who perform it and to those who register what has been done. It may be understood as directed to some end beyond itself, fulfilling some externally imposed requirement, conveying a message or expressing a sentiment of some kind. A person's action may, on the other hand, be seen as meaningful by others who feel they can draw inferences from it over and above any intention to convey information in performing it. There are however kinds of action, and we shall come across many in this book, which puzzle on reflection even though normally they are practised unreflectingly. They seem sometimes to be the most meaningful of all; they may indeed be defined by some as a distinct category labelled 'ritual' on the basis of their alleged 'expressive' or message-bearing nature. Yet observation shows that they are unlike ordinary action in that those most closely involved are often convinced that they do not know what meaning their actions have. They are performed with no more intention than to do what is appropriate. The major and continuing task is to explore this situation, not in the abstract as a kind of philosophical pursuit – if one embarks on the task of getting straight an epistemological framework for enquiry one risks never getting through the thickets of philosophical scholarship to the practical task of telling people about people[5] – but in the context of people acting and conceptualising and explaining their own actions and those of others.

The basic purpose of this book is to record and to make the record available, but beyond this it carries therefore a message of more theoretical relevance as to the nature of such cultural phenomena as rites of marrying. It is the meaningfulness of such rites that is inherently problematic. Interpreting them is a common though by no means inevitable human activity, significant more for the part it plays in cultural creativity than for any explanation it can offer.

Chapter 1

Contexts of Scottish marrying

Looking back on the early 1980s with the benefit of figures not yet published at the time, it is clear that marriages were decreasing in Scotland: the number celebrated fell from 38,501 in 1980 to 34,942 in 1982. Four out of five were first marriages, but decline in these was not apparent at the time. Marriage seemed locally buoyant, in the face of economic difficulties being experienced at the period and a flood of assertion from the mass media, based largely in the South of England, that living together unmarried was replacing more traditional arrangements.

What was happening was that the average age of marrying, after remaining steady throughout the 1970s, was rising fast. For women it rose from 22·0 years in 1980 to 22·4 in 1982, for men from 23·8 to 24·2. This proved to be a new trend which would run throughout the 1980s; average ages would be back to levels last seen in the 1950s by the end of the decade. It was teenage marriages, a popular scapegoat for marital instability, which were declining most dramatically. From a peak of popularity in the early 1970s when there were 33 per thousand men and 90 per thousand women married before their twentieth birthdays, by the late 1980s it was down to 6 and 20 per thousand respectively.[1] However, after the decline of the early 1980s, the total of marriages at all ages stabilised at around 36,000 a year. The decline had been due therefore partly to delays in marrying in the economic difficulties of the period (Kendrick 1981, p. 38), rather than to the abandonment of marriage as such. Certainly, however, and perhaps paradoxically, sufficient marriages continued for the wedding industry, already flourishing at the time of the research, to expand strikingly in subsequent years.

The legal framework

The basic fact to understand about the law of marriage in Scotland is that it has been progressively simplified and many of its former implications for the rights of the married stripped away. In the early 1980s, two major pieces of

recent legislation determined law and practice. These were the Divorce
(Scotland) Act of 1976 and the Marriage (Scotland) Act of 1977. Legislation
reaching back to the Marriage Act of 1567 was repealed, important changes
were made, and the intention was to provide a thorough and comprehensive
framework for the future (Clive 1982).[2] To these was to be added during the
1980s the Law Reform (Husband and Wife) (Scotland) Act of 1984. Though
brief, this was yet another significant contribution to the ending of long-
standing legal implications of marriage.

Reform has been powered, through a long series of Acts of Parliament since
the mid nineteenth century, chiefly by a fundamental change in values.
Throughout that century members of the higher social classes commonly
made marriage contracts to protect wives against the consequences of
medieval property law, of Roman origin, which was still then in force. This
distinguished for married women three kinds of property. There was her own
personal paraphernalia, her clothes and jewellery and the like. This was hers
absolutely, to dispose of as she wished. There were then immoveables, land
and buildings, which a wife might own but which she would have no right to
run. Unless it was specifically excluded, her husband took over whatever
rights she might otherwise have had in this respect. Third was all the
remainder, moveable estate, including produce and profits from the lands and
buildings, and all household goods and supplies. All these belonged to the
husband. There were doctrines about community of ownership in the
moveable estate between husband and wife, and these issued in the entitle-
ment of widows to a share of it on their husband's death. They would receive
– and changed assumptions may make this seem at first sight a perverse
scheme though it retains a place in the law even today – a third if there were
children to inherit too, a half if there were none. They might also receive the
same if the marriage were ended in some other way, as long as it was not their
own adultery which brought it about. The property law was symptomatic of
the legal relationship of husband and wife more generally, with the wife
under her husband's authority and almost entirely eclipsed as an independent
adult person by him. This was the legal position; we should keep in mind the
distinction between law and the varying practical realities of relationships
between individual personalities in differing circumstances.

The value change which began to make this legal position appear
unreasonable was centuries in the making. It began to issue in legislation for
Scotland in the Conjugal Rights (Scotland) Act of 1861. Starting with the
feeling that women were unfairly disadvantaged by marriage, legal
disabilities of wives as compared with husbands have been gradually
removed. The right of the husband to decide where the 'matrimonial home'
should be was eliminated only in 1984. This process has had the effect of
reducing the legal significance of marriage in one respect after another until
now little remains. As this has occurred it has become increasingly possible to

imagine marriage as a relationship between two equal people, equivalent to one another in every respect except the sexual characteristics of their bodies. Concern to ameliorate the lot of wives has therefore provided the basis for a shift in the understanding of the nature of marriage. It has become possible to understand equality between the partners as the fundamental value. As will be seen below, even this is far from new; it is grounded in a main strand of Christian thinking about marriage which has always been in tension with husbands' official dominance, and usually their practical dominance too, in the secular world.

However, at the same time as this equality has been increasingly espoused by the law-making classes, with its implications of independence for wives and the declining legal significance of marriage, welfare concerns were generating a whole range of new types of legal significance for marriage. The long-standing concern of communities and subsequently the state that a man should be responsible wherever possible for the material support of his wife and children blossomed under twentieth-century welfare thinking into a new range of benefits legislation largely framed, until recently, in terms of marriage and of families based upon it.

In the most recent period there came therefore to be a measure of conflict between two progressive values, between the value of improving conditions for women as wives and the value of pursuing equality in the relationship of marriage. The dilemma tended to be resolved by dropping the increasingly enfeebled institution of marriage. Equality would be judged in relation to people's practical circumstances, in particular whether they had dependent children to look after, and if so whether on their own or with the assistance of the other parent. Whether or not people were married had come, that is to say, to be regardable as some kind of incidental, no longer the basic determinant of their nature as people and of the rights and duties applicable to them which once it had been. It could even be excluded from an account of their 'practical circumstances'. A kind of marriage had now been created which retained so little legal significance that the utility of recognising marriage at all could begin to be questioned. Why, asks Clive (1980), Professor of Law at Edinburgh University and author of the standard text on *The Law of Husband and Wife in Scotland*, should marriage be of more concern to the law than friendship or entering a religious order?

The state does, however, still determine[3] directly who may enter into a relationship which will be officially recognised as marriage, how this is to be done, and under what conditions and by what means people may escape from the marriages they have entered into. In Scotland two people can marry one another as long as they are of opposite sex, neither is currently married to anyone else, both are sixteen years of age or over, and they are mentally capable of understanding what they are agreeing to. Whether and what they actually do understand is perhaps a different matter. In addition, they must not be already related to one another in a number of specified ways: neither must be parent or grandparent or great grandparent to the other, nor brother or sister, aunt or uncle, nor an adopted parent, nor a former spouse's parent, grandparent, child or grandchild. It makes no difference whether relationships are legitimate or not, and relationships through one parent count as if through both. This list represents no single theory as to what such prohibitions are for; it is rather the result of a gradual whittling down in successive legislation of the prohibited degrees which the medieval Church developed on the Biblical basis of a passage in the eighteenth chapter of Leviticus (Scottish Law Commission 1980). The age for marriage was set at sixteen in 1929, being then raised from the twelve for girls and fourteen for boys which dated back to the first regulation of such matters by the medieval Church. Until recent centuries parental permission was usually expected to be obtained, but it was never required for a valid marriage and has never been incorporated into secular marriage legislation in Scotland, even for minors (Kilbrandon Committee 1969, pp. 11-12).

There are preliminaries required before a marriage can be made, and there are required procedures for its actual making. Both are legacies left to the state by the medieval Church. A system of advertising intended marriages was instituted by the Church in the thirteenth century. Banns of marriage, so called from the beginning, were to be proclaimed in the parish church at the time of Sunday worship for three successive weeks. The intention was to ensure that marriages from which the couple in question were known to be disqualified would not be celebrated. The system did not always work as designed but it remained in place in Scotland, latterly co-opted by the state, for over six hundred years. From 1878, giving notice to a registrar and obtaining a licence to marry from him became an alternative to banns, though it took time for the Church of Scotland to accept it and for banns therefore in practice to die out. From 1977 notices have been compulsory for all marriages and banns have finally disappeared.

Those wishing to marry must therefore apply to the office of the District Registrar, normally of the district in which they plan to be married, at least fifteen days in advance. They need to submit birth certificates and a fee, and if either has been married before, documentation for the ending of that marriage. The registrar will record their details and display somewhere around the office their names and the date on which they are intending to marry. If anyone should see this and think that they know some reason why the marriage should not occur – that one of the parties is still already married perhaps – they have the right then to inspect the full record and, if appropriate, to make their objection known. This is, however, peculiarly unlikely to happen. Notice of intended marriage can be given wherever the parties wish, and this may, if this is what they want, be far both from homes and from anyone likely to know them.

No objection having been made, there is further action to be taken, depending on whether the couple want a civil or religious marriage. If civil they will need to make the booking and other arrangements with the registrar, if religious to collect the essential document, the marriage schedule, from the registrar once the fourteen-day waiting period has elapsed. This document is, in the first place, a licence from the registrar to the chosen celebrant to conduct the marriage. It is indeed a criminal offence to conduct one without the appropriate schedule, a surprising sanction to be imposed on such worthy folk as ministers and priests but required by the fact that a marriage conducted without a schedule would be entirely anomalous. It would produce a modern form of an ancient problem by being at once illegal but potentially valid.

Regular marriages in Scotland can, therefore, take two forms, termed 'civil' and 'religious'. Only a registrar or assistant registrar expressly appointed to 'solemnise' marriages, who must be over the age of twenty-one, can conduct a civil marriage. Such marriages were introduced into Scotland only by the Marriage (Scotland) Act of 1939, various expedients having been adopted previously to achieve a somewhat similar effect. Civil marriages can normally be performed only within registrars' offices. In the 1980s they accounted for about 40 per cent of all marriages, a proportion slowly rising though absolute numbers were fairly steady.

There is no set form of marriage required of registrars, though the committee set up in 1967 under Lord Kilbrandon to look into Scottish marriage law, whose work led eventually to the Marriage (Scotland) Act 1977, recommended that one should be prepared (Kilbrandon Committee 1969, p. 39). Registrars may choose their own words and procedure, but two witnesses, a declaration from the couple that neither of them know of any reason why they cannot be married, and a clear expression of consent to marry one another are all required. They will pronounce the couple married and have the marriage schedule signed. This permits their primary task, the registration of the marriage, to be performed.

Civil ceremonies therefore vary but within narrow limits; the religious have wider scope. The schedule permits a named person to solemnise the marriage before two witnesses on a given date and at a given place. This is not necessarily within the registration district even. Two alternative principles are adopted to ensure sufficient regulation. One is the recognition of well-known religious bodies, with the Church of Scotland and its ministers in first place, as fit to attend to the choice of celebrants and forms of marriage for themselves. They are not told by the state how to do either, and no further requirements are imposed on them. The other principle is that would-be celebrants belonging to other religious organisations can apply to the Registrar General for Scotland for personal recognition. This may be on a regular basis, for periods of three years at a time, or it may be on some more limited and temporary basis, even for the conduct of a single marriage. Such recognitions may be granted on whatever terms the Registrar General sees fit but with the additional general requirement that the form of marriage must include a declaration of consent by both the parties and, following on it, a pronouncement by the celebrant that the parties are therefore married.[4] In both cases the schedule must be subsequently completed and signed by the couple and their witnesses and returned to the registrar. Though the English custom of the wife taking her husband's surname crept into Scotland in the early nineteenth century, there has never been any legal requirement for this; indeed, maiden names are never in legal eyes lost in Scotland even today.

It is regular marriage which has so far been considered. There is also a way in which people may become married in Scotland without going through any such procedure. This is the one form of irregular marriage which was not abolished by the Marriage (Scotland) Act 1939, marriage 'by cohabitation with habit and repute'. It is of little practical relevance to the vast majority but has always been regarded both as inoffensive and sufficiently useful on occasion to deserve preservation (Kilbrandon Committee 1969, pp. 42-4). If a couple in Scotland live together in all respects as if they were married and are generally understood by others to be so, and if they are legally eligible to marry one another, then they may on petition to the Court of Session be declared to have been so married from some appropriate date in the past. Those who live together but make a point of announcing themselves unmarried are not therefore in any danger of finding themselves actually married by default. The arrangement is sometimes useful in that it allows doubts which may arise as to the existence or propriety of a marriage ceremony in the past to be overridden. The most usual case is where a couple have begun to live as man and wife when they were not free to marry one another and failed to take any action when they subsequently became so. There are, however, rarely more than one or two cases in a year.

To summarise: contemporary Scottish marriage requires no parental consent and may take place anywhere in the country, regardless of where the parties live.[5] It must be either religious or civil. The former allows great freedom of choice, not only of celebrant and in effect of form of service, but also, since there is no legal specification of appropriate times or places, of where and when the marriage may be held. If a religious service is to be avoided, there is less choice. Marriage will normally have to be before a registrar in his or her office. There is a considerable choice and variety of these though. It is still perfectly possible for anyone to be married at Gretna Green on a day trip if they make the necessary arrangements with the registrar there in advance; it would even be possible to be married in the Old Smithy if a willing authorised celebrant could be found.

The relationship so established has, however, in legal terms become considerably enfeebled. What the state continues to regulate is therefore an ancient but increasingly content-less notion that by marriage a fundamental, if now mysterious, change is brought about in and between the parties, a change which is irreversible; yet in contemporary circumstances, an acute awareness of divorce is inescapable. It may be wondered, at least as a hypothesis to be considered, whether the elaboration in the twentieth century of the rites to be discussed in this book may not be linked to the increasingly immaterial nature of any difference made by the act of marrying.

The Churches in Scotland

The two main strands in Scottish Christianity are represented in this study by the Church of Scotland and the Scottish Catholic Church. The common Church of western Europe focused on Rome was replaced in the second half of the sixteenth century by a reformed national Church taking its inspiration mainly from the Genevan Church of Calvin. The new Church was led by John Knox, a Scottish minister who had been a leader of the Reformation in England and subsequently an exile on the Continent when Queen Mary Tudor returned her country to allegiance to Rome. It was characterised by a rejection of priesthood as any kind of special religious status – Calvinist churches have ministers, not priests – and by a system of church government shared between lay elders and ministers. There are four levels of church courts, from kirk sessions at the parish level, in which elders are chaired by the minister, to Presbyteries, Synods and the general Assembly of the Church at the higher levels. In all of them elders and ministers sit together. The Church of Scotland was subject to dispute and fission from the seventeenth century onward, and spectacularly in the Disruption of 1843. A small family of Calvinist Churches resulted. These continued to be subject to some further fission but they also undertook major recombinations. By the early 1980s, besides the Church of Scotland, only four separate and fairly small Churches persisted, the Free Church, the Reformed Presbyterian Church, the Free Presbyterian Church and the United Free Church.

Meanwhile the Catholic Church in Scotland survived intermittent persecution either though the protection of local magnates or by sheer remoteness, particularly in the North-East. In parts of the Gaelic-speaking West it was also re-established and nurtured by Irish missions (Macdonald 1979, pp. 56–7). A more widespread and ultimately much larger Catholic population began to be established by immigration into the western lowlands in the eighteenth century, and from the 1790s onwards it was increasingly possible for the Church, cautiously and with setbacks from time to time, to make its presence visible in the country at large. A handsome church seating over 2,000 was built in a conspicuous position on the Clyde waterfront in Glasgow and opened in 1816. Two years later it was being used, successfully if not without controversy, for concerts to raise money from the non-Catholic bourgeoisie for the support of Catholic funds. The Emancipation Act of 1829 set the seal of official approval on the re-emergence of Catholicism.

The famine years in the 1840s in Ireland changed the nature of emigration from that country to a refugee flood. Those with the means tended to cross the Atlantic, those without to go only as far as Scotland. The bulk of the new immigrants were at least potentially active Catholics and they settled mostly in the industrially burgeoning area around the Clyde. An identification in the eyes of established Scots between poverty, Irishness and Catholicism was combined with a strong streak of Irish nationalism amongst the immigrants themselves, and particularly their priests, to produce an explosive situation. It did not fail on numerous occasions up to the 1880s to ignite into popular violence and riot. Within the Church tensions between Scots and Irish clergy culminated in clamour and discord which had a focus in a Glasgow newspaper, *The Free Press*, and the appointment of an Irish Bishop, James Lynch, in the 1860s. This, however, led ultimately to the restoration of a Scottish hierarchy in 1878. A normal ecclesiastical organisation of territorial bishoprics, which had in effect been destroyed at the Reformation, was set up. Most of the country from the Northern Isles to the Borders was covered by the province of St Andrews and Edinburgh, headed by an archbishop and four bishops, but the immigrant areas in the western central lowlands were held separate as the Archdiocese of Glasgow, subject directly to Rome. Only in 1947 was the distinction moderated, with the elevation of Glasgow into a normal province of three diocese. With the notable exception of the first Archbishop of Glasgow, an Englishman who had overseen the re-establishment of order in the West and the restoration of the hierarchy itself, bishops and archbishops of the Church in Scotland have subsequently always been overwhelmingly Scots-born. Despite the ancestry of so many of its members, the Church has identified itself as Scottish with ever-increasing unanimity (Handley 1964; Aspinwall 1982; Walker 1972; McRoberts 1979).

The Anglican Communion, which can perhaps be seen as straddling the Catholic–Reformed divide, is represented in Scotland mainly by the Scottish Episcopal Church. This is another survivor, with roots both in the immediate post-Reformation period and in two periods in the seventeenth century when Stuart kings of Scotland and England replaced the presbyterian government of the Church of Scotland by an episcopal one. Although its Scottish distinctiveness has been asserted over the centuries, the Episcopal Church has repeatedly been open to influences emanating from the Church of England (Herring 1973). It has often been keen to emphasise its 'catholic' stance: its bishops refused to join the Reformed Churches in celebrating the four-hundredth anniversary in 1960 of Scotland's Reformation (Highet 1960, p. 32).

Though one or two other Churches emphasise their indigenous origins, most are in-comers, mainly from England and more recently. None are particularly prominent, but Baptists, Christian Brethren, Congregationalists, Methodists, the Salvation Army, the Society of Friends, Unitarians and others are represented. Scotland has rarely proved favourable to the growth of new religious movements (Highet 1960, pp. 17–53).[6]

Of these Churches the one with the largest following almost everywhere except the Western Isles is the Church of Scotland. In the mid-1980s it had 1,745 congregations, some 1,400 ministers, and was organised into 46 Presbyteries and 12 Synods. It is the official Church in Scotland, to which the sovereign belongs, and its General Assembly meeting annually in Edinburgh is the nearest thing the country currently has to a parliament. Its debates receive considerable media attention. Though its membership has been declining, in 1982 it could still number 918,991 communicant members on its rolls, almost a quarter of the adult population. Besides these, many with no currently active religious affiliation would consider themselves in some residual sense, as when asked for their religion in hospital or when considering where to be married, Church of Scotland. In many areas over half of all marriages, and a much larger proportion of first marriages, were in the 1980s still being conducted by its ministers. Using this indicator,[7] it is apparent that the Church of Scotland was particularly strong in the North-East, with over 60 per cent of marriages in Grampian Region excluding Aberdeen City, and over 50 per cent even within the city itself. Otherwise it claimed high proportions in such mainly rural areas as Argyll and Bute in the West, the Borders in the south, Tayside outwith the city of Dundee in the East, and Orkney in the far North. In the major cities and conurbations apart from Aberdeen the proportion of marriages provided by the Church was smaller – with Glasgow going as low as 28 per cent – but numerous congregations of considerable size were nevertheless to be found in such areas.

The Church of Scotland can also be regarded as a national Church in drawing its members from across the range of social classes. The evidence from the few studies which are available suggests a pattern for the 1960s. The legacies of secessions and reunitings had produced, in towns at least, a complex pattern of churches without any clear territorial separation. Secessions produced new congregations which built their own churches, often close to the church which members had left. Over the years, each developed its own character and traditions. When new members were then recruited it would necessarily be in terms of such established differences. Each congregation would nevertheless continue to draw from the same general area and, when members moved yet maintained their membership, as happened not infrequently in cities, the boundaries of its catchment area would be still further extended. A reuniting of churches, such as took place most spectacularly in 1929, would then bring back into the same Church these

varied congregations and their buildings. As has been frequently acknowledged, it became for this and for other reasons impossible to specify what
was typically Church-of-Scotland, either in style of worship or in type or
social identity of congregations. Within a single area there would often be
found a great variety of Churches of Scotland amongst which any newcomer
might choose (Sissons 1973, pp. 26–30; Panton 1973).

Since the 1960s a number of factors are likely to have modified this
situation. The movement of population out of inner-city areas and a general
decline in church membership from a high point in 1956 have meant that, in
larger places, new churches have been established for populations in peripheral housing schemes and old ones have been extensively amalgamated and
closed and a clearer pattern of parishes established. It is probable therefore
that patterns of affiliation have been simplified somewhat and that the
location of a church has become, in many cases, a better indicator of the
character of its congregation. Nevertheless the social range encompassed
within the Church of Scotland is still a marked characteristic.

The only other Church with any claim to be considered in the same league
is the Scottish Catholic Church, also declining but still with 1,127 priests in
1982. It estimated Catholics in the country as a whole in the same year at
824,400, 16 per cent of the total population (Catholic Directory for Scotland
1988; cf. Derragh 1979, p. 225). This is a much smaller proportion than the
Church of Scotland figure cited above, since the latter excludes children and
the religiously inactive.[8] The distribution of Catholics was also far less even.
With the major concentration in and around Glasgow, there were districts,
Clydebank to the West and Monklands to the East of the city, in which
Catholic churches hosted more marriages than Church of Scotland, up to one
third of the total. In addition there were well-known Catholic islands in the
Highland and Islands of the West, such as Barra, but the size of these
populations was, as suggested by numbers of marriages, tiny; in 1982,
whereas Glasgow city reported 1,397 Catholic marriages, the entire North,
including the West and Aberdeen city, recorded only 185. On the whole,
where the Church of Scotland was particularly strong, the Catholic Church
was very weak.

Although there are undoubted differences in character between Catholic
parishes, there are many fewer sources of variation than in the Church of
Scotland. It was, since the re-emergence of the Church, always possible to
develop and maintain a straightforward system of parishes,[9] amongst which
those established for public-authority housing schemes became in the post-
war period prominent. Though upward mobility in the post-war period has
been conspicuous, the predominantly working-class identity of Catholics up
to the first half of the twentieth century, particularly in the West of the
country, means that the Church still has a large working-class base. If it was
still in the 1980s relatively weakly represented in the higher professional

classes, amongst the new middle classes this was certainly no longer so (Gallagher 1987, pp. 244 foll., 305 foll.).

After the two major Churches, themselves unequal, only the Scottish Episcopal Church accounted for more than 1 per cent of marriages. It was relatively well endowed with clergy but had less than one-twentieth of the communicants of the Church of Scotland. All other religious organisations were much smaller. Though numerous, together they accounted only for about 5 per cent of all marriages. The religious scene in Scotland is therefore dominated by the two contrasting Churches. It is on them that the present work concentrates.

Antagonisms between them in the past were formative. It was in reaction to the medieval Catholic Church that Reformed Churches such as the Church of Scotland came into being, and it was in reaction to the challenge of such developments around Europe in the sixteenth century that the Catholic assumed the form and tone it maintained from then until the twentieth century. In Scotland 'papist idolatry' was taken only too often as characterising a supposedly threatening enemy against whom the possessors of Reformed virtue and truth should close ranks. The Pope could readily personify foreign priestly autocracy against a true and Scottish order ruled by the virtuous amongst the people. 'Idolatry' similarly would stand for everything in worship that might be currently rejected in favour of a simple hearing of God's word. Allegiance to such 'foreign' causes could readily be seen as denying local and patriotic loyalties. Persecution as a hated minority, sometimes officially but more often by the mob, was at least informed by and perhaps partly the result of such views.

From the other side, Catholics have rarely in Scotland been in a position to mount comparable hostilities, but at a Church-wide and theological level the antagonism to Reform was acute. The Catholic was the one true Church, maintaining the one true faith and led from Rome. Its firmness of boundary, in the West, and its dogmatic character were certainly reinforced over the centuries by hostilities and rivalries across Europe. There was no question of recognising that the Church had fragmented and perhaps needed to be mended. Once the extirpation of heresy had become impractical as a policy, the best that could be hoped for was a return of the separated and deluded brethren to the true faith. In Scotland the handful of Catholics could continue to pray for the reconversion of their country.

This difficult legacy still cast shadows in popular consciousness even in the 1980s (Gallagher 1987). The 1918 Education (Scotland) Act provided for the absorption of Catholic schools into the system of state education, with financial support on the same basis as other schools in return for adherence to standard curricula. Since that time there have therefore been, in parts of the country with sizeable Catholic minorities, two kinds of state school, the Catholic and the non-denominational, the latter sometimes termed in opposition 'Protestant'. The former have been named for saints, the latter generally for their locality. Separation between Catholic and 'Protestant' has therefore for most people been reinforced by, or even grounded in, their school years. One consequence has been that knowledge of the name of the school attended has generally been sufficient to place anybody on one side or the other of the divide. Football, particularly the 'Old Firm' opposition of Rangers and Celtic in Glasgow, carries the opposition forward from school days and constantly brings the ancient division to general attention. What is surprising therefore is that its implications have not been more serious. Residential segregation, however, was never strongly marked in the city itself, and population movement in the post-war period greatly weakened even the identification of particular areas with one side or the other. In the employment field, rumours of discrimination are heard but in general people interact at work without reference to the distinction. Even in Catholic schools there are a substantial minority of non-Catholic teachers. In leisure activities similarly, segregated organisations such as the avowedly Protestant Orange Lodges with their colourful marches are a minority interest.

The proportion of 'mixed marriages', which in Scotland means marriages between Catholics and others, is an indicator of interaction, whilst their existence is an accumulating cause of it. Figures were collected by Derragh (1979, p. 237) for mixed marriages in which the Catholic Church was involved, i.e. excluding those in which a partner in some sense Catholic ignored the Church. These showed that even in Motherwell diocese, lying to the east of Glasgow and probably containing the largest surviving local concentrations of Catholics, a third of all Catholic marriages in the 1970s were mixed. In the other two west-central dioceses, with more extensive movement and resettlement of population, proportions were rising towards half, whereas in St Andrews and Edinburgh and in Dunkeld, the other two diocese for which figures are available, it was two-thirds. This was a growing phenomenon – all figures are higher than those for the 1960s – but by no means new. They show, not one separate population from which bold and rebellious individuals venture out in marriage – let alone two, Catholic and Protestant, facing one another – but increasing numbers of mixed families for whose children it is essentially accidental whether the partners they themselves choose have the same religious affiliations as themselves. Individual mixed marriages can still cause strife and dismay, but normally they do not. They are too familiar. For the averagely undogmatic, the difference is of rather little practical moment anyway.

If the level of separation and antagonism between ordinary people is, despite persisting symbols of difference, low, between Churches officially and between many individual clergy relations had by the 1980s become positively amicable. Behind this lies in part a fundamental shift on the Catholic side from an 'exclusive' theology concerned, as one expert and closely involved

Scottish witness has put it, with 'the demarcation of frontiers that was characteristic of the time of "siege" after the Reformation', to an 'inclusive' theology. It became possible to look for shared basic belief and practice without the compulsion to stress whatever was not (Quinn 1979, p. 207). At the same time an awareness of common interests in facing similar problems grew. Doubtless there was, underlying both, the changed position of the Christian Churches in western Europe. In the twentieth century they have been faced, not by challenges from one another, but by a fading away of the assumptions and interests which, at least on the part of ruling classes, in the past supported institutionalised Christianity in European societies.

One leading common interest has been Christian marriage, necessarily heightened by the increasing levels of intermarriage noted above. There has been concern with its theology and with more directly practical issues in the changed contemporary context. The Churches have now to celebrate marriages as agents of a civil authority in no clear sense Christian, in the context of increasing divorce rates and for people with neither much knowledge of nor interest in time-honoured Christian understandings of marriage. A joint working group of the British Council of Churches and the Catholic authorities for England and Wales and for Scotland, set up in 1966/7, reported in 1971 on 'The Joint Pastoral Care of Interchurch Marriages in England, Wales and Scotland'. Within Scotland itself, since 1968 the annual General Assembly of the Church of Scotland has been inviting official Catholic Visitors to attend and on occasion to address it. A Joint Commission on Christian Marriage held the first official talks between the Churches since the Reformation and in 1980 produced a leaflet on *Inter-Church Marriage* for the guidance of couples belonging to the two Churches. It sets out the continuing differences, stressing the requirement on the Catholic partner to obtain dispensation in order to marry a non-Catholic, but also the possibility of further dispensation to be married in the Church of Scotland and the willingness of at least some ministers and priests to partici- pate jointly in marriage celebrations. As the leaflet said, 'There are still genuine differences between us, but relations have grown much more friendly'. The term 'inter-Church marriage' is itself intended to suggest the more positive and ecumenical spirit in which the former 'mixed marriages' are now to be approached.

Christian marriage and Scottish liturgy

By its conversion to Christianity, begun in the early fifth century, the area which was to become Scotland became heir to and a participator in the thinking and practice of the Church in relation to marriage which reached back to the first years. Already then it was grounded in Jewish thought and practice, and this endured because it was enshrined in the Old Testament, the foundation of the literate and literary, historical and critical tradition which characterises both Judaism and Christianity. It had indeed been accentuated by western Christianity's formation on the Jewish foundation but within the Graeco-Roman world (Stevenson 1982, pp. 3–12; Brooke 1989, pp. 39–54). Together these meant that, from the beginning, marriage and marrying were things recorded from pre-Christian times in scripture as well as occurring in an environing world not yet Christian. It was within a multicultural context that Christianity created itself, its practices and its ideas.

There has never been any way in which Christianity could altogether monopolise marriage. What Christians as such should do in a variety of practical circumstances, whether they were bound by the rules of others, what their response to their own conversion or their spouse's paganism should be, such issues necessarily from the beginning turned thinking towards defining the truly Christian (Martos 1981, pp. 399 foll.; Helmholz 1978, pp. 27–9). The search culminated in two main ideas. Christian marriage was the representation or playing out in human lives of the relationship of Christ with his bride, the Church, a notion which itself has very clear Jewish roots in the special relationship between God and either Israel or Jerusalem (Sampley 1971, p. 43). It also came in the somewhat longer run to be understood as a 'sacrament', a means to spiritual 'grace' provided for each spouse by the other. Both ideas were to prove immensely problematic but they did provide ways in which Christian marriage could be seen as a higher form, the existence of lower forms never being forgotten. They set ideals but it has never been possible to imagine that everybody would subscribe to them, certainly not to subscribe knowledgeably and unequivocally, or even that those who did subscribe would in practice not frequently infringe them.

The complexities of this situation and the need to relate to changing practical circumstances produced repeated rethinking, and this in turn produced in Europe at large the long history of liturgical experimentation and development which is of direct relevance to the present study. From Scotland itself it is not until late medieval or early modern times that substantial evidence for Christian thinking about marriage and practices in relation to marrying exists. The major sources for the pre-Reformation period are few[10] but they present a powerful picture of the distinctiveness of Christian thought and an impression of the great time-depth of themes which are still with us today.

What is particularly striking is the symmetry and equivalence in the way the partners are discussed, except in so far as biological differences affect definitions, as in the case of impotence. Marriage for Hay, a theologian who lectured on the topic to students in the 1530s, was the giving of their bodies to one another by two individuals, a man and a woman (1967, pp. 131, 71). It was a giving which created a 'debt' (I Corinthians vii, 3), payment of which could properly be demanded by either party in the form of the use of the other's body for 'carnal copulatioun'. Marriage was made, first, by the consent of the two parties to this mutual giving as a permanent arrangement, and then by its fulfilment: 'And eftir ye consent, quhen yai coinjoine togidder in carnal deid, marriage is consummat & endit' (Hamilton 1882, p. 168). The first purpose of marriage was reproductive, as it was considered always to have been since the Creation, but the avoidance of sin was not far behind in importance. The first thing that Hay says about marriage is that it 'has efficacy to regulate and determine the proper circumstances in which the pleasures and pains of touch, that is the sexul acts, may be lawfully and properly performed without mortal sin' (*op. cit.*, p. 3). Given that most people would require sexual intercourse, marriage and specifically 'the debt' was how they would get it without the sin of fornication. It was, according to Hay, as a protection against sin that the Church had set the ages for marriage, twelve for girls and fourteen for boys, so low: 'to avoid fornication, to which the young are very much inclined, and so easily incited to lust, and also because the carnal appetites usually awaken about that age' (*op. cit.*, pp. 151–5, 113).

Hay expresses, therefore, a concept of marriage which lies behind the more explicitly Christian ideas noted above. It was a matter for two individuals, of opposite sex but otherwise with the same needs and problems. With one another's assistance they would be able to face and overcome them. These needs and problems were essentially to do with sex, not any need to repro- duce – that is not thought of at the level of individuals – but the compulsion to sexual intercourse. The exclusiveness of the relationship was of its essence. It was perhaps reinforced by specifically Christian developments in ideas about sin and particularly sexual sin, but it was rooted in the pre-Christian words of Genesis ii, 24, translated and glossed in the Catechism as:

> The maryit man sall laif his father and mother, sa that he sall nocht be oblissit to dwell with thame, & he sall abheir and dwell with his wyfe, and thai sall be twa personis in ane flesche, because that thai sall bayth concurre in the generatioun of ane barne. (Hamilton 1882, p. 165.)

It is this ancient idea, surprising as to its first part in the comparative perspective of anthropology, and in its second echoing the Genesis story of the creation of Woman out of Man as his help or helpmate, which seems to found the distinctiveness of western marriage.[11] Quoted and affirmed by Jesus as reported in Matthew's Gospel, repeated in apostolic times (Ephesians v, 31) and on innumerable occasions ever since when Christian marriages have been celebrated, it can scarcely be surprising to find 'one flesh' becoming a cultural axiom.

It has until recently been possible to imagine the liturgy in which such ideas are given expression as something fixed, an unchanging legacy of a distant past fossilised in print and therefore of minimal interest to students of living society. Two remarkable phenomena fostered such an illusion: in England the *Book of Common Prayer*, a monumental production of the sixteenth century, stood almost unchanging until the mid-twentieth century, and so in a wider world did the seventeenth-century Roman liturgy of the Catholic Church. In Latin which few but priests would understand, the latter could become even more remote from the thinking and action of ordinary life than the former. Looked at in a wider perspective they are, however, unusual. Up to the period of Reformation and Counter-Reformation from which they date, liturgical exploration and hence variety are everywhere apparent, and from that period on, a proliferation of new Churches explored possibilities which were temporarily being denied in the old. In the twentieth century a need to renew liturgy has been sensed generally, even in the Anglican and Catholic bastions of conservatism, and has resulted in almost universal revision, experimentation and innovation.

Rites of marrying have shown a particular dynamism. Christian thinking about marriage has always faced dilemmas resistant to any final resolution, partly generated by the systems of religious and legal thought themselves, partly by the interface which marriage necessarily represents between this thinking and such basic and partially independent human realities as sex, procreation and interpersonal relationships in families. Unless blocked by authority in some way, this has always stimulated liturgical creativity. Established practices have been looked at in the light of new ideas and new circumstances and have been found in need of modification. Writing and subsequently printing allowed new solutions to be offered to others and to spread widely. Their preservation in this form not only allows the history of liturgical effort to be traced; it also builds up bodies of precedent from which ideas can be drawn and new selections made. With such resources to hand, new liturgies can be constructed with little or no need to challenge tradition, the authority of the past.[12]

Sources for pre-Reformation Scottish marriage liturgy are, as has been noted, few, but it is clear that by the fifteenth century Scotland had its own versions of the liturgies to be found at the same time in England (Galbraith 1984). Rathen is one of these, in the Sarum tradition. The Manual gives an account of a complex and intricately patterned ritual, with three spatially separate sections. In the first the couple, supervised by the priest, marry one another at the door of the church, using forms of words in vernacular Scots. They then move into the church for a nuptial mass in which, though it is in Latin, they participate through their movements at the different stages. The long sequence in the church ends with a blessing of food and drink brought for the purpose, and a sharing of them amongst those present. The proceedings are completed when the priest visits the marital home to bless the marriage bed and the newly married couple in it. The movement of the ritual sequence here, first out of the secular world, then held separated around the altar for a procedure conducted in a special language, and finally back into everyday life again, is such as to delight every admirer of Van Gennep's theory of 'rites of passage' (1909). It was. it should however be noted, not a spontaneous creation of the human spirit but the laborious product of centuries of experimentation and change (Molin & Mutembe 1974; Stevenson 1982).

How widely such complex and presumably costly procedures would have been practised cannot be known (Cowan 1982, pp. 3–4, 152–5 & *passim*). They were in any case almost entirely swept away by the Reformation. They were replaced by the liturgy which John Knox had drawn up for his congregation at Geneva, made up of exiles, like himself, from the restored Catholicism of Queen Mary's reign in England. The main sources he used were Cranmer's second Prayer Book of 1552, radically simplified, and Calvin's French form. Imported into Scotland it constituted a revolution, though not, in its English dress, an entirely foreign one. Swept away were all the movement and ritual elaboration of the old order. The new was not to be a free-standing service, let alone one which reached outside the church itself into the home. It was to be a section inserted into the normal Sunday morning meeting for instruction and prayer, and instruction was to be the keynote of the inserted section too. The couple were instructed on the nature of marriage and on what they were assenting to in marrying one another. This they did in a simple form of words without actions of any kind. There was to be no giving away of the bride and the ring which had become well established in medieval times was explicitly banished. One short prayer of blessing at the end provided the only lightening of the heavily didactic load (Church Service Society 1901).

Knox's liturgy, as it was then called, remained in place for eighty years. Alternatives were proposed and made their own contribution to the politico-religious turbulence of the first half of the seventeenth century (Cooper 1904). In 1645 it was officially replaced by the Westminster Directory (Leishman 1901). This was more a handbook for the practice of congregational religion than a prescribed order for services. It was drawn up by an assembly commissioned by the English Parliament to attempt, with Scottish participation, to unify worship throughout the two kingdoms. As has been usual through history, unification meant for Scotland a surge of English influence. Knox's minatory tones were replaced with pastoral advice and exhortation, and there were vows which were once again clearly descendants of Sarum in both the words and the accompanying actions, though there was still, and pointedly, no ring. A pronouncement of marriage by the minister, which both Knox and the pre-Reformation order had avoided, was for the first time prescribed.

This was a major significance of the Directory for Scotland. It provided backing for a new conception of marriage as something done by the minister to the couple. Apart from this it was to contribute to breaking down any sense that there was a single prescribed order for marriage in Scotland. Its legal standing lasted only until the Restoration of 1660, though it was again recommended by the General Assembly of the Church of Scotland in 1705. In effect, from the seventeenth to the nineteenth centuries Knox and the Directory were twin but increasingly remote sources for a practice which came to depend heavily on the preferences of individual ministers. Prescribed forms of any kind were devalued in favour of extemporisation, often of extreme simplicity, by the minister. By the nineteenth century bride and groom were commonly asked no question nor given the chance even to say 'I do'.

Idiosyncratic ministerial control over proceedings was further accentuated by the removal of the congregational context which had been so important to Knox. From the first half of the eighteenth century, marriages gradually ceased to be celebrated in churches at all (Sprott 1882). By the later nineteenth century, either the manse or the homes of those marrying were widely understood to be the proper locations for Scottish or Presbyterian marriages, and this was assumed to be traditional in Scotland. In the earlier part of the twentieth century the hotel, the restaurant and the public hall were added to the places where ministers commonly officiated. Marriages were subsequently brought back into the churches, but they were not congregational or even public services and the move served to make almost complete the control each individual minister was able to exercise. Despite a necessary preoccupation with ensuring that whatever is done meets the few requirements of Scottish law discussed above, neither the minister's right to choose nor extemporisation have been superseded as values in the Presbyterian churches even today.

It was against this background, in sharp contrast with the authoritative regulation and book-based liturgy of the Church of England, that a movement for liturgical reform finally started in the nineteenth century (Murray 1984). This was couched in the form of an appeal for the restoration of a liturgical tradition, both Scottish and universal, which had in Scotland been submerged to the point of being forgotten. It was usually clear however, in relation to marriage particularly, that the Anglican marriage service was at least a standing provocation and even at times, despite the considerable ambivalence about things English which Scots must feel, a model. From 1867 a succession of new orders and then new editions of these orders began to appear. They came to be called *Books of Common Order* by analogy with the Anglican *Book of Common Prayer*. In the Scottish context they were more or less free to compete for the favour of individual ministers, but they gave rise to considerable contention in the Church of Scotland. It was not until 1940 that the General Assembly of that Church joined fully in the process and issued its own official though not in any sense mandatory book.

A free-standing marriage service, to be held in church, was in all of these envisaged, its pattern increasingly similar to Anglican practice. The ring came back before the end of the nineteenth century and to the relief of all (Cooper 1904, p. 291). Its use had never disappeared; it had merely been denied a place in the service itself. Reappearance allowed the central event to be once again supported by ritual action meaningful to those involved. It came increasingly to be surrounded also by prayers and readings and blessings and music. A newly revised *Book of Common Order* had only recently been published at the time of the research, in 1979.

Since the Marriage (Scotland) Act of 1834 it has been lawful for Catholic priests to celebrate marriages, but little indigenous Catholic liturgy seems to have been published until the period following the Second Vatican Council. Before that, forms prescribed originally for England or Ireland and mainly in Latin were often borrowed. These provided either for the insertion of a marriage rite into the middle of a mass, a pattern quite different to the pre-Reformation one noted above, or for a small and simple free-standing service. In a largely working-class population, the latter style certainly predominated. A version which was published in Glasgow in 1936 had simply a consent in English followed immediately by the Tridentine priestly pronouncement, like the rest of the service in Latin: *Ego coniungo vos in matrimonium*. There then followed a blessing of the ring, its putting on and prayers, and a nuptial blessing might follow this. By the 1950s less sparse forms from England, with increasing use of English and printed with parallel English text, were available. It was one of these which then provided, on an interim basis, the first entirely English forms as required by the reforms of the Second Vatican Council in the 1960s.

Current marriage liturgy for Scotland is published in two books, one for priest and the other for the use of congregations, primarily at nuptial masses which are now the expected form of service.[13] They are necessarily large and complex rituals, amalgamating as they do the procedures of marrying with a performance of the central rite of the Church. It is this which distinguishes them most sharply from the marriage services of the Church of Scotland and other Protestants. It is made apparently even more complex in its printed form by the offering of choices at many points. Compared with its current English equivalent, it as at once a more conservative and a more permissive document. It conforms to the new practice of the Church generally in eliminating the priestly pronouncement of marriage but it is more conservatve in retaining ritual action around the ring and in including older forms; it is more permissive in offering alternatives and in the scope even for *ad hoc* innovation which it allows. It also provides for more lay participation than does the English. Their differences demonstrate the tendency of liturgies, given any opportunity to develop in their own ways, to diverge.

As will be seen, written liturgy is one thing, performance often quite another. Performances and their preparation in both the Church of Scotland

and the Scottish Catholic Church are discussed in Chapters 3 and 6 below. The distinctive Christian conception of marriage underlies the discussion throughout.

Chapter 2

Engagement

Getting married

The decision to marry acknowledges the cultural distinction between single and married. Here it is a decision placed on each individual, to be taken finally by two eligible people of opposite sex in agreement. The need to refer to eligibility emphasises the fact that it is a culturally defined and regulated decision. Unless the parties meet the various conditions set out in the preceding chapter it is not a decision they are allowed to implement.

Marriage contrasts therefore with 'living together', recognised as an alternative way in which people of opposite sex can have a domestic and sexual relationship but with none of the further significances and resonances of marriage. It is 'just' living together, avoiding marriage and remaining single or married to someone else as the case may be. To the extent that the behaviour of the parties resembles a conception of the proper marriage, i.e. with stability over time, companionship, mutual faithfulness and perhaps bringing children up together, it may be treated as tantamount to marriage. Real marriage, by contrast, is neither more nor less marriage whatever the behaviour of the parties, though such behaviour may give grounds for divorce. By the 1980s, however, it was commonly thought that a major change had occurred, that people could take for themselves the benefits of domestic and sexual partnerships for which previously they would have needed to marry but without doing so. In principle this was so, as indeed it had always been, but in practice, as was clear in this research, such relationships were still far from equally available to all and had affected marginally, if at all, the fundamental western conception of marriage which has already been outlined.

People were continuing to marry, as they had always done, for a variety of perhaps typically tangled reasons, acknowledged and unacknowledgeable, admitted to all or not even to themselves. The multiplicity of reasons they would give could only be summed statistically and only then in the most superficial of ways. People say such things as 'we are getting married because we love each other', or 'to make it legal', or 'for the sake of the children'. But these are all standard justifications for something which is normally so expectable and acceptable as not really to require justification at all. They reveal little therefore. The experience of the research does however allow the practically relevant possibilities to be outlined.

Some were marrying to be married. The attractions of being married come in a variety of forms. Some see their peers marrying and feel that they are being left behind. Parents see their peers' children marrying – weddings perhaps being held for these children – and the children themselves marry, rather than just moving in with a partner, for the sake of their parents or for the considerable material advantages liable to accrue. Some also marry to escape their families. Escape may take the form of a bid for moral independence or for the practical, daily independence of having a separate home: marrying is for many young people, as will be seen, by far the most practical and advantageous way to achieve the transition to a home, even a comfortable, well-equipped home, of their own. Even those who are already independent may get married in order to simplify and routinise dealings with family members, particularly those of older generations, with whom and for whom such matters as sleeping arrangements would otherwise be a source of difficulty and embarrassment. Many still identify being married as the route to a desired future with a home and family of their own. For active Christians, marriage is God's way and the traditional value of confining sexual relations within marriage remains important. Marrying to be married therefore takes a variety of forms.

Marrying for the sake of the particular other is the main alternative. Individuals may want to commit themselves and create a bond, to try to bind the other to them. They may want to have children with such a person and see marriage as the appropriate and most secure basis for that. They may want to secure financial advantage and status from particular matches. They may be flattered by the attentions of the particular other and be prepared to go along with his or her plans for the two of them. They may simply be afraid to lose them. Love will motivate or at least provide a language in which the complexities and idiosyncracies of personal relationships can be expressed and presented in immediately acceptable form (cf. Sarsby 1983, pp. 108–10, 115–16).

All these, and no doubt other and more idiosyncratic purposes and hopes and fears, lead people like those included in the study into marriage. It is important to be reasonably realistic about this, but what is of major importance for the kind of understanding of marriage and its procedures which is being sought here is the way in which getting married meets – or appears to those concerned to meet – a wide variety of interests and circumstances. As long as this remains so, people will do it. It is in any case what they were doing, rather than the more elusive why, which is the focus of enquiry here.

The engagement

It might be thought that engagement is an agreement by a couple eligible to marry to do so in the future. In practice it is more than that, but it may also in a sense be less. It is a present state into which people enter in anticipation of marriage, but anticipation may mean different things. When the marriage itself is clearly envisaged and firmly dated, engagement may be chiefly a matter of making the intention public and getting down to arrangements for its fulfilment. Anticipation may, however, indicate a wish to get married which cannot for one reason or another immediately be set into motion. The couple may feel they need to save for a house, or that one or both should complete a course of further study – perhaps entailing their separation – or finish an apprenticeship, or get a better job, or get a job at all when unemployed. The anticipated future may even be so vague as to have little reality even for the couple themselves. It may seem that engagement is being carried out almost for its own sake, the next step perhaps when a steady going-out relationship has been established for some time and others are going beyond it (McIntyre 1977, p. 148).

A sixteen-year-old schoolgirl from one of the large peripheral housing schemes of Glasgow whose first boyfriend, a young scaffolder of eighteen, became her fiancé after they had been going out together for two years represents what is a mainly working-class pattern here. The engagement happened when she was beginning a three-year teaching course. Looking back, she remembered enjoying everything enormously. As the anthropologist recorded her story, 'it had felt really good to be engaged, safe; her life seemed to be settled; she had a boy who was going to look after her. And Terry was good. He understood that she had to work late in the library at exam times and he would come and wait for her.' But they were not in the event to move ahead to marriage; indeed, it was being offered a council house for which they had applied when they were first engaged which precipitated the break. 'Terry was not the one she really wanted to spend the whole of her life with. She had wanted too much to be married, for security, love, and had been kidding herself.' It was emotional security she had been after. She felt, she said, quite unsure of herself as regards relationships. Terry had been the only one and she had the feeling that it would take too long to get to another such relationship with someone else. So she finally decided 'that she cared for him but didn't love him. To have gone ahead and married him would have been the easy way out. They could have had a good life, a normal life.' But she wanted something more.[N6 1]

Though it did not do so here, engagement largely for its own sake may ultimately lead to marriage as an eventual next step. A lengthy engagement broken off, however, will often set in train a well-known pattern of events: someone else is soon met and quickly married. The same person is then acting out a very different engagement, one in which the present state is subordinated to the event to come. Here engagement is little more than the decision to get married, though it is always possible to speak of getting engaged and the decision to get married as different things, requiring two decisions rather than just the one.

Engagement in fact normally acquires a life of its own, with other people inevitably becoming involved. It is possible to deny this, and couples with an acute sense of it being their own private business may, initially at least, be inclined to try. It is possible even to get married without being first engaged, but to do this it is necessary to avoid not only the giving and wearing of a ring which others will see and understand as an engagement ring, but also to avoid anything else which can be construed as an announcement of the forthcoming marriage. A couple in the study did try earnestly to avoid getting engaged. They had been firmly together for some time though they were not actually living together. One of them had indeed previously lived with another partner. They saw, they said, no point in getting engaged; or rather, the point they saw they did not like, namely that it was tantamount to asking for engagement presents. But they did mean to get married and inevitably people had to be told that there was to be a wedding. Despite their disclaimers about engagement, they did then begin to be given the presents they had sought to avoid.[T8] Only by forgoing normal wedding preparations altogether, as did a couple who were married without any prior indication to families or friends in a romantic 'elopement' from Glasgow to the registrar's office at Gretna[N4], can engagement be altogether avoided.

Rings and announcements are, however, the expected steps through which a mere and perhaps private agreement acquires the public standing which takes it beyond the control of the parties themselves. Others, again perhaps mainly in working-class circles, may expect to be warned in advance that it is to take place. They will be mildly resentful when, very often, they are not. Even those getting engaged may be affected by this: June, an assistant in a chemist's, was an extreme case of timidity here.

> I never told anybody. I didn't really know till about the week before it and I thought I'm no going to tell anybody. [...] Tracy [her best friend], I never told her. See, we got the ring on the Saturday and Robbie's sort of said something to Gordon [Tracy's fiancé]. He never really said that we were getting engaged but, eh, he, you know, kind of told him. And Gordon had said to Tracy, 'I think they might be getting engaged.' And Tracy came into the [pub] on Sunday night. She says, 'I was sitting like this, you know, to see if you had a ring on.' And I was sitting like this with it turned round [she laughs]. And she was frightened to say anything, and I was frightened to say anything to her. And she's like that: 'C'mon

to the toilet with me,' and I went into the toilet and she's like
that: 'Let me see your finger.' And I felt terrible. She says, 'I
wasn't sure if I seen a ring or no, and I didn't like all of a
sudden to say to you.' It's a good laugh now, right enough, but
it was terrible at the time. [T25 2]

That was only the beginning of her troubles. The following day she took
the ring in to work to show the girls[3] but didn't dare to wear it. And then
she was asked by one of them who knew that she and her boyfriend had
been going 'up town' on the Saturday what they had got there. 'Nothing',
she said, and after that could not even produce the ring. That evening she
did put it on. She went to a keep-fit class with a lot of other girls she had
been at school with and the girl from the shop was there too. Faced with
this same girl,

I wasn't embarrassed but I was awful kind of ..., didn't know
how to ..., just to say it. 'Cause I never told anybody that we
were even getting engaged, then just to suddenly say to
somebody. And I just went kind of like that [thrusting out her
left hand], and she went 'Oh!', and she went away and told the
rest of them. 'That's terrible you never told anybody.' But I, I
mean ..., I wish now I had said, because it was worse for me. [T25]

Even in her case, eventually the news was out. It was then, as eagerly as
it almost always is, acknowledged with presents. Standard announcements
in newspapers, in the names of the parents, express more formally, in the
relatively few and largely middle-class cases in which they occur, the way
an engagement moves from being the business of the couple themselves, to
the families' business, and finally into the public domain.

Rings

It is possible to be engaged but not, or not yet, to have a ring, but the ring
stands so clearly for engagement that getting engaged is often tied to it. It is
rarely tied in what is commonly regarded as the old-fashioned way, with
the ring bought by the would-be fiancé and presented romantically to his
admired as part of an unheralded proposal of marriage, though this can
still happen. Margaret reported a case:

She was on the phone to her sister, and she was saying to her
sister, um, 'He just went out and got it, you know, and ...'. And
Lawrence said to her afterwards, 'Why is everybody so
surprised that I just went out ...?' [she laughs]. And she said,
'Lawrence, most people don't do that!' [she laughs]. 'Most
people sit down and say, "Well, I think we'll get engaged", and
they go for the ring together.' But Lawrence thought that ... .

He arrived with the ring and a bunch of flowers or something.[T108]

And he was not thought of as being romantic, merely comically out of touch. The only actual participant in the study to whom anything like this had happened was so bemused when the man with whom she already had every intention of living produced an engagement ring that she did not at the time even register what it was or what it implied.

As these examples suggest, engagement, like marriage, is now normally expected to evolve out of an increasingly joint relationship, in which equipping oneselves with a ring or rings is one of the most significant joint projects. An expedition to the city centre, and especially to the Argyll Arcade, is very often the form that this takes. There, eight jewellers provide a couple, or individuals anticipating such a special expedition, with an almost continuous run of bright windows which can be gazed into in comfort, while possible rings are spotted and compared.

Margaret.	It took us, from the day we picked the ring, it took us seven weeks. We were going to get engaged whenever we had the money for the ring.
James.	Actually, we had the idea ... . Well, the 25th September was my birthday, so we had an idea we would try and get the ring for then. Plus, we would finish ..., we would both finish working by that time because we would have to start back at the university. So there was no way we could save any more money. We had saved money before we actually went to look for the ring. It was £265. That was quite reasonable, compared to what else they had.
M.	Just three small diamonds. We decided we didn't want anything ... . We could have got ones at that price which would have looked bigger, because they were all done up or something, but we wanted something authentic. A lot of them have very tiny wee diamonds in them, but all built up round about, and we decided we would rather have it looking smaller. It would just be the diamonds!
J.	There was a period ... . The day we picked the ring, put money on it, Margaret took a kind of 'let's get engaged now! we must get engaged!'
M.	I was desperate to get the ring that day.
J.	So we actually went down and looked at a wholesale place which Margaret had a card for. You can take it and pay it later. She was sort of looking at things, you know, she didn't really like but was going to take.
M.	Because we had thought about it – by that time, we had thought about it for about two months, and I was thinking, 'Och, we're

never going to get the money. It's going to take us months to·save
up for this ring.'[T26]

But instead, they went elsewhere, found the £265 ring which they really liked
and put a deposit on it.

J.   We made the final payment on the ring on the Friday morning.
This was the 24th. Margaret decided that she couldn't wait, she
wore it on the 24th, but we officially got engaged on the 25th.[T26]

In this case therefore there was one ring only and it was an entirely joint
enterprise up to the point of actually wearing it. Any idea of giving and
receiving had here quite disappeared, but matters are often more ambiguous
than this. Though the woman will expect to take the lead in choosing the ring
she is to wear, the man may pay for it. The significance of this is modified,
however, to the extent that there is already a sense of financial sharing
established by the time such an enterprise is undertaken.

Catriona. Well, Mark sold his car. We didn't spend it all. He sold his car and
we got ... . We spent four hundred on the ring and he got twelve
hundred for the car, and he paid off loans with it, and things
... .[T20]

Where marriage is clearly in mind, the implications for their future joint
finances of not setting reasonable limits are only too clear.

The giving and receiving of the ring, to the extent that they occur, and in
any case its wearing, become symbolic in the clearest sense of that expansible
term. Such a ring stands explicitly for one thing at least, the fact of the
engagement itself. In Glasgow it is often engraved, as was Margaret's, with
initials and the date. It announces the engagement in a way that no-one can
mistake, and it asserts its importance too. The diamonds such rings invariably
featured at the time are for most young marriers simply the best. Largely on
account of them, rings are conspicuously costly; James and Margaret, looking back from their very different circumstances after the wedding, expressed
astonishment at their willingness then to spend their £265 on a ring.

Whether it can also be taken to represent other qualities which are
associated with it is more problematic since meanings of any further kind are
seldom discussed or even implied. Rings might be chosen to suit a particular
hand, for a practical reason such as not to project too far, or for personally
meaningful reasons such as Margaret's 'authenticity'. One girl needed a ring
with a different number of stones to her mother's which she had never liked.
These few points effectively exhaust the topic of meaningfulness as it was
expressed in any direct form in the research conversations. But a ring
surrounds and contains. It could therefore readily be seen as representing
bonds, indeed as bonds freely and happily assumed. Bought by the couple
together, it could be seen as a joint investment in their future; bought by the

man but chosen by the woman, it could stand for his capacity to give her what she wants most of all.

These are all trains of thought available to anyone with an understanding of the culture and relevant circumstances, but none was 'found' in any direct sense in the research. However, add the fact that the ring is worn by the woman on the finger destined for the wedding ring and few would probably dispute that it becomes a clear announcement of her husband-to-be's commitment to her and of hers to him and their future marriage. The identification of symbolic meaning has often an element of ambiguity in practice, and using a sense of cultural possibilities to go beyond anything for which there is, strictly speaking, evidence is often almost inevitable.

A single engagement ring is envisaged here. As long as marriage could be comfortably viewed as a partnership of complementaries, the fact that only one party would wear a ring, or would buy one, was unremarkable. But as notions of equality and symmetry in marriage have come to the fore, so a logic which was always potentially present has become relevant.

James.   The reason people wear rings, it's obviously a social signal, [...] like, a girl was wearing an engagement ring because a guy would be more likely to chat a girl up than vice versa. So a girl wearing an engagement ring would be a sign, a social sign that she was already, if you like, engaged. I always assumed that was why you wore the rings, to give social signals.

Margaret. That was the way I'd always kind of thought of the rings. And that's why girls got engagement rings and men didn't.[T116]

But if the woman is to wear such a mark, what reason can there be for the man not to wear one too? In contrast to the wedding ring to be discussed later, such a logic of equality has not quickly produced a male variant of the established female ring, though a modest change is to be observed. Since about 1970, in the estimation of a jeweller of long experience in and around Glasgow, an established kind of male ring, the signet ring, has been adopted for this purpose, to the extent that one has been adopted at all. It becomes an engagement ring by being bought as such and by being worn on the same finger as the woman's, i.e. the fourth of the left hand. This is where its main significance lies, in its equivalence of definition and position. Its physical distinctiveness has no meaning, though the small diamonds with which such rings are sometimes set do suggest that the search for equivalence of form is operating here too.

Announcements and parties
Getting engaged takes off first and foremost through the ring or, much less often, rings. Those who wear them carry around with them an announcement which they may initially be shy about others noticing, but usually are soon

keen to show off. Putting the ring on is almost always a private matter for the couple themselves, perhaps to be performed without ceremony of any kind, as Margaret did, but sometimes provided with an occasion and a setting:

June.   Before we went to Ambrose's that night for the party in the house [a joint engagement party with a cousin], we went to a restaurant, and we put the ring on. We just went for a meal and did it that way. I think it's sort of between the two of you to put the rings on and everything. It's a sort of special moment. You have to ... just sort of keep it to yourselves.[T61]

Putting on the ring may be seen as 'making it official' or it may be a subsequent event involving others which is regarded as doing this, or the latter may be seen as 'just celebrating'. There are three groups of people who may be involved in varying combinations on one or more other occasions: the couple with immediate family, for a meal or a 'night in the house'; the couple with 'family', close and more distant and particularly of the older generation; the couple with friends, perhaps with a disco and sometimes on a large scale; and finally, as Margaret and James chose, all together.

'Just celebrating' would mean, strictly speaking, an event indistinguishable from any other party. In practice, however these occasions are done, there are likely to be at least hints of what Van Gennep identified long ago as 'rites of passage' (1909). Such a celebration is bringing in others and institutionalising a recognition by them of something new. Congratulating the couple, drinking to them, giving them presents are the everyday minor rituals of the culture, here applied to recognising the new pre-marriage state of the couple. Such happenings may be dispersed through a period of days or weeks, occurring at odd moments in various places, but to the extent that they are brought together on a particular occasion they can immediately be seen as making a point of transition. It may even then seem appropriate to represent this point by putting on the ring which marks the new state, though any such develop-ment is often inhibited by a sense of privacy appropriate to the moment. When an engagement cake at one family's celebration was decorated with a ring in a box, a young brother's imagining that this could be the real thing was regarded as a comic mistake. But such a putting on, whether in a larger setting or just between the couple themselves, need not be in reality for the first time. A first time is not of itself a rite of passage; it is the representing of transition which is, and for this a putting on of the ring is strikingly appropriate.

'Representing' is not however entirely adequate as a term. Van Gennep himself stressed that such a rite was not symbolic of the new state; it was what actually brought it about. It would bring it about here, not in terms of the decision to be married or even to be engaged, but by constituting the state of engagement for the couple in question. Their own decision about their future is transformed into a state of being engaged – they become fiancé(e)s – by their own and others' recognition of such a state and of the particular couple as now entering into it. To the extent that a rite of passage develops – and in the field studied it was no more than incipient – every occasion of its performance becomes a key part of the machinery of assertion and recognition which makes engagement part of the particular cultural furnishing of life.

People may therefore decide to marry and even wear an engagement ring, become engaged in this practical and even symbolic sense, yet still feel it appropriate to follow up with a rite of passage of this kind.

James.   Margaret decided that she couldn't wait, so she wore [the ring] on the 24th, but we officially got engaged on the 25th.

Margaret.   And the party was on the 26th.

J.   We were both working on the 25th, but on the night of the 25th we came over to my house and had just a kind of family thing, with Margaret's mother and father, and my mother and father and sister.

M.   That was just on the actual day. We just had a couple of bottles of wine. Just had an impromptu celebration.

J.   We were going to have a family party. We decided on this idea of having this family party ...

M.   ... which probably wouldn't have worked anyway.

J.   But anyway ... Margaret's brother said, he said: 'When we got engaged we didn't have a party. Have a party,' he said. 'You'll get lots of presents.' And we said: 'We may as well.' And we had a party and got lots of presents![T26]

M.   It was nice. We had a good selection of friends and there were people there – it was on holiday that James and I met – and there were people there who had been with us on holiday, and. . . . . It was quite a good party and the families mixed well.

J.   There were about twenty who were family, and then another twenty five who were friends.[T26]

They drank and they talked, and a friend who was a DJ had prepared a programme of tapes for them which got everybody up dancing. And there was singing.

M.   I don't know if that's a common thing. To get a mixed company like that is quite good, because the older people all start singing. They get the singing going. Whereas if you have a party full just of young people, you tend to get more ... . I always think it's a more inhibited atmosphere, whereas, you know, ... Like my dad sang, and James's mum sang, and you sang – basically did their party turn.[T26]

The party may provide a context for more serious and purposeful action too. Fairly late in the evening James's father had come up to Margaret and asked her to dance. He had then said he wanted her to know how pleased he was about the engagement. It was some months later before she learnt what had been going on:

M.   We were sitting talking and my mum was saying, and I never knew right up to then [...], she had said to James's mum and James's Aunt Aileen – by that time they'd all had a wee drink – she'd said to James's mum and Aunt Aileen how I had felt that James's dad didn't like me. And James's Aunt Aileen got right up and told James's dad. She said: 'Look here! Margaret thinks that you don't like her' [she laughs]. Which was probably why he came up to me and said to me then ... . I wondered why he came up in such a rush.[T113]

It was therefore an occasion for resolving relaionships. She may not have understood at the time just what had happened but she had indeed registered the effect. Soon after the wedding she explained:

M.   I'd always felt kind of awkward with James's dad. I always thought your dad didn't like me when we first started going out. But once we got engaged, em, I think he saw ... . You know, it was an example of somebody seeing the relationship differently then, and ... . I mean, I'd realised by that time that he didn't ..., it was not that he didn't like me; it was just that he was getting used to the idea of somebody in the family being seriously involved with someone else.[T110]

Larger scale and greater elaboration are possible too, with halls hired, and caterers, discos or even live bands. There is no required form for such celebrations but they tend to pick up features such as a cake which point forward to the wedding, as the presents clearly do, since this is what is in people's minds.

Presents

Margaret.   We had tremendous presents really. We were astonished by the presents.

James.   Yes, really good. [...] It was quite embarrassing for a few weeks after.

M.   We would go into department stores and come across things that we had been given, and see the prices.

J.   You were weighing yourself up in people's affections: only £8.99 from Aunt ... [he laughs].

M.   We did not!

J. No. We used to see things that someone had bought you, and you'd turn and run before you saw the price.[T26]

M. Some of the things we couldn't put down as essential, you know, things we really need ...

J. That ornament.

M. ... like the tea's-made, and that ornament! [she laughs]. I suppose it's nice to get the things but ... maybe you wouldn't spend money on it. Most of them were quite ..., they were, I suppose, fancy accessories, ... Things.

J. Sometimes you get things like table cloths, and matching table mats, dessert forks, and glasses, and a ... .

M. We got quite a lot of dishes as well,

J. which are quite practical,

M. and we got tea sets and coffee sets,

J. coffee-makers, electric irons,

M. and four clocks!

J. Four clocks!

M. All different kinds of clock, right enough. [...] We also got some money. We got £50 from various people. It's quite a done thing now. I think it's quite good in a way, because it means you can maybe put it together, that money, and buy a piece of furniture that you might need, as opposed to having lots of gadgets that you won't ..., aren't absolutely essential to you. I don't feel bad about getting money [laughing]. We've actually used that money – we'll need to replace it – because both of us are still waiting for grants. So we used that money in keeping ourselves going, which we will replace.[T26]

SC. So what kinds of thing are you expecting for wedding presents?

M. Well [laughing], we're hoping somebody might give us a house![T6]

Engagement presents can therefore be numerous and lavish. Their timing certainly depends on how the engagement is announced and celebrated, their number rather less so. The enthusiasm for giving presents which is still more apparent at weddings and the birth of babies is often already apparent here. Even those with whom connections might be thought slight may wish to give. It is predominantly women of senior generations who act in this way. It might be understood as a means of claiming a relationship with the recipients; this would be in line with general anthropological thinking about gift-exchange. In most cases, however, neither they themselves nor anybody else construes the action in this light. What they are doing seems, rather, to be using the present as a way of actively identifying themselves with the event, the birth, wedding or engagement, which in itself and almost regardless of who is performing it is important and satisfying to them. In everyday life it is the same phenomenon as the flood of presents from complete strangers elicited in Britain by the equivalent royal events.

Engagement presents are overwhelmingly the same kinds of thing as the wedding presents to come. They are items for the couple, and especially the wife to be, viewed as in the business of setting up a home. If the present occasionally takes the form of money, this is not properly to be treated as a contribution to running expenses, though it may be what actually happens. Presents are unlikely to be co-ordinated in any way; they will be seen by their donors as first small offerings in the direction of equipping a household. 'Small' has however to be understood as relative to the giver's relationship to one or other of the couple, to their means, and to what they might give as a wedding present: one theory expressed was that the engagement present might be expected to cost about a third of a wedding present. Couples regularly express surprise at the number and quality of the presents, which are sometimes already making a substantial contribution to the home to come.

Being engaged

Being engaged may be a state into which one settles, little more than a formalisation of a steady boyfriend–girlfriend relationship.

Margaret. Quite a few of my friends have been engaged now maybe two or three years. That's their attitude: when they got engaged, they got engaged. They'd maybe known the person for a couple of years by the time they got engaged, and then they said 'well, we'll maybe get married in two or three or ... .[T26]

In the early days they will be asked when they are getting married, but if they do not respond to the mild pressure then, they will soon be left to get on with being simply engaged.

For others, like James and Margaret themselves, engagement is from the beginning transitional, but the nature of that transition depends greatly on individual circumstances. Whether the parties have grown up together in the same milieu or have met only recently; whether they are living with parents at home or have their own homes separately or together; whether or not they are earning, and how adequately to their needs; what the demands of their jobs or other activities are; whether both are in the same situation in such respects; whether they live close, at least in the same city, or are in different parts of the country: all these are bound to affect the significance of engagement, and indeed of marriage itself. For Margaret and James, recently met and both living at home but on opposite sides of Glasgow, when they looked back from the perspective of marriage, engagement seemed to be the time when a need to go out to be together turned into spending time together at each other's homes.

Margaret. I think it was quite an active time really, because it was really taken up with getting to know each other's families and things like that. [...] By that stage your families recognised that you had this relationship, so you do spend more time in each other's houses together. I mean, apart from anything else it was the time when, em, like **you** were either staying at my house or I was staying at your house. Probably one of the big things about being engaged is that people begin to react to you as a couple. You know, people ask you places together and just generally see you as James and Margaret, rather than ... . Your families begin to do that as well. [...] That was something I quite enjoyed, I think. It was the feeling that ... . I suppose in a way it confirmed to you your relationship. You know, by getting engaged you were making this statement about your relationship. It was a kind of public statement, and people were acknowledging that, which was quite nice, I think.[T110]

Family events have a major part to play here. At Christmas, James and Margaret were with her family for midnight mass at their church and with his on Christmas Day. The biggest series of events was in connection with James's parents' silver wedding. This is something which, given average ages for marriage, occurs with some regularity around the time of children's own weddings. When it does it provides an opportunity to link the generations together in a particularly striking manner. There is no set form, but a deliberate echoing of the wedding day is not uncommon. Margaret's own parents' pattern a few years previously was a special service, a mass, followed by a meal in a hotel to which family, friends and the original celebrant were invited. At hall or hotel 'receptions', some might even have a top table; the original best man and best maid might be included and given a special place in the celebration; there might be a cake, with clear wedding echoes, to be ceremonially cut; and there would certainly be presents.

James's parents' celebrations were more numerous but less formal. There were five separate 'nights' at various people's houses or going out for meals, and Margaret and James were involved in several of them.

M.   Remember the night you had in the house? People were kind of ..., like, saying to us, 'Oh, it won't be long ...'
J.   Yes.
M.   ... you know, 'to your turn!', and all that kind of thing. Our wedding was kind of entering into it a bit. I think ..., did we not sing that night? Did some people not sing 'The bells are ringing'

for us, or something, as the night wore on? And that night in the house people spoke about our wedding. And when I went up to the women's night in Julie's house, people were all talking about the wedding then, and ...: 'Oh, it won't be long till June,' and 'It'll pass really quickly', and ... [T110]

The incomer here was very clearly becoming one of the family, at the same time necessarily encountering the ways of that family, its own particular variant of the wider culture which both sides shared.

One thing, significant for Margaret, which it meant here was that she was becoming not just a member of the family but one of the women of the family. This was not entirely welcome.

Margaret. A couple of weeks ago James's aunt and uncle came round, his Aunt Joan and his uncle Ian who happened to be his godparents, but that's by the by. They're really nice. That's the first time I met them. They're really nice people, really friendly, and ... um ... but after about an hour, James's dad suggested that they would go over to the pub for a pint. So your dad and Ian and you and Joseph [James's brother] went over – which is not something we would normally do, do that kind of thing, go out separately or anything. And, you know, I was left with your mum and your Aunt Joan which didn't really bother me. That was fine, talking to your mum and Joan. But what bothered me was this idea of, here the boys go off to the pub for the pint and we're left to talk about ... . The fact that your mum had a bottle of sherry which we about polished off is beside the point [she laughs]. We were left to talk about things, the show of presents and this kind of thing. [T91]

I couldn't imagine either of my [married] brothers, their friends coming and them ... . I think they would all go out for a drink or they'd have a drink in the house. I don't think there is such a definite distinction now, for a start, between what the men are going to talk about and what the women are going to talk about – because the women are not going to necessarily sit and talk about all the wee housewifey things... [...]

J.   We ended up talking about politics, in the pub [he laughs]. [T91]

M.   Well, I think, likes of your Helen would resent, and I would resent, and Anne would resent, and Christine would resent, the fact that it would maybe be assumed that they are not going to want to talk about politics, and they're not going to want to go to the pub, or you know, that they should just accept that sort of stereotyped role. And I think it is a lot less in young couples. Maybe still some, but ... .

SC.   Don't you find that even if they start together, men and women often separate out?

M.   Ah ha, I noticed that at your mum and dad's silver wedding very much. It's very much the kind of male thing and female thing. I think that's inherently wrong. I mean, what are couples about? I don't think you have to live exactly in each other's pockets, and one of the positive things about the relationship is that it allows each person to grow in lots of ways on their own. But surely it's still about ..., in a social situation or whatever, it's still about – I don't know – being together and communicating.[T91]

    To be absorbed by this other family necessarily therefore meant patterns of interaction often clearly marked by gender. This was not merely something to which an educated and independent young woman in the 1980s might well take exception. In the first place it conflicted directly with the values of jointness and inter-sex partnership so strong in the engagement period – such conflict is indeed to be a theme of the wedding preparations in general. But in addition it was not part of the micro-culture of her own family to the extent that it was of James's. She was therefore encountering its effects within a family context for the first time. There is almost nothing that the period of engagement in all its diversity is bound for every couple to represent, but this beginning to come to terms with the different micro-culture of another family is often likely to be important. Where there are major cultural differences, these may make the engagement period highly problematic, but that is beyond the scope of the present study.

Chapter 3

Learning the lore: planning and the wedding industry

James.   We decided on a period in June from one weekend to the next, including the two weekends, and then we looked at the hall which we were going to book for the reception. We sent the dates and asked them if they could put us in [– this was about nine months ahead –] and we got 25th June from that. We said anywhere between one Saturday and the other, and we were lucky to get a Saturday.

Margaret. And then we booked the church after that. When we went to see about getting it we thought maybe the time for the wedding may be about half past two or three o'clock, and there was already a wedding booked for three o'clock, that had been booked for quite a while, so we had to take it earlier. We're having it at one o'clock. That's quite early.[T26]

J.   The last wedding I can remember really was my aunt's, a long while ago. There have been weddings since, cousins and so on, but I missed them. My aunt's was a long while ago. It was, as my Dad says, the last wedding he was at when there was free drink – the old style wedding actually, when all the drink was free from start to finish.[T26]

M.   We've booked a band [she laughs]. Again, they played at this friend's wedding and they were quite good for ... . They played quite a wide selection of things. They were good for getting people mixing, which is obviously quite good at a wedding. We don't want the two families staring across the hall at each other. So we've decided on them. It was my father booked it. I don't know who it is.

J.   The cake's already ordered, isn't it?

M.   This friend of my mother's, [...] she's making us a cake. She's giving us a cake as a present, you know. [...] She was a neighbour years and years ago and her daughter and I were very friendly, and then they moved away but always kept in touch. She got us the address of the cars as well, which are working out quite reasonable, more reasonable than we thought they would be. [...] So we've booked the wedding car, the bridal car, and we're still trying to make up our mind whether to have a second car, for bridesmaids and parents. The car's costing about £50 odd and if we get the two, that's a hundred.

SC.   What about a photographer?

M.   We're thinking of one that one of my brothers had, who is good. From Hamilton. They're quite well known – they're well known out our way anyway.[T26]

SC.   Will your father be paying, Margaret?

M.   He is. We're doing ... . I'm buying my dress and things like that, and we're trying to get some of the drink, but they're basically doing it. Well, I'm the only daughter and the youngest one of my family, so it's just a wee bit, you know ... – whenever I got married, it would I suppose be something like that. And my father has retired this year, just taken early retirement, so ... he's got a wee lump sum [she laughs]. Which is disappearing rapidly – his security for the rest of his life![T26]

This conversation rehearses a typical series of early decisions and some of the key terms in which they are taken. The decision to set a date launches a couple into a new stage of preparation. From merely talking about it, perhaps only between themselves, they begin now inevitably to involve others in their enterprise. The others are of two kinds. There are family, friends, colleagues, in short their own associates, and there are those who are professionally or as a business involved with marriage and weddings, in short the wedding industry. It is possible to eliminate the former altogether, but the latter are represented at the very least in every marriage by a registrar. The Gretna marriage mentioned in the last chapter shows how a marriage can be made with outside participation limited almost entirely to the people in a registrar's office. More commonly, it is close family who are first involved, then the people who will provide the key services listed by Margaret and James, then other associates who will be actively participating and supporting the couple on the day, then the wedding industry again. Finally the wider range of associates who will be the guests are brought in. And they in turn, through the services they require, call upon the industry again. Pre-wedding events often bring in still more associates, and on the day itself new representatives of the industry are encountered. A wedding, that is to say, is an enterprise which typically draws in an expanding range of people over the period, often lengthy, of its preparation. As an event it is created and shaped by the inputs of all those who become involved and the interactions between them as they collectively progress towards the wedding day.

Escalation is the typical experience through which a normal Glasgow or Scottish wedding is achieved. If it were left to couples themselves there would be many more 'quiet' weddings.

SC.   Is there anything you would like to do differently?

Catherine. Probably a lot quieter. I think I can sincerely say I would have liked, you know, a much quieter and smaller wedding, but again ... – because the alternative was for us to be **paying** for a big wedding and that just seemed out of the question, whereas now it's happening that it's my mum and dad that's giving me my wedding – there are times I'm really looking forward ..., that I'm enjoying all the attention, kind of thing, you know. I mean I'd be fibbing to say otherwise.[T67]

There are some small weddings of course; there are also intending brides and grooms who want from the start to make a big event of it. There may even be the occasional real-life example of the girl who is actually after a wedding more than a husband. But in general couples want one another and to be married, and these are their priorities, whereas for others involved the manner in which these ends are achieved has a relatively much greater significance. This applies even to their own families but more necessarily to the many people who make their living, or a part of it at least, from the wedding industry.

Escalation means increasing cost. It is well known that weddings are expensive, but there are few who go into the preparation of a wedding with any real sense of the enormity of the costs which build up as each apparently small detail is added into the plan. If couples are paying the main costs of the event themselves, more resolute attempts to hold back the escalation are likely to be made. They can scarcely help realising that resources spent on the wedding are resources not available for their future married life, in particular for that major preoccupation of the engagement period, housing. But they are often caught in a double bind here. They may wish to defend parents and others from costs which they see as incurred on their account, but those people themselves are reluctant to rein in their own expectations of the wedding or to be other than conspicuously generous in helping with it. In the event therefore, for much that happens others are paying, even where bride and groom have initially intended otherwise. Any direct relationship between wedding expenditure and impoverishment for the couple which might influence the performance disappears. Indeed to the extent that expenditure on the wedding is balanced by the inflow of household goods and cash in the form of wedding presents – this will be discussed in Chapter 5 – the wedding itself becomes a part of a system of indirect dowry.

Escalation of the scale and complexity of the event is facilitated, therefore, by the way its cost is shifted largely on to others; it is the involvement of these others, and their interests in the occasion, which drive ahead the expansion. In deciding to marry, couples are often initiating a process the control of which moves progressively out of their own hands. This may happen very speedily. Carol had got engaged in July and wanted to be married fast:

SC.   Was that a problem, getting everything arranged so quickly?
Catriona.   Well, if you've a mother like mine it's ... . We got engaged on a
            Saturday and my dad said 'What about the [...] Hotel?' 'Um, very
            nice!'. So we went down on Sunday [– this hotel was outside
            Glasgow –] and it was all booked by the Sunday night. 'Cause we
            wanted to get married in October and that was it. And the [...]
            recommended people, and that was everything. And we didn't
            want to be married in the church, so ... it was easy enough to
            marry ... .
SC.   And the hotel happened to be available?
C.   Well, we're getting married on 22nd. We suggested the 15th. And
            they said 'No,' but had one free the next week. My mum's a
            teacher and it had to fit in with her school holidays, her con-
            venience.[T20]

It may happen a lot more gradually and less strikingly than here, but one way or another a pattern of who will do what in setting the wedding up needs to be established. Once this has happened the couple themselves do not necessarily find themselves playing the dominant or even a leading part.

As well as the personalities concerned, the pattern is affected by who is available and who can and wants to pay. The bride's mother has the main claim here. She may well feel it to be her responsibility, particularly if she also has the practical and financial support of a husband, the bride's father, to call on. Where the mother does not have full-time paid employment and the bride does, or lives in Glasgow or wherever the wedding is to take place and the bride does not, she is likely to be particularly important. Since the young and unmarried are often not invited to family weddings – for reasons to be discussed in the next chapter – mothers are likely to have relevant experience which their daughters lack. They also, as in Margaret's case, far more often than their daughters have associates who are in one way or another relevant and potentially helpful in making arrangements. It is indeed often suggested, and not altogether in jest, that the only wedding a woman gets to arrange as she wants it is her daughter's.

Most often, however, it is some balance of mother and daughter as a team who lead the wedding operations, with roles for others, for the groom, the father of the bride, associates of the mother, and others, to be worked out around them. Where a bride has no mother, or no mother who is able to take an active part, parents on the groom's side are likely to feel a responsibility for helping, at least financially. It is indeed always possible that the groom's family will feel that they should contribute, though the bride's father often then feels honour bound to resist any such suggestion. Outcomes, just who in the end is paying for what, are highly variable, but the bride's parents, as well as being by convention the givers of weddings, were still at the time of the research in most cases the main contributors to the cost of them.

Whoever begins to get things organised quickly finds themselves in greater or lesser degree in the hands of the wedding industry. There are highways and byways here which different organisers explore in varying degree, but for most they fall into three main sections, each with a key figure in charge. The celebrant, the photographer and the reception manager control, or at the least seek to direct traffic through, the stages of the day itself. They all depend upon being chosen initially, the celebrant only slightly less freely than the other two. What they will provide is potentially a matter for negotiation, but they have the confidence of experience and their own clearly formulated procedures giving them a firm basis for persuading clients to want what they will provide. On the day, they command the territory through which the wedding flows and thereby shape its course.

This chapter proceeds by discussing in necessarily brief and abbreviated form the setting up of the first and third of these three major sections and the range of other services needed to support them. For photography there is little to be learned or arranged in advance and the topic is more conveniently treated in Chapter 7 below.

The reception

Dates and times

Once there is an idea of when the wedding is to be held and the kind of wedding it is to be, finding a venue is likely to be the first practical arrangement to be undertaken. Deciding the kind of wedding means establishing whether it is to be religious or civil, whether it is to be celebrated with a reception in the usual Glasgow understanding of that term, i.e. with meal and dance, what kind of numbers attending are to be considered, and what day of the week is wanted. An exact date cannot be fixed without somewhere to hold a reception and someone to conduct the marriage, and, unless the reception is to be at home which is rarely even considered, the former strikes most people as the main constraint. It therefore needs to be dealt with first. Though there are many possible venues, and weddings could be held almost any day of the year and indeed at any time of the day, in practice both cultural expectations and practical advantages lead to a concentration of choices. There is then perceived pressure: 'weddings have to be booked at least a year ahead'. Indeed they do if the reception is to be held on a date and at a place that many others are likely to want too, but a willingness to adjust dates and to choose other than peak periods of the year allow arrangements to be made much more quickly.

In the Glasgow area the pattern of weddings around the year in the early 1980s was simple. It was registered clearly in the bookings of major suppliers in the industry, a leading wedding-cake manufacturer and car-hire firm for instance.[1] From a quiet beginning in December–January, numbers built up steadily to April. In May however, when expectations of good weather and the increasing appeal of holidays might be expected to boost figures, they fell back in what was indeed the usual pattern:

Jan.   We were going to get married in May, and Shuggie's mum went mad and kept saying 'When you get married on the first of June', didn't she?

Shuggie.   That's it! 'Marry in May and rue the day.'[2]

J.   And we said, 'We're marrying in May,' because we had our hearts set on May. Because we'd said it, it kind of stuck in our minds, and also when she started saying 'Marry in May ...,' it was like ... a bit of defiance.[T8]

They stuck to it and were not the only ones to alarm their elders in this way, but the figures show clearly that not all are so bold. After this, numbers rose in June to their high summer level, interrupted only by the Glasgow Fair holiday in the second fortnight of July. With potential guests more likely to be away then than at other times during the summer, some saw this as a time to be avoided. During September there was a definite decrease in activity but business usually held up through October before falling off sharply in November, back to the low mid-winter level.

People may get married on any day of the week, but churches are not available on Sundays and Registry Offices not on Saturdays either. Fridays and Saturdays are the most favoured days, with Saturday the busiest in the churches and Friday in the Registry Office, with two-thirds of civil weddings performed on that day. There is little difference between the remaining days of the week. Friday and Saturday are the normal times to hold parties, and they make sense for a celebration going on late. If guests who need to travel are important to the planning, Saturday allows time for them to arrive and return home again over the weekend. A weekday wedding inevitably asks those invited who are in work to take a day off it, making what is already an expensive event for them a good deal more so. There may be idiosyncratic reasons for choosing an earlier day in the week, or people may be led into it when the place of their choice is not available at an appropriate weekend, but it is Saturday which makes most sense to most people.

The preferred timing for weddings was strikingly illustrated by the practice, until 1983, of the Glasgow Registry Office. Performing about two thousand marriages in the year, the time of the week most in demand there was a Friday evening session from 5.30 to 7.00. This generally booked up first and weddings then were timed at a rate of four per room per hour. For the rest of Friday it was three per hour and for other days two only.[3] The pattern represents a general requirement for a time which will allow participants to go straight on to a dinner-like meal, to be followed by an evening of drinking and dancing. Four o'clock, a typical time for a church wedding, even allows local guests to attend on a weekday at the cost of only an afternoon off work. At an earlier period of greater poverty, evening weddings would allow the couples themselves to attend after work on a Friday and take advantage of the weekend for all the honeymoon that could be afforded. The long-established pattern here had a partial exception for Catholics who wanted a nuptial mass. Before the reforms of the Second Vatican Council in the late 1960s, this necessitated a morning wedding; once afternoon masses were allowed, Catholics as much as others converged on the common timing. The main persisting exception, not so common in Glasgow, is amongst members of the Anglo-Scottish upper class who may follow English timings with a ceremony and reception around the middle of the day.

'The hall'

A number of widely advertised hotels within and around the city were, at the time of the research, the most obvious places for receptions. These might be large establishments with more than one 'function suite', and different sizes of suite, able therefore to accommodate a wedding of almost any size and even to host more than one at a time. The most successful of these were mostly on the fringes of the city or a few miles outside. Each of the generally recognised sections of the city, east, west and south, had its own major hotels of this kind. There was also a range of somewhat smaller but more varied establishments catering for different tastes and sizes of wedding party. In the north for instance, a modern main-road hotel near the edge of the city vied with an older town-centre one in a small, high-status satellite town and with a Victorian mansion in gardens and woods on the edge of the hills a few miles to the north. Each would be suitable for a particular size of wedding party; too much space could be as undesirable as too little.

For such hotels, weddings were a special variety of 'function' for which they would offer a range of menus at prices per head which would include self-contained accommodation for whatever kind of function was envisaged. For weddings they might offer special 'packages': one highly popular establishment, belonging to one of the main Scottish-based hotel chains, offered, for instance, their cheapest function menu, priced normally at £5.50, for a 'Champagne Wedding' at £7.60. This included, besides food and some drink, a changing room and 'toast mastering', a series of other items apparently required, for which someone else somewhere might think to charge separately. Toast mastering meant greeting people on arrival and controlling them through the fixed series of events with announcements. It did not normally mean in Scotland actually proposing the toasts or making speeches of any kind. This hotel's particular and obviously appealing speciality was its 'Complimentary First Anniversary Candlelit Dinner' for bride and groom. Such packages commonly required a minimum of guests eating. For this package eighty was chosen explicitly to push up the average size of wedding parties. This was the hotel's policy; they would indeed on occasion pressure people trying to book prime times far ahead into promising larger numbers than they had been intending. If this size of wedding party were really wanted, however, the £7.60 was undoubtedly a keen price for what was offered. Most hotels would also be pleased to see extra guests joining the party for an 'evening reception', since bar sales throughout a long evening were a major source of anticipated profits. Managers put their average bar-takings at weddings at between £3 and £5 a head.

Though, as will perhaps have been noticed in quotations, there persisted a verbal tendency to refer to the location for any reception as a 'hall', in spite of the industry's 'venues' and 'function suites', a hall was in fact the one clear alternative to a hotel. Hotel weddings and hall weddings were categories often, on a little further reflection, distinguished, though individual establishments might be tricky to fit into them. Clubs, restaurants and the kind of hotel which is primarily a pub might provide some or even most of the facilities offered by the major hotels. Smaller parties which could not, or would not want to, constitute a separate dance of their own might find more suitable accommodation, for instance, in a restaurant. A wedding-cake order list showed about a hundred different venues from the Glasgow area, the bulk of them falling into this intermediate group. Since most were, however, achieving no more than occasional wedding business they accounted for only a small proportion of the five thousand or so weddings to be catered for annually in Glasgow city alone.

Halls of one kind and another are numerous in the city. They belong to the corporation, to tenants' associations, to masonic lodges, to sports clubs, to churches and to bodies of other kinds too. They vary greatly in their attractiveness, the condition in which they are maintained and the facilities they offer. Church halls might seem the obvious choice for wedding receptions, located as they generally are close to churches in which weddings may be held. In practice few were ever used. Many, Catholic halls particularly perhaps, were in such regular use for activities and groups affiliated to the church as to be rarely available, whilst Church of Scotland and most other Protestant halls were ruled out for most people by an official exclusion of alcohol, occasionally of smoking too. To hold a wedding there you would need, as one women who had done so put it, to have 'orange juice toasts and things'.[T24] Teetotal weddings are no commoner in Glasgow than elsewhere.

The main difference between hall and hotel is that all the catering and provision for the meal and for a bar has to be brought in. There have long been caterers in Glasgow specialising in moving into such places, as well as earlier into private houses, and providing full meals and appropriate trimmings for whatever particular event is to be held there. Most halls have some provision for cooking and some have reasonable kitchens, but caterers would in any case bring in whatever may be required. Suitable accommodation for a bar is standard. The final result is not necessarily greatly different to a hotel, but there are two views of the comparison. For many, hall weddings have clear associations of low status, with poor facilities and none of the image of luxury or even extravagance which may be important in the context of a wedding. Others, for whom status is not a major concern, may on the other hand value the hall wedding as freer, as well as more economical:

Jim.   Most of the weddings I've been to ..., I've enjoyed the ones where it's been, you know, halls and people have hired the hall theirself and you're free .... It's, you know, your own thing, as far as things go. Hotel weddings tend to get very ... – the hotel runs the show, you know.

Lisa.   Maybe more relaxed. [...] I think the hotel's a lot ..., you're paying a lot for nothing. You could do it a lot cheaper and just as well. That's what I felt. I think you could get ripped off a lot more easily in the hotel, if you didn't watch.[T44]

Though there are benefits there are also, however, hidden costs in extra organising and jobs needing to be done. For the bar there is certain to be a very considerable saving over hotel prices, but a licence has first to be obtained and someone to provide the stock and to run it arranged. For food similarly, prices will be lower but more arranging will be needed with an outside caterer than with most hotels. The hall wedding is a way therefore of getting the same kind of event but somewhat more economically, at the cost of leaving rather more for the parties themselves to arrange. Hotels were at the time undoubtedly winning out over halls. A casual survey by a local caterer at the time suggested that as many as 20 per cent might contemplate a hall wedding; those who actually held them were probably not more than half that.[4]

Food

Menus will not generally need to be fixed until a few weeks before the wedding when invitations will have gone out and numbers are more or less established. After cost, a major consideration is the unknown but probably various tastes in food of the mixture of guests expected. Both factors combine to keep menus simpler than the plushness of their surroundings might otherwise lead one to expect. The 'Champagne Wedding' package noted above offered an unpretentious meal, though this fact was almost hidden at first glance in an efflorescence of fancy typography. The combination was no doubt carefully calculated: 'Farmhouse broth', roast chicken and apple pie would be acceptable to most, and the addition of 'Coffee and Mints' gives the list a semblance of four courses. In fact four courses had come to be widely expected; to provide only three might be seen as mean.[5]

Here a 'Florida Cocktail' could be added for a few pence more. Lamb would cost an extra pound, beef an extra three. For two pounds more than the basic the menu would break into French. Another hotel of the same group but with a more expensive image offered a similar package with more ambitious menus at much the same prices but with no drink included. The offerings of caterers, though they might tend to be less pretentiously described, were in no way fundamentally different. In such a context any contrast based on class-related values was bound to be limited, though greater financial resources would allow more and more expensive items to be included, and some of the latter might be such as to appeal more to middle- than working-class taste. The measure of difference is suggested by the menus for two receptions attended, one a definitely working-class wedding with a caterer serving the meal in a hall, the other equally middle-class, held at a non-'package' hotel on the shores of Loch Lomond. The former offered a fruit cocktail, a good homemade soup, roast beef cut thickly and served with plenty of assorted vegetables, and a chocolate gateau; the latter, responding in part to ideas of the hostess, added to this pattern a lemon sorbet, called on the menu 'Intermezzo', before the main course of turkey, provided 'Fresh Loch Lomond Salmon' in place of the soup and 'Fresh Strawberries' in place of the gateau.

Drink

The special and various drinks needed for the wedding would also begin to be clarified by dealings with hotels and caterers. An enthusiastic customer for the 'Champagne Wedding' quoted above explained, if not quite accurately:

Carol.   You have sherry, or whisky, when you come in, and there's a champagne toast to the bride ... . It's not champagne; it's sparkling wine. He [the manager at the hotel with whom they had been booking] let that slip. I don't think ...

Angus.   Asti Spumante.

C.   I actually was going to say to him 'I don't like champagne. Could you have Asti Spumante or something like that?' And he actually said, 'It's sparkling wine. It's not champagne.'[T17]

In fact his package included this 'champagne' for a first toast at the cutting of the cake, then table wine for the meal, then the sherry and whisky, and the inevitable orange juice, for the main series of toasts with the speeches at the end of the meal. The quantities for such packages would generally be firmly and somewhat minimally stipulated. 'Champagne' here was an English influence, there being in Scotland little of the automatic association so well established in England. Carol, in reporting what she thought was going to happen, was in fact reverting to the more usual pattern for first drinks.

There are therefore, the planner discovers, four lots of drinks to be thought about. There are drinks when the guests first arrive at the reception. These may be tied to a receiving line: when guests have formally greeted the wedding party, they may be given a drink which is intended to last into the next event when bride and groom cut the cake and are toasted by the company. There is then a question of drink for the meal. It is possible to provide none, guests being left to obtain their own drinks from a handy bar such as is likely to be available in a hotel. More usually though, wine will be provided for the tables, a choice of red or white, either as glasses or bottles or carafes, with varying implications for the lavishness of the supply. What will always be needed, however, is another round of toast drinks. The set of whisky, sherry or orange juice is likely to appear again here; certainly it will be different to the ordinary drink for the meal.

The fourth and final lot of drinks for which provision will need to be made is a bar for the rest of the evening. Drinks might be provided free – this was encountered once in the course of the research – but most people regarded this, as did James quoted at the beginning of the chapter, as no longer a possibility.

Jean.   My father and I were kind of wrestling over the fact that he was wanting a free bar, because in the past **all** his family done this, you see – you know, all my cousins. I mean, I've got cousins older than my daddy, so to speak, and they all done this at their weddings – free bars. But I mean it's a different kettle of fish doing this these days, 'cause it's awfully dear. [...] If the whole of Murdo's side appeared, the bill at the end of the night would be sky-high. I'm not saying they're particularly ..., but they can drink. It doesnae really bother them. They'd just be continually going up to the bar. So we still havenae come to a final agreement, because I don't really agree with **that**. As I say, it's dear enough, maybe two drinks and wine at the table – no' that my family are great wine drinkers but ... – even three drinks. That's a lot of money. So we haven't come to any ... .[T76]

With the elaborate series of drinks around the meal and many people's tastes in drink having become more varied and exotic – some suggest, as drinking has become heavier – the likely cost of all that people will wish to consume has certainly increased to a point considered beyond the capacity of most wedding hosts to provide. Guests must therefore normally buy their requirements for the rest of the evening, at prices which many are bound to regard as inflated if the event is being held in a hotel. Half bottles of spirits may be smuggled in. In a hall, friends or acquaintances might be recruited to run a bar, but it would then normally be difficult to provide anything like the array of possibilities which drinkers had come to take for granted. There was some nostalgia for 'the old days' when a barrel of beer would have sufficed.

The cake[6]

A wedding cake to be cut is, even ahead of a wedding dress for the bride, perhaps the most generally known and essential requirement for celebrating a marriage. No more than a reminder of the cake will therefore need to be provided by hotel or caterer, though the knowledgeable may delay ordering until they have decided on the bridesmaids' dresses so that they can link the cake trimmings to the colour of these. A complete three-tier cake cost, in the early 1980s, from £70 upwards.

The nature of a wedding cake could be clearly specified. Three individual cakes of the same shape but declining size, each made of a dark, rich-fruit mixture and covered with a layer of almond icing or marzipan, with smooth, royal icing covering that, would be the ideal. The iced surface would be white or almost so. On it there would be piped ornamentation in either white or a colour, generally pale, and a number of further ornaments called 'favours', this time inedible, would be attached. The three individual cakes would be mounted one above another on inedible pillars in tiers of declining size, uniting to form **the** cake. The top would be finished with an ornament, centring either on miniature figures of bride and groom or on flowers, artificial or natural.

No actual cake had to conform absolutely to the specification in order to be a wedding cake, though most at the time of the research did so rather closely. Two or four tiers were readily acceptable, and even one tier if decorated in characteristic style would be clearly identifiable. The shape of the individual cakes varied too. Round, the traditional shape as the wedding cake developed between the seventeenth and the twentieth centuries, was still popular, but square had replaced it as the most often seen. A range of other more eccentric shapes were available too, though their generally higher prices might curb enthusiasm for having them.

A wedding cake might be made at home by a keen baker but providing it with decoration of the expected elaboration and polish would defeat most home cooks. There was also a technical problem which the amateur might or might not realise until it was too late: the lower tiers and their icing had to be sufficiently strong to support the pillars for the upper tiers and to do so without making an icing so rock hard as to be impossible to cut. Homemade cakes therefore, and for good reason, formed no more than a small minority of those used.

Music

Music for dancing is the last requirement for the reception to be considered here. For some, matters were simple: a band was what you had and it was just one more costly arrangement which someone had to make. As one young man reported his own and his fiancée's experience at the hotel,

> they said 'Have you got a band?' 'No.' She says, 'Well, we can suggest a couple.' And we were going 'Oh good! We don't know ...'. We didn't even know how much it cost. And she says 'It costs roughly about £125, for four hours of a reasonable, middle-of-the-road band. They'll do almost anything.' And she says, 'If you want, we can arrange one for you.' At which we went 'Ah yes!'[T53]

'Middle-of-the-road' means mainly the ability to play music for any kind of popular dancing. The alternative is something more specialised, a ceilidh band for a Highland style of dancing and participation, for instance. Generally, however, there would be a need for waltzes at beginning and end, often for one or two Scottish country dances such as the Gay Gordons, for a few wedding set-pieces danced almost exclusively by women – with such unlikely names as the Slosh and the Alleycat – and for recent disco-dancing styles. A good band from this point of view is one that 'gets people up'; how busy the dance floor is becomes a major measure of the success of a wedding. Since it is the band leader's responsibility to control this side of the proceedings, his role is crucial, though this is not often explicitly realised at the stage of making arrangements. It is the band as a unit with which people are then concerned and, if they are interested in music at all, with the kind and quality of its playing.

Wedding music is bound in any case to be quite a mixture. For the many who do have an interest and definite tastes in popular music, this presents problems. Experience of dreadful wedding bands is much discussed. One strategy is to go for a disco which will be playing professionally recorded and inevitably more polished music. The selection to be played can also be planned and controlled in advance to a much greater extent than is the case with a live performance. There were at the time of the research disco operators who bid for wedding business, who argued that they could do all that a live band could, and better, and who did get chances to show it. However, bands were still preferred precisely for this live quality, the capacity to respond to the company on the night, a company which is generally acknowledged to consist of people other than the bride and groom and even perhaps like-minded friends. Bands also have what seemed to many with working-class origins another advantage. They readily accommodated the songs which some guests might like to perform and which for them and even for others were often a significant part of the enjoyment of weddings and other party occasions. Since bands necessarily take a break in the middle of the evening, this becomes a moment for guests to have their turn. In addition, many groups are willing, within limits, to do their best to provide backing for singers. Conversely, for those trying to avoid their relatives' contributions, the fact that a disco does not need a break and gives no encouragement to amateurs can be a positive advantage.

For many, however, the problem of wedding music is set precisely by the mixture of generations and tastes in the company to be assembled. A common response, perhaps after hankerings for a disco, is to look for a band, but one of which the couple and the older generation, represented in the first place by their families, can approve.

Jean.   It sound a really dead-pan attitude for your wedding, but it doesnae really matter to me. I would like a disco, because I like disco music and all the rest of it, but I cannae see some of my aunties at sixty-odds getting up to a disco, even if it was an Engelbert Humperdinck or something like that. So, as I say, we've got a few names, but ... .[T76]

The ceremony

A basic decision, and usually perhaps the first one to be taken, is whether the ceremony is to be religious or civil. Most first-marriers go for a religious service, either because they believe in Christian marriage or, being indifferent to religion themselves, see no reason either to forgo a standard part of the procedure and the associated photographs or to disappoint their families in the matter. Taking one's turn at the Registry Office, with its restricted accommodation and often far-from-picturesque location, generally needs rather more justifying.

A civil ceremony, if that is chosen, is always brief and relatively simple. It may be slightly elaborated according to the inclinations of the particular Registrar, but there is nothing about it for the couple to decide beyond whether to have a ring or rings. Though not legally required, they are expected. One registrar would say: 'These rings are given and received as pledges of love and fidelity. They are tokens of accepting the responsibilities of marriage.' What such responsibilities might be would necessarily remain unexplored. Some further echoes of traditional Christian language are likely, in what one registrar described as 'padding', additional to the simple declarations and pronouncement legally required. There will be no vows as such. After his pronouncement of marriage, the same registrar would tell the groom he might kiss the bride – but not if they were Muslims, he noted.

Setting up a religious ceremony is an altogether more variable and some-times complex procedure. The celebrant is not responsible for ensuring that a couple may legally be married – that is for the Registrar – but he or she has to be willing to conduct the marriage. The first step is therefore seeing a minister or priest with the request. It may even be necessary to book church and celebrant as long ahead as the reception, though for two reasons the pressure tends to be less. In the first place, the parish system spreads demand rather more evenly across the facilities available, and in the second, since the ceremony takes much less time than the reception, further bookings for the same day can often be fitted in before or after. There are, however, exceptions here. Mainly because of the pattern of past migrations in the city, there are areas with concentrations of people of marrying age, and hence churches busy with weddings on summer weekends, and other areas with few potential marriers in which a wedding is seldom seen. A few special places such as the cathedrals and the University chapel have particular attractions for the organisers of such events and may therefore sometimes need to be booked far in advance.

These exceptions aside, for Church of Scotland marriages it is usual to go to the minister of the parish in which the bride lives, but there is no compulsion to do so. Indeed, in older established areas of the city parish boundaries are far from obvious. As was discussed in Chapter 1, historic patterns of division and amalgamation, movements of population, and the characters of particular churches and particular ministers mean that regular members of congregations often live outside the official boundaries. Ministers in their manses are often outside too. In this situation the emphasis comes to be on the minister rather than the parish, and ministers with whom either party has a personal link of any kind are likely to be favoured. Any minister may therefore be approached and may agree; if this is not the parish minister, he should be informed. This will be necessary in any case if the parish church is to be used. There are fees to be paid, locally set and sometimes distinguishing between members and non-members. Typically these are for the Church Officer or Beadle who looks after the practical arrangements on the day, for an organist, for a flower arranger, to whom the whole business of providing flowers for the church may sometimes be handed over, and for heating and lighting too. The celebrant appears to be making the charge, and only those well informed on church matters are likely to realise that he or she receives none of it. It can on occasion be a bone of contention: faced with a demand for £50 at the rehearsal the night before, one financially hard-pressed and non-church-going couple argued the fee down to £20. A better informed and perhaps middle-class couple may sometimes make the minister a small gift.

Catholic weddings are free, though here a small gift, discreetly contained in an envelope, is far more regularly handed to the priest. With a few exceptions, the bride's parish priest – the 'PP' – has the right to celebrate. He will, in large parishes, often delegate the right to one of his assistant priests, and he may give permission for another priest of the couple's own choosing to perform the marriage elsewhere or in his own parish church. There are no prescribed formalities for arranging a Church of Scotland ceremony, but for a Catholic there are. A 'Prenuptial Inquiry' has to be completed, generally by the priest who is to officiate. This will establish whether dispensations of any kind need to be obtained from the bishop, as in the many instances where one party is not a Catholic, 'mixed marriages' that is to say.

Couples who are in such a situation or who are out of touch with the church may be apprehensive in approaching the minister or the priest, not knowing what kind of reception to expect.

Barbara.   I phoned up the Catholic church where my parents live, the one which my primary school was actually attached to, and I got the housekeeper, not a priest. I phoned her to say I was getting married and would like to come down to chat to a priest and she said 'Fine! Come down and bring your baptismal certificate and your fiancé's. He is a Catholic?' I said, 'No.' 'Oh well!' I thought, if that's the attitude of the housekeeper, I'm not interested.

Donald.   She probably rules the roost, eh.

B.   Yes, she probably does rule the roost, a wee Irish lady ... .[T13]

Experience with priests themselves is usually very different.

Shuggie.   I went in one Sunday after mass, to see him. He's hardly ever met me but he knew my name, because he'd ..., they have their own wee beats. They patrol certain parts of the parish. And – well, not patrol but they go and visit the houses now and again. But we're part of 'the lost quarter', but he does know my name. And, when I walked in and gave him my name, he just matter-of-fact looked at ..., took all the details. And he asked about Jan, and said 'Is she a Catholic?' And I said 'No,' and I thought, here we go! Crunch! But he just matter-of-factly wrote down all the details, said 'That'll be no problem. Come back and see me nearer the time.' And that was it. So all we have to do is get all the ..., Jan's got to get her baptismal lines from somewhere. And I've got to dig mine out.[T8]

They were told to go back again a month before the date. When they did:

Jan.   He was really nice, wasn't he? He was really nice to us.

S.   He went all through ... . There are various forms you have to fill out.

J.   He explained it all.

S.   He's a pretty nervous man himself, but I think he went out of his way to make us relax.

J.   We were in there for over an hour, weren't we?

S.   Yes, ages.

SC.   What was there to explain?

J.   There wasn't really all that much. The main thing he stressed was that marriage must be insoluble.

S.   Yeah. He was very certain about the insolubility thing. He was also talking about, you know, any children we have should be brought up as Catholics, kind of thing. He has to be clear on that as well, but he was pretty ..., you know, he wasn't heavy handed or ... .[7]

            He's an Irish priest and, you know, you fear the worst when you go to see them, but he was really good.[T57]

He also, on this occasion, talked to them about the service and gave them a copy of the Nuptial Mass book. A rehearsal was arranged for the evening before the wedding.

This is the other part of what may transpire. That there are choices offered in the text of the Nuptial Mass and official encouragement to personalize the rite was noted in Chapter 1 above. Priests may or may not in practice encourage couples to think about alternatives and discuss preferences, and couples may or may not be keen to do such things. There is potentially a lengthy and complex service here; it can be expanded still further or considerably contracted as the couple and/or the priest – and far more often the latter – feel appropriate. As will be seen in Chapter 6, James and Margaret were keen to elaborate their service in just the ways that Brenda wanted to avoid:

Barbara.   I just want the thing kept really simple, and I don't want there to be too many people doing different things, you know. I mean, I've been to weddings where you've had, you know, your best man and your ushers, and then somebody else comes from the congregation to do a reading, and then someone comes from the back of the church to bring forward the offertory procession, and then three wee cousins are all altar boys ... . From having something which is supposed to revolve round the two people, you've got this show of twenty-five folk doing the cabaret. It really does just get out of hand. So, I mean, we've just kept it quite simple.[T42]

Seeing a minister is likely to be a somewhat different experience. Though priests are very aware that many coming to them are not religiously active, and may indeed have two generations of no more than nominal church membership behind them, being Christian is for their Church essentially a matter of having been baptised. The system of Catholic schooling in the West of Scotland also ensures that most of those who are in any sense Catholics will have had some contact with priests and with Catholic belief. They tend therefore to assume the religious suitability of those who come to them unless conclusively shown otherwise. Ministers tend to be more aware of the very marginally Christian qualifications of many coming to them, though they vary in their response to it. Some feel they need to ask outright of strangers who appear, usually at a 'vestry hour', a minister's surgery held one evening in the week, whether they believe in God. On occasion someone will say no, or make clear in the course of some less direct enquiry that this is the case. The minister will then feel obliged to refuse to marry them.

For some, however, it is not so much basic belief as Christian marriage which is the focus.

Minister.   There is no profession of faith in the service. They don't have to be Christians in that sense, but they must be intending to establish a lasting home and willing to acknowledge God's place in it.

Or as another minister put it, they must 'see God as coming into their marriage somewhere'. Many will, if in doubt, refer to the rival attractions, and greater economy, of the Registry Office. But, either because people do have residual Christian beliefs, or because in such a situation they are mostly ready to play along with requirements which most ministers will not pitch too high, causes for outright refusal are rarely experienced. Sometimes an obligation to attend church in the weeks preceding the wedding may be laid on the couple; occasionally they themselves feel this is appropriate even where the minister is not pressing them to do so. It would be 'cheek' just to take advantage of the church for the celebration and to ignore it otherwise.

As regards the second part of seeing the minister, the preparation for the service itself, the 'personalising' theme so clear in the Catholic case appears, but, lacking official backing, less often. Ministers, indeed, are less likely to draw attention to the text to be used. If choice is offered at all it has one clear focus in the vows. These may in the Church of Scotland be recited clause by clause after the minister, as in the Catholic Church, but they may also be put in the form of a question from the minister to groom and bride in turn, to be answered by each, 'I do'. The latter is easier for a nervous couple, minimising the contribution they are required to make. If offered, it is often thankfully accepted. Some ministers may also use their freedom to invent text to try to put in something which will be particularly meaningful for the couple. One minister keen on making the service really 'theirs' gave an example. If in talking to a couple he found that the experience of looking at one another across a crowded room and feeling on exactly the same wavelength was precious to them, he might include in the service: 'As they look at each other over the years ...'. This would mean something special to them but not seem odd to all the sisters and cousins and aunts there. He would also try to select biblical readings which would be meaningful for the individuals concerned, though there might also be consultation about this.

The stress even in this case was on the minister's decision. 'Leaving it to the minister' is perhaps the most general theme. It is perhaps almost inevitable in dealing with those who have little relevant religious background. As Sandra, herself religiously inactive but from a Catholic family and marrying an equally inactive Protestant, explained:

> I asked what kind of service it was going to be, you know. But he never said, like, you know, 'You'll need to pick your hymns', or anything like that. He just said, it's just going to be a straight-forward service. And it'll no be any chitchat or anything. It'll just be ...

DM.   What does he mean, there won't be any 'chitchat'?

S.   You know, like a big long sermon thing. It'll just be a normal ... . We'll come in and he'll say a few words, and then he'll marry us.[T87]

But even with the well informed the line may not be very different.

Richard.   We had two meetings with him beforehand to discuss it. The first one was just generally getting all the details. The second one was a meeting to go through what happened in the service. And he told us exactly ..., he says, 'Don't invent anything. **Do exactly what I tell you,** You will stand where I tell you. You will move when I tell you. I will lead you in. I will lead you out. It means you don't have to worry about getting anything wrong. Just do what I say.'[T53]

A final aspect of seeing the minister is a much greater likelihood than with priests of encountering someone who feels a responsibility for the arrangements of the wedding outwith the episode in church. Ministers in parishes where weddings are at all numerous often have typed sheets of hints and requirements which they give out to those who come to book a date with them.[8] As well as the matters to do with the service itself, these are likely to cover the procedure for the Registry Office and for the rest of the celebrations. They aim to provide a substitute for the kind of wedding etiquette books to be found in libraries. These, as one such sheet noted, 'do not describe accurately the normal Scottish practice for either service or reception'. This is hardly surprising since they emanate from England, and 'at the best of times lead folk into more expense'. They 'should now be totally disregarded as being out of date and misleading'. The same document recommended not throwing money on the road 'on the grounds of road safety'; it discussed arrangements for inviting the minister to the reception and for speeches there; and it emphasised the need for a supply of soft drinks, for those who do not want alcohol, for the 'under age', and for those driving: 'It is a sad end to a wedding where some guest is killed by a drunk driver.'[N13]

Music is normally required for a wedding and the general pattern is much the same in both Catholic and Protestant weddings. Indeed, in so mixed a religious community as Glasgow it is possible sometimes to find the same organist playing for both. The general expectation is that the organ will be played before the service when people have assembled but are awaiting the bride. What to play is normally left to the organist and varies considerably according to her or his particular taste. Music for the bride's entrance, for hymns, and for the procession out after the signing of the documents are, on the other hand, usually offered to the couple as choices to be taken in consultation either with minister/priest or with the organist. Even people who would feel entirely out of their depth if asked to select a reading may be happy to choose a couple of, perhaps favourite, hymns, though there are those who baulk even at this. Occasionally hymns are chosen because they appear on some printer's standard Order of Service or on a hymn sheet which someone happens to have available to photocopy. Some couples, on the other hand, want to develop this side of their wedding much more extensively. This may emerge from a scheme of meaningfulness of their own, such as choosing items to make a link to parents' weddings or particular tastes, or in terms of their own sense of the importance of the music, or, perhaps most commonly, just to make a grander event of it. There is rather more scope for such elaboration in the procedures of the Nuptial Mass than in the much briefer Church of Scotland service, though there a sung blessing was becoming increasingly popularly, adding an extra, if short, musical item to the regular pattern.

Despite the often successful efforts of organists and ministers, the Bridal March from Wagner's opera *Lohengrin* and Mendelssohn's 'Wedding March' remain the most popular choices for entrance and exit respectively. Choosing anything else is always choosing against this established pair. Hymn singing is always a problem with non-religious congregations; the wedding with vigorous singing is therefore quite an exception and ministers may even congratulate congregations on it when it occurs. In the Church of Scotland it is indeed often the minister's voice alone which avoids total inaudibility. In such circumstances ministers, if given the chance, encourage simple and widely-known hymns and may try to curb unrealistic musical ambitions.

And all the rest

Ceremony and reception are the main elements of the day to be planned. As has been seen, they may be planned in careful detail for the particular marriage or much may be left to the main professionals involved, the celebrant and the hotel manager with a 'package'. Around and between these events photography and transport always need to be separately arranged, and there are other items too, flowers and stationery in particular, which are bound to be partially separate. Photography, as was mentioned above, is to be held over to Chapter 7. Stationery was chiefly notable for the ever-lengthening list of items on offer and for the scarcity of designs with any reference to or even appropriate for a Scottish wedding. Specialised stationers in England had been learning from transatlantic practices to promote this very length. Suites of specially printed items, harmonised in design, had been developed and were marketed via sample books in the same way as wall-papers. They involved special printing techniques, embossing and the use of metallic foils, and were ordered in small runs economic only for printers specializing in such work. At least partly for this reason, nearly all came from England.

Flowers demand more attention. They are needed for the church, for tables at the reception, for bouquets for the bride and bridesmaids, and for corsages and buttonholes. Providing for the church may mean simply paying a small fee to the ladies who normally arrange flowers for services. This would then be used to supplement what would have been there anyway. Many middle-class mothers of brides and indeed brides themselves for whom flowers are important are, however, keen to go further. They may belong to or have friends who belong to local flower-arranging clubs who will be keen to put on a good display in the church; alternatively, they will pay professional florists to do the job. Since large numbers of flowers are needed to make an impression within the spacious settings of most churches, this is inevitably costly. For tables, floral decoration may well include artificial flowers, of which very limited use is made in church. Most often they will in any case be provided by the hotel or caterer as part of the package. Bouquets, corsages and buttonholes are part of the proper equipment of the actors for the day and will be noted again in the following chapter. There may also be flowers decorating wedding cakes and on the back shelf of wedding cars. Flowers are therefore a major requirement for weddings and there is one clear pattern here. The materials for fulfilling it are, however, not so uniform. Indeed, this is one of the few areas in which values clearly correlated with social class diverge.

There are two approaches, associated with working-class and middle-class orientations respectively. On the one hand flowers can be seen merely as contributing to a colourful and lavish show. There need be no scruples about the use of artificial flowers, foliage and such spectacular additions as large feathers in bright colours to make up what are essentially visual ornaments. A florist with a predominantly working-class clientele reported that four out of five bouquets he prepared were artificial. Magi-silk was the in thing, he said, and had many advantages. You could match shades exactly to bridesmaids' dresses; with fresh flowers, you might order pink roses for a Friday but you could never know exactly what shade would arrive. Artificial flowers could be kept and used as ornaments; you could even wash them. Fresh flowers, in contrast, begin their preparation by losing their stems. They then have to be wired and stapled, and are therefore dying from the moment they are made up. All the flowers had to do, he thought, was to contribute to the overall appearance on the day. Freshness and scent are not important to people.

Middle-class enthusiasm, on the other hand, does focus on the freshness and fragrance of flowers. Artificial flowers are to be avoided as far as possible and feathers are anathema. A florist in the suburban and largely middle-class west of the city had a contrasting story to tell. This shop would do artificial flowers only if there were some exceptional reason – such as the bride suffering from hay fever. They were not generally asked for them anyway. They might occasionally mix silk lily-of-the-valley into bouquets of real flowers. This was useful in the winter. They would tell the bride about it, but nobody else would notice the difference. In contrast to some other sections of the wedding trade, here they were clear that those with most money spent most on this particular contribution to the wedding. As for church flowers, a single arrangement, a large vase, cost at the time £20 or £25, and to make a real splash as many as five big arrangements and flowers for the ends of the pews would be needed. The cost would be in the order of £170. In the working-class area the florist had bemoaned the fact that **his** customers begrudged even £10 for the church flowers.

Flowers are used, therefore, to create a show and to mark the specialness of the event, though the importance attached to decorating the interior of the church varies. It may be that, for those who never enter a church except on such occasions, there is neither a need for decoration to make it special nor much sense that the setting itself is part of the show. The middle-class orientation, it may be noted, is also attaching to flowers an additional dimension of meaning which is otherwise absent. This would not be articulated, particularly in the wedding context, and is difficult to pin down though it has a rich expression in the literary heritage. It is the sense of fragrance, fragility, impermanence, the sense of flowers as living things which bud, blossom and, unavoidably, die. It is this that gives 'fresh flowers' a value over and above the display objects and material for artistic creation which they undoubtedly also are.

We saw at the beginning of this chapter that Margaret and James were hoping to get away with one wedding car only. More usually, and even when distances are very short, the moving around of the principal actors is thought to require at least two cars. The main one is 'the bridal car'. This is decked out with white ribbons from windscreen to bonnet across the front and a white sheet over the back seat. There are also often plastic flowers arranged on the back shelf, though, as will be expected, firms aiming for a more middle-class market may avoid this. The bridal car transports the bride and her father, or whoever is giving her away, from home to church, and the bride and groom between the church and reception, sometimes by way of a photographic session in some picturesque spot *en route*. This car always arrives last at the church and leaves first. Firms making a speciality of providing wedding cars compete chiefly in terms of the eye-catching nature of this car. One may offer a vast limousine in which, in contrast to the ordinary car in which the bride will need to squeeze and shuffle along the seat, she can walk to and from her place 'with style and elegance'. Another may offer a white or a silver Rolls Royce, another a vintage one; another chooses maroon bodywork, the better to set off the white-dressed bride. One Glasgow company had the ultimate in number plates: WED 2. Drivers are invariably uniformed and may be equipped with such accessories as large white umbrellas for rainy days.

Besides this obviously special car, another car or cars will ferry the other principal actors, particularly the bride's mother and the bridesmaids who have to leave home before the bride. Such other cars usually match the bridal car in colour and uniformed driver but are clearly less special. A bus is very often provided too, to take guests from the church to the reception. Even if they have cars – and Glasgow is a city in which the proportion of cars to population has always been relatively low – it is expected that, with alcohol certain to flow freely at the reception, many will want to leave them at home.

Cars are one of the wedding businesses in which it is common to remark that money and a willingness to spend it do not necessarily go together. This is not simply a matter of smart cars being of most interest to those who have least everyday experience of them. One firm bought a vintage Rolls in 1981, thinking of it as an attraction in exploiting the middle- and even upper-class end of the market. They found it going out in fact as often to the vast and almost entirely working-class peripheral housing schemes of Glasgow, to Castlemilk and Drumchapel, as to the leafy suburbs of the west and south.

Conclusion

This chapter has seen the enterprise initiated by the decision to hold a wedding move out into the multifarious hands of the wedding industry. Learning what is involved in holding a wedding is at the same time a matter of coming to terms with the wide range of those who have established for themselves a piece of the action and who have a constant interest, in an overwhelmingly commercial society, in expanding requirements. At times there is consumer resistance, but the need to do things properly and to make a show is the industry's ally. Its secret weapon is the spreading of the cost away from the couple marrying on to others predominantly of the senior generation and in particular on to parents who will be spending not only for themselves, but for their child too.

Chapter 4

Casting, dressing and participation

The bride and her dress

Margaret. My mum came with me. She was sitting there with tears in her eyes [she laughs]: 'With those tears in your eyes, I'll take this one! It must be the right one.'[T59]

A bride is a woman in the process of getting married. This is an adequate operational definition; it would be sufficient to enable someone to use the term correctly in English. It is quite inadequate, however, for the cultural significance of the term. At the cultural level a girl – almost always so termed – becomes an embodiment of an important symbolic idea, the bride, when she is appropriately dressed and on her wedding day. In this sense the outfit is essential to the bride. Securing the outfit is a fundamental requirement, and its main component, the wedding dress, becomes very special. This is widely recognised in the way it is treated when it is being acquired, before the wedding and even after. Occasionally it is even put into words:

Mother.   It was a beautiful dress.
SC.   It's a pity you can't enjoy it several times.
Mother.   That would defeat the purpose!
Catriona. They're holy!
Mother.   That's right. They're a kind of symbol. It's different.
C.   It belongs to the day.[T43]

A wedding dress is not therefore simply a dress in which a woman is married; it is a dress uniquely associated with her as a bride on that occasion, a dress which is a key part of the way in which she embodies the idea of a bride. The characteristics of the dress are crucial therefore. A woman getting married does not have to wear such a dress. She can distance herself from the bridal frame of reference by avoiding any hint of such a dress. It will not then be a 'white wedding' she is having; it will almost certainly be a 'quiet' wedding. A woman may also play with aspects of the bridal scheme, by having an outfit which makes reference to it but avoids adopting the full specification. Whatever she does, however, will be seen in relation to the standard, meaning will be read into it and her actions will be judged accordingly.

A standard of this kind was certainly alive in the thoughts of people participating in the study and in their discourse. It was constantly reinforced by experience. It was of a particular kind of dress, that is to say a garment with a fitting top and an attached skirt. The skirt would be long, reaching down to the wearer's feet, and the whole garment would be made of white fabric. It was to be worn with a veil attached to the top of the head, usually by means of some kind of circlet, and providing an extra diaphanous layer of fabric around the back of the head and falling to the shoulders or below. A woman would be instantly recognisable as a bride in such an outfit. The majority of first-marriers were conforming to it without question or qualification.

Such a standard is, it has to be stressed, an idea. It is not any particular specimen created on the basis of the idea. It cannot have the fixity or the possibility of duplication which is a characteristic of objects. It is necessarily susceptible to changes of emphasis, to greater or lesser elaboration and to shifting boundaries. The implications for variation, interpretation and change are important.

It means in the first place that much variation is possible without exciting any sense that the idea of the wedding dress is being challenged. The shape of the skirt for instance, though important for the general appearance of the bride, seems able to vary over time by a process of largely unremarked drift. When variation is remarked, however, it may evoke two kinds of response. Permissible variants or ranges of variation may be recognised, treated as exceptions which prove the rule. Colours departing significantly but slightly from white are an important instance to which we shall return. Other kinds and degrees of variation may on the other hand generate unease:

Cathy.   It's nice, it's nice, but it's no ... . It doesn't – I don't know – it doesn't look like a bride. D'you know how a bride, you expect a long dress, all the trail and veil and all that. You expect that, I mean ... . You see someone with three-quarter length, it does look different, but it's nice. And she'll be ..., she's petite, so she'll be, she'll be a nice bride ...[T38]

A dress shorter than the standard is felt here to be testing the boundaries of the wedding-dress concept.[1]

Responses of this kind are part of constraints which limit variation, a price in qualified approval which anyone choosing to be different in such a way will soon find themselves paying. At the same time they cause observers such as Cathy, herself a bride-to-be, to think about and formulate their conceptions of the standard, thus reinforcing it for themselves and for others. Change may by such means be held back but never altogether prevented. Eccentric examples may impress others to the extent of producing imitation, even at some cost in withheld approval; today the media and advertising are the most obvious sources for such innovation, though their influence is often less in practice than their pervasiveness might lead one to expect. In such a way individual initiatives and chance innovations may graduate from being sources of unease to acknowledged variants or even directions of change for the standard itself.

Colour offers, as has been noted, a prime example of acknowledged variants. Any radical divergence from white destroys people's sense that what they are looking at is 'really' a wedding dress. But the kinds of near-white which are called ivory, off-white, champagne or cream represent permissible variation. Very pale pink or blue or peach would be marginal. What this means is not that the former can be used on the same basis as white. Permissible variants may indeed be used without raising doubts as to the nature of the garment, but, whereas no justification for having a white dress is called for – that choice can be made without a second thought – justification will be needed for anything else. People can be expected to try to read a reason or purpose behind what will be taken to be a choice against white, and a need to explain is generated.

Special force is given to this particular need by the presence of a pattern of ideas which associates the white of the dress with purity or virginity. Whereas wearing a white dress is predominantly following custom rather than making any statement about one's own condition – though a visibly pregnant bride in white may excite unease, distaste and even snide comments – choosing not to wear white risks being read as indeed asserting that the purity of white would be inappropriate for the self wearing it. It is often commented, with something of the same implication, that such a dress will be indistinguishable from white on the photographs. The need to explain, that is to say, will not go beyond the day itself, but up to that point explanation is felt frequently to be called for. Incorporating 'antique' lace which is not white, or being made of 'natural silk' which was often said not to be either, were two particular explanations encountered. By far the most popular line, however, was that the shade chosen for the dress was kinder than sheer white to the complexion of the wearer, that the girl in question 'did not suit white' and that this therefore was the only conclusion which should be drawn from her failure to wear it.

A wedding dress is therefore far from merely personal clothing, and the ways in which it is acquired tend to be very different too. It is striking how often buying the dress brings the bride back into dependence on her family. Shopping for the dress with one's mother may, as was sometimes suggested, have become less common than in the past, but that brides who have been buying their own clothes for years before getting married should so often involve their mothers at this point is highly significant. Catriona's mother was at home recuperating from an operation when she went with her sister to choose her dress. As soon as one was found, she summoned her mother by telephone. Arriving in a taxi at the shop door, she then sat while her daughter paraded before her and secured her approval.[T20, 40] Paying, likewise, does in the end frequently involve the family in one form or another. There may be a certain competition here. Girls reason, though not presumably to their parents, that only by paying for the dress themselves can they be free to choose what they really want without either worrying about the amount they are adding to their parents' burdens or having to bow to their mothers' preferences. Fathers, however, are sometimes particularly keen to pay for this so obviously special and personal item of their daughter's wedding expenses. It may also be simply absorbed into the family's contribution to wedding expenses.

Other aspects of the way in which the dress is bought also show its exceptional nature. A girl is expected to identify closely with her dress, to choose the one which is just right for her, but the bases for this choice and identification are a little mysterious. It is such an exceptional garment and has such slight connection with anything which would be chosen and worn for any other occasion that individually meaningful criteria are few. Colour is almost eliminated as a factor, and shape, length and what it is to be worn with are largely predetermined. It is indeed often bought far ahead of the event and in a different season. Fashions do of course change.[2] Every spring, the trade tries to generate excitement with allegedly new styles, but the significance of this is limited. In the first place there are many designs designated 'classic' to suggest that they are unchanging; in the second, few outwith the specialised trade and possibly photographers have the experience and interest to register such changes of fashion anyway. Choosing a dress is not therefore the normal process of choice guided by some balance of taste, fashion, the sense of self-presentation, the need to fit items together to make an outfit, and expectations and limits as regards cost. As with all other items of specialised wedding expenditure, people here are almost always moving beyond the zone in which they normally operate and make judgements on the basis of their own experience. Buying a wedding dress is something quite different.

The wedding trade had, at the time of the research, become increasingly specialised in order to capitalise on this distinctiveness. Wedding dresses were no longer for the most part one of the many lines carried by large department stores. They had become the central item in outlets designed to celebrate the specialness of the wedding dress and to draw maximum profit from it. The ways in which the choosing, buying and the subsequent handling of the dress were conducted no doubt took their cues from already existing attitudes and expectations, but they themselves added substantially to its ritualisation.

Margaret had bought her dress in a smart and successful city-centre shop.

The owner gave her view of the choosing process:

> We try to impress upon the girls that they should just be enjoying
> themselves. I mean, it should be fun. And we do have a laugh! And
> we just say to the girls, you know: 'Look through ...' – we've got
> catalogues, eh, albums that we've made up – 'look through all the
> dresses. Try on as many as you want. Enjoy it! Don't be sort of
> uptight and scared to try them on, or whatever.' So we have a
> great time.

Often many are tried on, with assistants attending to customers sometimes
for hours at a time. Trying on may take place in several shops on a number of
occasions. What, however, was again striking in the research was how often
girls returned to the first or almost their first choice. Where the grounds for
choice are few, the first dress tried may perhaps become a standard by which
subsequent possibilities are judged.

But the dress tried first has not been chosen at random. It may have been
picked out in a magazine or at a wedding show and sought in the shops. Since
manufacturers are not numerous – labels are more so – any given dress may
sometimes be found in a number of different shops. Less consciously, resonances set up with dresses seen in the past, whether at weddings attended, or
television weddings, or even royal weddings, clearly also have a part to play.
This became clear in Margaret's case. Anne, a childhood friend, had been
married two years before. Her very successful wedding provided, as far as the
reception was concerned, a direct precedent for her own. Anne's mother was
indeed the donor of the wedding cake and helped in many other ways with
arrangements; with the dress, however, she had nothing to do. But it turned
out that

> M.   We'd exactly the same style. In fact I tried Anne's on in the shop. It
>   was ... . I tried two on, and one I got and another one which is
>   exact..., well, almost the same style, trivial differences except it
>   was made from different material. Anne's was made from heavy
>   embroidered cotton, and mine was made from tulle. The tulle was
>   kind of lighter and kind of sparkled a wee bit. And, em, after I'd
>   bought it – although I knew it was the style of dress I wanted –
>   after I'd bought it it occurred to me that it was like Anne's. [...]
>
>   I remember thinking it was funny that, you know ... . Mrs
>   McDonald at the time Anne got married was saying how she got it
>   in [another branch of the same shop] in Aberdeen, her dress, and
>   she went into the shop and she tried it on, and the woman had said
>   it was just her dress, just her dress. I remember thinking when I
>   realised that it was the same dress, thinking this is really funny,
>   because Anne and I are totally unalike. You know, Anne's tall and

dark, and very different features from me and I'm much smaller and fair. Anne and I would never have worn the same kind of clothes. And here we were with almost identical wedding dresses. And of course in [the shop] they had told me that it was just my dress as well.[T116]

The selling process is therefore working to create an identification between the particular woman and her dress, a relationship for which, with mass production of particular models, the bases available are slight. The process continues too. In this particular shop, the dresses to be tried on were used as patterns; **the** dress was to be got in fresh. Two fittings at intervals would ensure its exact adjustment to the girl for whom it was meant. Even if the procedure is not everywhere quite this elaborate, the dress is usually then kept in the shop until near the wedding date and when finally it is taken away by the bride, sight of it is more or less carefully controlled. Keeping the dress from the groom until the day is a common theme; the shop he will probably have kept clear of anyway.

Margaret. I'd left James outside. I felt I couldn't take him into a bridal shop, you know. I mean, all in all we're not too bothered, but I thought I couldn't take him in. I thought I just had to go in and collect it, but the woman had taken out the wrong Rafferty. And they give it an iron before they give it to you, so I had to wait while she ironed it. [To James] You had to wait outside.

James. Very embarrassing, hanging about outside a bridal shop. Because the two shops on either side of it ...

M. ... there's nothing you could look at.

J. [...] It's OK for girls to gaze into [the bridal shop] window.

M. Of course it's OK for girls![T91]

J. I've never got to see the dress though. I've not seen the dress properly.

M. You did see the dress. I showed it you in the house.

J. We kept that tradition going for a long while.

M. Yes. Well, there wasn't really a chance for you to see it because it was in the shop. But you saw it yesterday. [This was ten days before the wedding.][T91]

A bride, therefore, is expected to identify strongly with **her** dress, but the evidence suggests that this is not, as sometimes with other clothes, because it represents her taste, her personality, her choice. It is special for her because and almost exclusively because it is the dress for her wedding. Her special relationship with it is asserted in the ways which have been considered from the time that she first comes into contact with it. Since it is the unity of her in the dress which is going to make her in the fullest sense the bride, this is not surprising. It is this unity which is in reality being kept for the wedding day; most grooms would in any case be hard pressed to distinguish one wedding dress from another. But the dress can stand in anticipation and again in retrospect for the wedding-day bride, an important and widely meaningful cultural creation. For the particular woman who became its latest exemplar, the dress can stand for her pre-married independence, for the way all must wait on her appearance in the church, for her starring role on that day and the excitement of it.

Such a pattern of ideas and practices inevitably makes anything other than buying a new dress of one's own problematic. Even buying a bargain dress may be a matter for mixed feelings.

Aileen.   I got to the wedding dresses – that was the last thing. And I just looked through the rails [in a large city-centre department store] and I didn't see anything I liked at all, and the woman said, 'Oh, what about one of these over here?' and I saw it, and I liked it. I shouldn't really tell you how much it cost, but I will tell you and you won't believe it – £15.

DM.   You're joking!

A.   [...] I mean, I was prepared to pay for my dress, 'cause I thought, well you can't really afford to scrimp. I wasn't going to go £300 or anything, but you know, I thought, well, I'll have to pay quite dear for a ..., but when I found out how much it was .... And I mean I really liked it – I wouldn't have taken it if I hadn't liked it, you know. But the fact – that was a bonus – the fact that it was .... So we just took it [- she was with her mother]. I really hate telling people, you know, 'cause I feel ... – you know £15, you can't even sometimes buy a day dress for that, you know an ordinary ....

DM.   Exactly.

A.   But ... so long as you sort of keep it a wee secret.[T37]

The alternatives to buying new are either a secondhand dress or hiring. Secondhand means either handed on within the family or bought. At the time of the research, advertisements for dresses did appear in the small-ad columns of local newspapers, and for some the possibility of selling afterwards was a way they were able to reconcile themselves to the cost of a new dress. Relatively few dresses appeared to be being recycled in this way though, since most brides wanted in the end to keep the dress. Dresses might also be hired, but whereas male dress-hire was entirely open and widely displayed, female hire, and particularly of wedding dresses, tended in the city at least to be a little surreptitious. The hiring out of high-quality and expensive dresses, as a way not of saving money but of obtaining something to wear which was more exclusive than could have been bought, hardly as yet existed. What were available were dresses of similar prices to those being bought, which could be hired at about one third of the buying cost. The range might be somewhat limited since only styles suitable for altering and re-altering would be suitable for hiring out, and some manufacturers were reluctant to sell to hirers anyway. In the circumstances, dress-hirers in the city were facing an uphill battle.

In addition to the dress, a veil and a 'headdress' which holds the veil were needed to complete the outfit. Veils are oval pieces of fine netting, of varying size but always attached towards one end, with a shorter piece to fall down in front of the face, and a longer and more bulky one to fall down the back on to the dress. Wearing a veil, whether the front portion is down over the face or put back over the head, contributes importantly to the unique shape and soft, gauzy appearance of the bride image. It is also needed to balance the dress. Without a veil, as the dress-shop owner put it, 'with the length and volume of dress, you can have this little pea head at the top. And really you want your face to be the focus – you, not the dress.' The headdress may be more or less conspicuous and is subject to changes of fashion. At the time of the research it was either a small circlet of flowers, usually artificial, or a tiara of some kind. Headdress and veil are often bought together with the dress, but the cost may suggest other strategies. New and appropriate shoes will also generally be needed, and perhaps gloves and a garter. Flowers complete the bride's scheme, but these are generally thought about in relation to the bridesmaids and their dresses and will be considered below.

Finally for the bride, as the day comes closer she will have little alternative to paying attention to hairdressing and make-up. Both are usually understood to have special requirements for the day. Hair has to fit with headdress and veil, make-up to take account of the probably unaccustomed colour she will be wearing. For most people it will also be needed if they are to fulfil the cultural requirement for brides, whatever their everyday mixture of charms and blemishes, to look on the day 'lovely'.

The bridal party

It is in working-class areas that large bridal parties are most often seen. At a church in the eastern peripheries of the city, a white-dressed bride was accompanied by three grown-up bridesmaids in pink dresses, two small girls in white dresses with pink sashes, two even smaller flowergirls in pink again, and two small boys as well. One bridesmaid is sufficient for many brides, some may relish more and others have more thrust upon them. Younger unmarried sisters have the least deniable claims, and large families tend therefore to produce big shows of attendants. Other young women with what are regarded as 'close' relationships with the bride are possible candidates too: friends, nieces, cousins, sisters of the groom. The distinctions available – between 'best maid', to be considered below, and other bridesmaids, and between bridesmaids and flowergirls – may be emphasised or ignored according to the relationships and ages within the chosen set. The concept of a 'matron of honour' is also available for careful use where age and married status make the term 'bridesmaid' and its connotations of youth if not innocence feel less than wholly appropriate.

When it comes to dressing the bridal party, the scale of the enterprise is very variable therefore. Providing such clothes is an expense of the wedding; it is not, that is to say, something which, even when the individuals concerned are adults, they are usually expected to supply for themselves. The clothes may be bought or made, in which case they may be thought of as presents for the girls concerned, or they may be hired. This latter strategy appeals quite widely, as the hiring of wedding dresses does not, though the range of colours and styles available at any given time will be quite limited. Dresses will usually be distinct from the bride's in colour or in being patterned, but echo it at least in length, except for very young girls. Colours vary widely and are subject to changing fashion from year to year. With a single bridesmaid to dress, the choice of colour and style is likely to be jointly taken between her and the bride, but for big shows a stronger hand at the centre is inevitable.

As has been seen, there is a term 'best maid', unfamiliar to the English it may be noted, which is the direct feminine equivalent of 'best man'. Of each there can be one only. They stand symmetrically beside the couple during the service and in some of the standard photographs; they commonly act as the two legally required witnesses; they sit symmetrically on either flank, or together, at the top table for the meal; they follow the bride and groom on to the dance floor at the first waltz; and they offer to bride and groom respectively their assistance before the wedding and at it.

There is, however, also asymmetry here which is in the context striking too. The best man's tasks tend to be of a more essential and organising nature. The best maid may or may not stand in partially for the bride at the show of presents; the best man is charged with looking after the groom at the stag night and, on the day, before the service. He keeps, and at the appropriate moment supplies, both rings if there are two; she at most assists with dress and veil and holds the bride's bouquet. He must rise and speak at the meal; she has only to sit and listen. Afterwards he may do any organising which is called for, of singing for instance; she may assist with the distribution of favours. In dress, bridegroom and best man make a pair, their clothing identical whenever, as is usual, something other than ordinary suits are worn; the ultimate in identification was achieved at one wedding in which groom and best man were identical twins identically dressed and the comic potential was enjoyed by all. The best maid, in contrast, is dressed not to match the bride but any other bridesmaids there may be.

The best maid's practical contribution is therefore relatively slight even when she is the sole attendant for the bride, but often she is not. She becomes merely the first amongst a set of bridesmaids, flowergirls and even small boys as pages. These extras have no role beyond accompanying the bride in church and in photographs. As a group including the best maid, their contribution is to the appearance of the event. To this end they are prettily dressed in colours which will make a harmonious frame for the white-dressed bride. She and all female attendants carry flowers, the bridesmaids' dresses providing the major cue for the bouquets to be carried.[3] The pattern here is such as to make the bride stand out. The bridesmaids' bouquets will match and will usually relate to the bride's but differ from hers in shape or size. Occasionally she may carry a flower-decorated prayer book instead. Very young girls will carry posies or baskets containing a flower arrangement, this latter being the recognised badge of the flowergirl.

Both practically and symbolically therefore, brides' and grooms' supporters are clearly differentiated. On the one side the stress is on being decorative and on highlighting the uniqueness of the bride, on the other on male control and organising.

The task of choosing the single, all-important best man might be expected to be more difficult. Brothers or best friends are the normal choice.

James.	I've got maybe four or five guys who are maybe my best friend, kind of thing – you know, from different situations – I think mainly due to the fact that I've been in my life ..., I've been in four or five different centres: when I was young, at college, and then when I was older, and people at home. It was going to be very difficult ...
Margaret.	... to choose a best man.
J.	... to say who should be my best man, because it was going to offend someone. So I just decided the best thing would be to ask my brother, as a way out of it.
SC.	Did that please the family?
J.	Yes, but it doesn't please him though!
M.	I think he's quite pleased about it really.
J.	I'm going to wear a kilt, you see, and he's not too keen on that – not too keen on this idea of wearing a kilt – but we'll get him round to it.[T59]

Male enthusiasm for wedding roles is in fact rarely conspicuous. Since the job of best man, even without wearing a kilt, is commonly regarded as something of an ordeal, feelings about being asked are mixed. Being likely to measure up to the requirements of being a best man may indeed even influence the choice that grooms make, a practical consideration of a kind unlikely to occur on the female side.

Richard.	I do have a brother but ... . I don't know why.

Pat.	He's not best man material [she laughs].
R.	He's not really the kind of guy that can stand up and talk in public. I don't think I really am that kind of person, or I **wasn't** then – I was the best man for my brother. I don't know whether he would have said yes or not. He's been best man before and he said at the time 'Oh! Never again!' sort of thing. And I'm very friendly with the best man I have, probably the guy I know best. So I asked him. [...]
P.	But he ..., your brother's an usher, so ...
R.	Tom is – he's one of the ushers. And Pat's brother's the other.[T18]

In this situation, men seem less likely to be upset at not being chosen. If there is a danger of it in the particular case, people can be asked, as here, to be 'ushers'. These are generally young men – only one girl usher was encountered in the course of the research, at a church with a woman minister – who are appointed to direct or show guests to their seats in the church and give out orders of service, if any. This is one of the aspects of wedding organisation at which the two 'sides', bride's and groom's, are generally represented. It provides therefore a representative but undemanding role to be offered as a male consolation prize, if required by the necessary uniqueness of the best man.

The bridegroom and the males of the company

Everyone dresses up for weddings, but there is no single rule producing uniformity of practice here. The only general principle is that people are setting themselves up to go on display. This leads to a characteristic well-scrubbed look amongst those participating in a wedding – with the exception of photographers – and a shift away from a man's everyday dress in a direction which is described as 'formal'. The more central the role a man is to play in it the more pronounced is this shift towards formal wear likely to be, but for most male participants the principle is adequately recognised by putting on a suit in a darkish colour and a tie. A flower for the buttonhole is in Scotland a very common additional marker.

The bridegroom himself and those close to him or to the bride frequently want, or feel that they should, or are persuaded by others to adopt one of the even more distinctive uniforms available for such occasions. The Scottish dinner-dance style of wedding makes evening wear an obvious possibility. Both dinner-suits, normally in black with white shirts and black bow-ties, and the 'Highland' equivalent, Bonnie Prince Charlie jackets, kilts and accoutrements, or even the fancier Montrose style, were common at the time of the research.[4] The kilts were indeed increasingly popular, even with those with little or no ancestral connection with Scotland, let alone a Highland clan. Though some would take pleasure in getting married in their own kilt of their own tartan,[5] most of those worn were being hired and were available in two or three patterns only, chosen for the colour effect, usually red or green. 'Tails', highly formal outfits characterised by jackets cut long at the back, worn with waistcoats and top hats, might be seen too. These were however picking up a different cue. They were mainly the variety called 'morning coats', usually in silver grey and reflecting an English or Anglo-Scottish upper-class pattern of morning or early afternoon weddings, without the evening celebration.[6] All these more specialised uniforms were largely hired for the occasion. Hirers were able therefore to exert some direct influence over male dress for weddings, and some were trying to enliven and expand the market by introducing and advertising new styles and colours of jackets and trousers and variations of neckwear.

This variety of possibilities meant that there was rarely the kind of uniformity of dressing which was to be seen amongst the morning-coated men of a southern English establishment wedding or the dinner-jacketed men of a Glasgow Jewish one. There was, however, a general sense that groom and best man should be matched in dress and this was normally in some measure achieved. They would not mix the varieties listed above: if the groom were wearing an ordinary suit, so would be the best man, but they would not then wear matching suits; if one wore a kilt, so would the other, but the tartans would be likely to differ; but if they wore one of the other uniforms they were likely to match closely.

Groom and best man might or might not be distinguished by the flower they wore in a buttonhole. Grooms invariably wore a white carnation, unless in Highland dress for which a sprig of white heather was generally preferred – the apparent link to the white bridal outfit was not commented upon. White heather – which is very commonly said to be lucky in whatever context it appears – or a white carnation might be worn by the best man and others too, or they might wear red or pink carnations.

Even this level of uniformity declined sharply with fathers, let alone other members of the couple's families. The father of the bride would be most exposed, since he would be bringing the bride into church. This pushed him more strongly than the father of the groom towards greater formality of dress. Those who envisaged the events of the wedding in planning it were almost bound, however, to see the two fathers as equivalent and to feel that their clothes should harmonise. They would be together in the procession out of the church; there would be photographs of them arranged symmetrically on either side of the couple; they would stand in a line receiving and greeting the guests; they would be seated symmetrically at the top table and might both make speeches; they would be expected to get on to the dance floor with their own and each other's wives for the ceremonial first waltz. But despite many feeling a need for uniformity here, it was less regularly achieved. This resulted not so much from any lack of communication between the two sides – the womenfolk generally knew well what the men were going to wear – as from the meanings men often attached to particular styles of clothing.

Margaret. Your dad hasn't gone for his suit. [This was only ten days before the wedding.]

James.   It's terrible! He won't wear tails. He just refused point blank to wear tails. Well, you see, Margaret's dad got tails, grey tails, but **he** won't wear them. He says: 'You may as well ask me to vote Tory!' You know, he's got this vision of the whole thing. He just laughs when you suggest it. He thinks you're kidding him on.

M.   I know, but I think he could submit on this occasion.

J.   He won't wear them. So he's going to get himself a suit. [...] he's agreed to wear ..., he's going to wear a bow tie and a suit. Maybe we can get ...

M.   A bow tie and a suit is not going to go with it, James!

J.   He might hire a grey suit without tails.

M.   You'd better try to get him to wear a grey suit, because it's going to look ridiculous in the photographs if he's wearing a black suit.[T91]

Or the problem may with some fathers be more basic still:

Jan.   He keeps saying he's not coming, because he'd have to wear a suit and your mum wants him to do something about his teeth.

Shuggie.   That's right. You see, they're all nicotine stained, and she wants him to get them all cleaned up, you know: 'Ah! Can't be bothered!'

J.   And he's got teeth missing. She wants him to get new teeth as well ..., for the wedding.[T41]

The mother of the bride and the female company

If the mothers of the couple have a dressing problem in relation to one another it is the opposite of the men's: they will try to ensure that they do not match. In this, as in other clothes matters, the two mothers express in a less differentiated way than the men the principles that apply to all guests of their own sex at the wedding. There is little sign of the formal as a criterion; hats, for instance, once required both for weddings and for church attendance generally, were at the time and place of the research almost entirely a matter of individual choice. The criterion of suitability for female dress was not formality but 'dressiness', allowing personal choice of colours and shapes and fabrics full play. A boldness and flamboyance of dress, and attention to the outfit as a whole beyond the everyday practice of the person concerned, were what seemed to be called for. Jean, reporting a wedding at which her mother-in-law had recently been a guest, exemplifies the usual attitude:

> She was wearing her wine woolly thing, knit, 'cause she was really skint. I think she was actually quite upset about that, 'cause she was moaning for weeks, 'I can't go to this wedding – I've got nothing to wear.' A new dress would have cost her a fortune. I think she should have worn the brown dress that she wore to our wedding. It's the nicest dress she's got. But she said she had worn that to our wedding and to Pamela's wedding, and she didn't want to wear it again. So that's ... .[T46]

But the mother of the bride would somehow have to afford it. Indeed, her outfit might well include a hat, even for women who would never otherwise wear one, and itself of a style unlikely to be worn on an occasion of any other kind.

Jane.   My mum put on this dress and it was really lovely, exactly what she had been looking for. She liked the idea of crossing over on the front – exactly what she wanted. So I mean that was ..., it was an expensive dress. Usually my mum's the sort of person that buys expensive shoes, not expensive ..., she doesn't splash out on other things. She'll pay a lot of money for shoes but not for other things. So she did ..., she really went her duster that day. I don't think, I still don't think she's told my dad how much it cost but ... . So the next problem was then her hat, and she got one the other day that is quite nice but was a bit big-brimmed. So she ended up getting two hats. She saw a hat the other day, she liked it better, so ... .[T9]

The groom's mother would often react very similarly:

Jan.   She's more excited about it than either of us.
Shuggie. I mean, she spent most of her holiday this year in every shop in Bournemouth trying to find her wedding outfit. She eventually saw the thing she wanted and she bought it. She looks fabulous in it.
J.   She looks gorgeous. She's not wearing a hat. She was going to wear a hat because that's the thing you do at a wedding, but she's got fabulous hair ... . She's got her suit and her shoes and her bag. She's got everything. She could go to the wedding tomorrow. She'd just have a bath and be ready, you know.[T41]

All such efforts would be in the cause of 'looking nice' and making a distinctive impression. The results would be evaluated as self-expression; for male outfits, by contrast, interest was likely to reach little further than whether or not they would conform. The female criterion of dressiness would rule out casual clothing, just as the male criterion of formality would.

Jean.   I think they were the only guests who didn't look dressed up at all. I mean, Christine turned up wearing this sort of white baggy shirt and her hair stuck back in a ponytail. She looked as though she was just going out to the pub [she laughs].[T46]

The jeans so ubiquitous otherwise for both sexes would be understood by all as inappropriate. Such an exclusion of casualness had, it is worth noting, become the more noticeable, exceptional and therefore potentially meaningful as it had ceased to apply in other contexts. At the time neither church attendance for normal services nor most other kinds of sociable gathering were felt to require any particular form of 'dressing up'.

For mothers of the bride the general principles apply most forcibly. They know that they themselves will be a focus of attention and that there will be widespread interest in what they are wearing. The bride's mother is bound to be compared with the groom's. Like their husbands, they will both be conspicuous in the procession out of the church, will feature in photographs, will usually be greeting all their guests in the receiving line, will be sitting at the top table, and appearing conspicuously on the dance floor. In addition there is the added pressure of knowing that this is her event. Even if she has not in practice been largely responsible for organising it, such is the standard expectation that she will be assumed to have been. It is sometimes said jokingly that when a mother sees her newborn baby girl, she sees a wedding, and, slightly more in earnest, that it is through their daughters that women have the weddings their own mothers denied them. Whether individual mothers seize the opportunity of stardom on the day or do their best to hide behind the even more often expressed cultural dogma that it is the bride, their daughter, whose day it is, the pressure for self-presentation is strong.

The guest list

Who should be invited to the wedding is a major problem and preoccupation for many. Its discussion also throws a valuable light on current thinking about the family and kinship (Strathern 1981, pp. 138–46). The basic difficulty is that there are too many different categories of desirable attenders and every likelihood that in some categories there will be more claims than can possibly be met. Even in the early days of planning it is obvious as soon as approaches are made to hotels and caterers that costs are going to be substantial and that there will be a ceiling on practicable numbers. An idea of the size of the event is needed in order to book accommodation and this provides a starting point for subsequent thinking. The capacity of the hall may itself prevent expansion; occasionally, by contrast, it is so large that it provides an incentive to keep numbers up. Thereafter, serious thought about the guest list will be required.

Thinking has to begin with the bridal party itself: the minimum standard number of people in it is eight. The categories of further claimants then rush in to augment this basic set. There are friends and there are relatives; there are people of the couple's own generation and of their parents'; and there are the sides, the bride's side versus the groom's, and even on each of those the mother's versus the father's side. Whenever there are more than minimal numbers of relatives to be found in the four parental families, there is already a problem. Principles and sentiments often compete too. Those who may expect to be invited according to general principles, in the main kin, are not necessarily the ones whom those doing the selecting most want to have with them on the day: friends may be 'closer' than many kin, and some kin are the subject of hostilities and resentments which may even lead to their exclusion.

It is not simply that there are many different claimants for attention; the couple and their parents are always potentially at odds over relative priorities. If the couple themselves were paying, what was essentially their list might prevail, but in practice the cultural expectation that it would be the bride's parents who would be paying remained strong. Only where this was manifestly out of the question would such expectations be abandoned. Otherwise the most that could be expected was some obviously subsidiary donation from the groom's family, such as paying for the drinks, and perhaps help with individual items such as the cake from others. Negotiation between the generations was therefore usually required, a negotiation in which the outcome was variable but rather commonly produced a gathering weighted heavily towards the older generation.

Once discussions between the two sides have been embarked upon, large families[7] and circles of friends make the limiting of invitations one of the commonest preoccupations in the run-up to the wedding. Since invitations are generally thought to need sending out only six weeks before the date, a long period is often available in which the matter can be repeatedly debated. Unless one side is manifestly not under pressure of competing claims, the idea of balance between sides usually comes into play again here. This overcomes any priority the bride's side, as the principal payers, might be expected to be able to exert. The parents on each side are likely to take and be given equal allocations to cover families and their own friends, with the couple themselves taking a third share for a few of their particular friends. Each side would then make its own choices and decide its own rules in the light of the particular problems facing it.

Margaret and James's problems and solution were not unusual. Four months ahead it was already on everybody's minds:

Margaret. We're getting a bit worried now about the numbers at the wedding, aren't we?
James.   Yes.

SC.   Are they creeping up?

M.   Well, they can't creep up above ... . They definitely won't allow above eighty. We've managed to keep it to about fifteen of our friends. People just won't be able to ...: some of our friends ..., we can't say to them all, 'Bring partners,' unless they are maybe actually engaged to somebody or something, because we just won't be able to have the numbers. And the rest of them to divide among the two families – which I'm not looking forward to deciding who's getting who, who's allowed to bring ... .[T59]

Margaret's father. I think in this case the parents probably have to bear the responsibility of seeing that, shall we say, obligatory invitations are sent out – relations that you feel should be there and probably that the young people have seldom seen. [...]

Her mother. We've got to sit and count. I have said, 'Well, let them have forty each,' but I feel, well, the young ones will have to get their choice of bringing friends, and Margaret and James **have** quite a lot of young friends they would like to have there – and I would like them to be there.

SC.   Are you members of large families yourselves?

Father.   Well, on my side there are a few; you know, I just have one sister. But Mary's family was a large family. There are eight of them still living.

SC.   That would fill up the hall.

Father.   Well, it would if you invited them all. But some of them are of course in other parts of the world, and other parts of the country.

SC.   Will they get invited even if they've no chance of coming?

Mother.   Well, we will invite them. I feel it might cause **hurts**, and I wouldn't hurt anyone. There's always someone hurt at a wedding, even if ... . We'll try and avoid that if possible. [...]

SC.   Your brothers and sisters have families presumably. That would make an enormous number of people.

Mother.   Yes. Well, you see, we'll have to avoid that sort of thing. There's only one brother who has asked us to all his family's weddings. Well, we'll invite that family.

Father.   Yes, that's Alan's family – Jack's family.

Mother.   Jack's family. We've been nearer to them, you know, friendly. They've always been very friendly with us. I'm not asking my married nieces and nephews other than that. As I say, you've got to draw the line. You could go on and on till it was over a hundred. [...]

Mother.   But if I can bring in James's parents – can I bring that in just now? Well, James's parents ... . I had a talk with his mum. She's very nice, very nice people. And she's from a big family, so she's not inviting **all** her brothers and sisters. She's leaving some of the invitations for her **friends**, whom she's very friendly with, people her and her husband go out together ..., things like that. They feel they want to include them. And she's got some brothers and sisters she seldom ever sees. How many did Margaret say were in her family, eleven?

Father.   Something like that.

Mother.   It was a big family and they're scattered all over, and she says, quite often she never sees them for years. So she's going to exclude them and put friends in in place of them. Which I think is quite a good idea. But of course it depends how she feels ... . [...] I wouldn't do it with my family. I feel I'd hurt them if I did. But Margaret was saying she's going to do that, because she couldn't ask all her family and then have her friends. And she feels she has so many nice friends she goes out with ... . I would think that's a dicey thing to do. It's a chance of hers.

Father.   Yes. You don't know what cross-currents, under-currents, there are in family affairs that you're disturbing ... .[T69]

But some of course do know fine, for it is not under-currents but open hostilities. Wedding slights are the ammunition as well as the injuries of family wars. In interviews such matters are likely to surface only gradually, if at all.

Bert.   I'd rather have friends, ...

Grace.   I know. I believe that as well, but you cannae leave your relatives out. [...] We had put a limit on eighty, and I mean, we did have to leave out a couple of people that we'd liked to have at the meal, but I just couldn't ..., couldn't say to my dad, 'I'm no inviting your sister.' Although, I mean, I must admit there is a couple of my aunties I can't stand, but it's my dad's sisters, and he's got all sisters – you know, four of them – and there's one in particular I just wouldn't invite if I had my own way, but I didn't want to hurt my dad. And I'm quite sure that it was the same for you.

B.   Absolutely. Really, it's the done thing: you've got to invite all your relatives, people you never see. You know, it's relatives that I know just lives a few miles away. I've no seen them since I was a schoolboy.

G.   Even worse than that, my gran just lives round the corner and they never come in to see us. And the lady that was in tonight lives out in Cumbernauld and she's down every week. That's my other gran. And if I had my own way I wouldn't have invited my gran. No so much my granda – my granda comes in. It's quite a ..., it's quite a long kinda saga, but ..., I'll no go into details, but I wouldn't have bothered inviting her, but for my dad's sake I will. I mean, I'm no her grandchild to her, you know, so ... .[T15]

Returning to James and Margaret's somewhat calmer waters, James explained:

> My mother's originally from Johnstone and she's been living in Paisley all her married life now, and her family ..., it's a large family. It's quite scattered, and a lot of her day-to-day friends have become more like family in many ways than ... . You know, I mean, a lot of my aunts and uncles ..., we'd quite a few people who were called uncle and aunt who weren't. They were always closer that way. There's three brothers in Australia, and some of them live in out of the way places like ..., fairly near but out of the way places like ...: one uncle lives in Bridge of Weir, and he didn't have any transport. So he sort of lived in Bridge of Weir and he was very seldom in town. Some of them would maybe go away for a period – like they were bricklayers, so a lot of them went away. They were away working for a couple of years maybe, moving about a lot.[T59]

After the wedding, James's mother herself spoke about what had in the end happened:

> The guest list was a real problem. Margaret and James had their own guests. And we were allowed twenty-five guests each – well, Margaret's mum and I. It was a problem because, to begin with, well James [senior] has two brothers and a sister – two brothers and a sister who are married – and then a sister who wasn't married. And I had ..., I've got five brothers at home, four of them with wives, and two sisters, and then I had friends who have always ..., who've known your family since they were small, who've been kind to your family. We had to work out the friends – that was a problem. But two of our friends, Maggie and Maureen, they couldn't come. They were going to a silver wedding. So that helped too. We managed it down to ...: we had two, four, six, eight friends – is that right? Steven, Julie, Thelma and Jim and Joan and Jack – that was our eight friends, and the rest were relatives, and us. Well, one of my brothers, I didn't ask him. He never goes to weddings. He just lives alone and I didn't want to put him to the bother of getting a wedding present. But I think there was a bit of ...; another brother was quite upset and said he wasn't going. [...] I mean, I was demented, really, trying to work out this guest list. [...]

> The girls [James's sisters] – I mean, Catherine couldn't get asking a friend. If I had ... . If she had asked a friend, well, I couldn't have asked some of the relations. Helen had a friend though. And Margaret didn't get a friend either. They never got a friend. Joseph [James's brother] didn't get a friend – he was the best man and he couldn't get a friend. That was really the problem, there were such a lot of other people. There were still a lot of friends we could have asked. We had to stop. You had to draw the line somewhere, and it was an imposition to make ... .[T106]

With pressure of numbers there is a general understanding that family have priority and in a rather definite order. The couple's own parents, siblings and grandparents come first. Then come the parents' brothers and sisters, followed by their children, the first cousins of the couple marrying. A 'couples' principle should then apply: for any attender who is part of a heterosexual couple, the spouse, fiancé(e) or even established boy/girl friend should be invited too. We have seen above the kinds of pressure which may lead to an infringement of the principle. It should be noticed though that it was members of the groom's immediate family who were being deprived in this way; they at least could be expected to understand the problem and not simply feel slighted by an apparent discrimination against them.

In practice, however, it is cousins who chiefly become problematic. There may simply be too many of them to fit within the quota, and they are in competition with parents' own friends. Their ages may be against them too. The only children commonly attending weddings are bridesmaids, flowergirls or pages, and brothers and sisters of the couple themselves who are not playing such roles. Receptions are seen as essentially adult events at which children, if they are not positively out of place, could scarcely justify the cost of including them. But even as adolescents or young adults, cousins do not compete strongly against friends of the older generation. It is here that a variety of principles may come into play. Only cousins with whom personal ties are strong may be invited, or only those to whose own wedding an invitation was previously received, or only those not already married, or a representative from each family. The variety of possible principles mean that those not invited cannot immediately know why they have not been included. They may then be inclined to mull over the history of relationships with the people concerned and take as a personal slight to themselves what is often no more than the consequence of having to take a decision impossible to get right.

Jean.   Mum knows how hurt I was at not getting invited to Anne's. I told mum, I said to mum, 'I feel really snubbed,' you know. I said, ..., and mum said, 'Oh, that's probably not Anne. It's probably Aunt Pam.' I said, 'I really don't think so. I think Aunt Pam would have

automatically thought of us', you know. I think possibly it was
Anne.

DM.   Did you say anything to your mum about Moira's?

J.   No, 'cause I was pleased, happy enough to get the evening invita-
         tion, 'cause I knew it was going to be in this swanky hotel, and
         obviously they're cutting down as much expense as they possibly
         can.[T46]

This is the simplest solution. Space permitting, cousins may be relegated,
with other young people, friends and associates of the couple, to the so-called
'evening reception'.

SC.   Will you be inviting extras in the evening?

Carol.   Oh gosh! About fifty probably. By the time I've invited all the girls
         who work beside me and their husbands ...,

Angus.   ... and the husbands' friends, and their friends ...,

C.   ... and then there's ..., like Fiona's, the bridesmaid's, partners. But
         that's no skin off anybody's nose. The whole world can come at
         night if they want.[T17]

The establishment of the evening reception as a standard practice, though still
at the time of the research contested by some, recognised the financial basis of
wedding celebrations and the constraints produced by it.

Seating for the meal

The final exercise of casting and design required, once acceptances have come
in, is the seating for the meal. Many find this a problem, but it is not to be
avoided unless the 'proper meal' pattern is abandoned. Almost always a plan
for the 'top table' at which the wedding party will be on display is required,
and generally one for seating for the rest of the guests.

In dealing with seating there are three general principles to be applied to
more or less recalcitrant sets of individuals. These are that couples are the
preferred unit and are normally kept together, that the sexes should be
alternated and that brides' and grooms' sides should be mixed. They have to
be applied in the two different contexts given by the distinctive layout. A long
top table accommodates the principals in a single line along one side only.
This is a form which has precedents going back at least as far as the medieval
feast but is more often thought of in terms of a platform party with a
chairman. In either case it is structured primarily in terms of a focal centre,
with the accent normally on bride and groom sitting together there but
sometimes on the celebrant, minister or priest, who acts as chairman, sitting
beside the bride and he may, with the minimum set of Chairman + eight at the
top table, be the central figure. All look out at the rest of the assembled guests

and can be looked at by them. These latter will be accommodated around tables of a variety of sizes and shapes and arranged in patterns to suit the room and the size of the party, to enable ease of serving and to allow the top table to be easily seen. Long tables at right angles to the top table are a common solution.

All three principles can readily be applied on tables with people sitting around them. Couples can be seated together but still both be in contact with people from the other side. Irregularities, guests lacking partners and uneven numbers of each sex, can also be readily absorbed. But problems there are.

Donna.	Nearer the wedding, remember, we had making out the seating plan. That was difficult. A lot of disagreements there.
Brian.	We sat ..., we spent about two nights over in your house with your mum and dad ...: who can we sit beside who? who talks to who? etc.
D.	That's right.
B.	And you found out, usually at one table you were trying to please just the one person. It was one person who didn't talk to somebody, and who didn't talk to this person, so you had to sit them there. Then this person didn't really like this person. It was usually one person who was the sort of catalyst for the whole thing, that started it off. There was only about ..., I think there was only about one table that fitted in really good. You know, I think there was ..., I don't think there was any members of the family in that. I think that was why. When you got to the family it was kind of bad.[T19]

Difficulties arise therefore from the need to place difficult relatives, to separate those known to be at odds with one another, and to try to match people who have never met and may not have much in common. They may also arise from the symbolic meaning which people are prone to read into their placing. Places are necessarily closer and more distant from the top table and from its focal centre, the couple themselves. Placing within this field is liable to be read as a statement of a person's relative importance to the couple and their parents. Most guests will doubtless not bother to think in such terms, but they are always available and are one well-known way in which fuel may be added to the fires of family animosities. There are multiple requirements therefore if the general table-plans are to be got right.

At the one-sided top table, there is often no way in which even a show of satisfying all principles simultaneously can be made. The bride and groom's place at or near the centre, with the groom on the bride's right, is the most constant feature. Beyond that, solutions vary according to the exact set of people to be accommodated, the preferences of professionals involved in the organization and their choice of compromise. One strategy is to divide the table by generation, with best man and bridesmaids on one side, with groom and bride if a chairman is at the centre, and the parents, usually in mixed couples arranged so that there will be a male at the end. An ideal pattern of this kind appeared in *Your Wedding*, a Catholic guide and one of the few distinctively Scottish recommendations published:

Best man	Brides- maid	Groom	Bride	Chair	Bride's mother	Groom's father	Groom's mother	Bride's father

Alternatively the parents may be placed on either side, usually again in mixed couples, each father on the side of his own child. The best man may be placed beside the groom, echoing the support arrangement of the ceremony earlier, but this infringes the principle of alternation by sex; the bride much more rarely gets the support of a bridesmaid. A plurality of bridesmaids is a further challenge to alternation and the balancing of couples. Celebrants who are not near the centre are almost certain to be at an end.

Such a patterning obviously puts a premium on a full, standard set of parents being available, though it does not require that separated parents should pretend to be together. Substitutes are possible. In particular, whoever has given the bride away may be expected to take the crucial 'bride's father' role. Whether new partners of parents should accompany them on the top table is one of the many matters of potential dispute. In one case in which the couple themselves successfully refused to allow it, it was argued that the partners of best man and bridesmaids have to sit separately amongst the ordinary guests, so a new husband should too.

There are of course other sources of variation too. All forethought and planning may always be brought to nought. Caterers who transpose the order at the top table or fail to bring the table plans are not unknown. For a small gathering it may even be decided that plans are unnecessary, with the likely consequence that those who already know one another will stick together. Mixing may also be forgone by conscious decision. Sharp class differences between the two sides may suggest that it would be too hard to achieve; at one such wedding where the problem was accentuated by very small numbers on one side, it was decided that they would be happier on a table of their own. There are therefore principles – there are also typical problems to be faced – and rather clear patterns may be observed as long as no mechanical following of any simple rule is expected.

The experience

Barbara.   When you make a decision to get married, [...] initially it's all very nice because people are congratulating you and you are making your initial plans and then, for us – because it hasn't been particularly ..., it's not been a long engagement but it hasn't been a particularly short one either – so there's a lull, and then things begin to pick up again. And once you start arranging the wedding and you've only got a few months to go and ..., everything ... , you become totally preoccupied with the organisation of it, and you find ... , well, you don't forget **why** you are doing it but you forget **what** you are doing. I certainly feel that way. Running about and buying things and doing this and that and thinking we must get the flat ready and that, I find it very hard to put my mind one step further again: we have to get the flat ready **because we are getting married,** and get back to that. You get totally swept along.[T42]

This bride-to-be reflects a common experience, though even at this level of generality not an inevitable one. Beyond it, so much depends on whether mother or daughter or both want the event to be theirs and whether they are able to co-operate amicably over it. Some daughters may be keen to persuade managing mothers that it is not **their** wedding; others may be pleased to have the responsibility largely removed from them. There are even mothers who retire thankfully into the background, though in that case so strong is the contrary expectation that others may conspire to keep alive an illusion of the active mother.

The experience depends also on the problems faced. The financial resources which can be made available are basic here. Large families and circles of friends of whom many are locally resident and therefore very likely to attend produce conflicts of interest and inclination which those with fewer potential guests may be spared. Couples if left to themselves would often choose simpler events on a smaller scale and therefore less costly. For them a sense of things escalating beyond control is a common experience. The cliché that it is 'the bride's day' may be invoked ever more frequently to mask the fact that both bride and groom commonly become pawns in one of the major ritual sequences of the society. It is a sequence powerfully and characteristically shaped by commercial interests too. Once within its grip their room for manoeuvre is usually highly circumscribed.

Chapter 5

Festivities before the Day

The presents

The arrival of the presents can be taken to signal the end of the preparations and the beginning of the celebration. Their significance, as with all gifts, is far from immediately clear however. Though normally hidden beneath the cloak of familiarity, two contrasting understandings of their nature were to be observed. A 'utilitarian' understanding focuses on the use or usefulness of the items given, and a 'personal' understanding stresses their symbolic significance.[1] The utilitarian was by far the most publicly vociferous, but the personal tended to be the view of brides. As such it had a central influence on the conduct of this first episode of festivity.

Utilitarian understandings were dominant, first, in the extensive literature of wedding advice which emanated almost exclusively from the South of England. This took the form of etiquette guides of varying degrees of specialisation, and of an annual harvest of magazine articles in the ever-burgeoning women's press and even in local newspapers catering to advertisers in the wedding trades. The guides have characteristically been issued and reissued long past the limits of their practical relevance, ever since the mid nineteenth century. In this literature, the list was the chief manifestation and instrument of the utilitarian approach. A new and avowedly progressive compilation at the period told its readers: 'There are really only two rules to remember: (i) Have a wedding list prepared for anyone who wishes to consult it. (ii) Be sure to write thank-you letters to everyone who sends you a present.' (Derraugh 1983, p. 30) A more conservative source, Debrett's *Etiquette and Modern Manners* (1981, p. 54), agreed that 'the bride's list' was crucial and explained how it was to be used. The easiest way to ensure that one received what one wanted was 'to make use of a service run by stores throughout the country. [...] The list is compiled a week or so before the wedding invitations are despatched and kept up to date as purchases are made from it. Many brides have lists in two or three stores.' The list is promoted as the instrument by which the couple, or more often still the bride – the organised modern bride – mobilises her army of eager donors into using their money to equip her home, as far as possible to her own specifications. Brides are encouraged to establish their colour schemes for each room, so that the colours of items to go into each can be specified, even towels for the bathroom. They should decide on patterns for their crockery, cutlery and glass, so that people can contribute to matching sets. The logic begins at some point to suggest that it would be simpler just to give the money and let the recipients do their own purchasing.

It is over money indeed that utilitarian ideas appeared most clearly, not just in the southern literature but in the Scottish field too. In the case of a young educational psychologist, the brother of a recent bride, such ideas had so far monopolised his experience of present-giving. Speaking with his wife he commented:

> It's usually been your family or mine, and I think that in that context we've been quite happy to ... – we've never actually given a *gift* as such. We've always given a cheque, haven't we? We kind of felt that left them completely free. You weren't giving them something they wouldn't like or wouldn't use.[T109]

Giving money is also seen as a practical way of financing items which are too costly for any single donor. Either way the giving of money is the ultimate expression of the utilitarian conception of wedding presents.[2]

The 'personal' conception is grounded in the more general culture of present-giving. A bride, a hospital technician, put it thus:

Barbara.   The appreciation of anyone's gift is for them to get a thank-you letter at the time, and then come to this house and see that we have put their gift into use. [...] I much prefer to go and see any present, gift, no matter whether ... . That goes for any gift to give to somebody: give somebody a birthday present – or a jumper – it's nice to see them wearing it. And I think equally it's true of a wedding present.[T42]

For her the model was the personal gift to be personally acknowledged. Like any other gift from this perspective, the wedding present is to be seen as an expression of a personal relationship between giver and recipient. It is what the former thinks the latter will like, and confirmation that this is so is, as in the quotation, the ideal fulfilment of the exchange. 'Just what I wanted' is the standard expression which catches the element of individualistic personal harmony here. This is a feature highly significant in British, North American and perhaps other European exchange cultures (Cheal 1987) but largely unfamiliar in the more highly prescribed types of exchange which have attracted anthropological analysis overseas since the days of Malinowski (1922) and Mauss (1923–4).

Whether it is altogether applicable to wedding presents is another matter. Where, indeed, they are commissioned on a utilitarian basis, any personally expressive element is largely eliminated. A sense that this has happened may produce a rather characteristic though mild embarrassment, to be overcome with a touch of good-humoured and standard facetiousness: 'How *did* you know that was just what I wanted?' In the serious context of wedding-present giving, such practices may occasionally generate stronger feelings. Lists in particular become for many the negation of their own preferred 'personal' interpretation.

Which perspective people would adopt was observed to be a function of their role in the wedding. Brides displayed a strong tendency to seize on the personal; for givers it was usually the utilitarian which made sense. In a striking refusal of the unanimous advice arriving from the South, Glasgow brides were, this is to say, resisting the list. Any attempt to direct present-givers would generally be seen as inappropriate. Initially indeed the whole business of being given such presents was often fraught with embarrassment. Brides are very aware that people's means are different and that wedding presents tend to be large. The combination of ideas sets up a distinct unease. The last thing that anyone wants to do is to presume on the level of expenditure that would-be donors may have in mind.

Barbara.   It's very difficult when somebody asks you what you would like for a wedding present and you don't know whether to say two wooden spoons or a tumble drier. So it's a really very, very embarrassing, delicate situation.[T42]

In this context lists are felt at best to be cheeky, at worst in bad taste. Despite Debrett's confident assertion that stores 'throughout the country' would hold lists, it was difficult to find any such stores in Glasgow.

Though there were some givers – to turn to the other side of the relationship – operating on an entirely personal basis, simply going out and buying what they themselves liked and what seemed to them right for the recipient, most were concerned with 'what is needed'. At least to try to avoid duplication they would often consult either the couple themselves or their parents. Most, including parents, would have been happier with a list. Indeed there might sometimes be substitute lists constructed in dealing with enquirers. There might be a list of engagement presents to help to avoid duplication with these. Sometimes a list would be compiled of things which particular people had said they would give and from which others might then be warned off. Though these could fulfil some of the same functions as 'the bride's list', they kept clear of the element of presumption so unacceptable in the eyes of most local brides.

Table 1 suggests the kind of collection being assembled at the time. This one was produced without a wants list, or even an engagement present list, though there was a good deal of consultation. There was none of the colour/ style co-ordination for which the approved utilitarian bride would have been aiming, but the cheques and the type of object which make up the bulk of the list do point in that utilitarian direction. In the event little serious duplication amongst the wedding presents themselves occurred here, though with the engagement presents there was rather more. The problem is sufficiently familar, however, for there to be a more-or-less specialised term for its results, 'doublers'. Doublers and what should be done with them at the show of presents (see below), and subsequently, are a regular topic of debate. The same two trends of ideas become apparent: recipients often have a sense of something close to betrayal in parting with them; for others, finding alternative uses is merely common sense.

Table 1 **Presents received for a wedding, June 1983**[N98]

Bed linen × 3	Dishes × 3	Rug
Bread bin	Dishtowels × 2	Settee
Breakfast set	Electric fire	Sherry glasses
Carriage clock	Food mixer	Silver (plated) tray
Chairs	Fruit bowl	Table cloth
Bottle of champagne	Glasses	Table lamp
Cheques × 14	Iron	Table linen
Coasters	Kitchen clock	Tea set
Coffee maker	Kitchen scales	Tea towels
Coffee set	Kitchen units	Toaster
Continental quilt	Mirror	Towels × 7
Crystal glasses × 2	Nest of tables	Tray
Cutlery × 4	Ornament × 2	Wall clock
Decanter and glasses	Ottoman	Washing line
Deep fryer	Oven gloves	Wedding cake
Dining table	Plant-pot holder	Wok × 2
Dining chairs	Pots and pans	
Dinner set	Pressure cooker	

As regards items suitable as presents, expectations are little more structured than by the basic idea that they will be contributions to the home and generally bought in shops, new, for that purpose. Recycling of presents occurs but would certainly not be advertised. Contributions to the festivities, such as the wedding cake and the bottle for the wedding night in the list above, are possible but not usual. Many items are, as this list suggests, merely useful. Proverbial dishtowels appear, together with such more original items as a washing line. The things that attract most attention, however, are those with something special or showy about them. The recipients of this collection distinguished between the 'everyday' and the 'good' amongst such items as cutlery and tableware. The 'crystal' which almost invariably appears in such collections has a strong element of display about it.[3]

On cost there is slightly more to be said. This is spoken of as a matter of size, how big or small a present is. There is a sense that those who are 'closer' will give 'bigger' presents. Closeness is a matter of personal relationships and/or kinship. In practice what this amounts to is limited since size is relative to means and these are variable. There can be no calculus to determine how much has to be spent on a present or even, usually, whether an appropriate sum has been. Though as an issue it certainly occurs to recipients and others, it is not a proper subject for consideration.[4] Particularly with close kin, there may indeed be the feeling that one donor has done well by the couple, or that another has been less than generous. As will be seen, the way presents are displayed makes some element of comparison almost inevitable despite being improper.

The size of presents is structured in one further way. Those fully involved in the wedding or wanting to give 'a proper wedding present', which 'will look something', needed to shop cleverly at 1983 prices to spend much less than £20. In china and glass it was difficult not to go well above that figure, and there were of course many who were able, and indeed keen, to spend a great deal more. Children and others not financially independent could, however, keep to lower levels, and for more peripheral donors the idea of the 'minder' or 'minding' was available. The minder is a wee something just to say that the donor is minding, or remembering, the recipient. The term is not restricted to the wedding context but it is particularly common there. It makes an explicit contrast with a proper – implying more costly – wedding present. It can also be used as a way of playing down one's own offering and suggesting its modesty: 'it's just a wee minder'.

A proportion of present-givers usually decide on money, the utilitarian implications of which have already been noticed. The proportion is generally small and people will sometimes explain this in cost terms. By clever shopping, it is claimed, one can hope to spend less on an object than one would have to give as money. But few have quite the forthrightly utilitarian attitude of the educational psychologist quoted above. Money is thinly disguised in most accounts as 'cheques', and often, as indeed in that quotation, it is verbally distinguished from a present proper, or 'gift'. Donors and recipients are often quite explicit that the money is a substitute. The infirm may be excused for giving it by their inability to get out to the shops: 'she would have got us something I think, had she been able';[T17] or it may be excused by the difficulty of sending anything else from such distant parts as Australia, or England; or because, in more clearly utilitarian vein, of 'not knowing what you really need'.

The familiar and unitary concept of the wedding present masks therefore a significant difference in assumptions, determined partly by one's current role in the wedding concerned. The two approaches are however also grounded, perhaps more permanently, in structural considerations. Givers of presents are far from uniform in the way they are placed in relation to the couple marrying. A convenient way of classifying them which begins to get at this distinguishes three categories: family and kin, other associates of the couple themselves, and associates of the parents. The tables show, first, the breakdown of presents received at four weddings and then the numbers attending these weddings.[5]

The most striking finding here is the tendency for those with little direct association with the couple themselves to produce substantial numbers of presents, often indeed more than either of the first two categories. There is something more complicated going on here therefore than the basically dyadic gift-giving which Cheal (1988) was able to concentrate on in his major study in Winnipeg, Canada. These are gifts which assert relationships, but the relationship which they are primarily asserting is not with the couple to whose home they are contributing, but with their own associate who has in turn some close connection with the wedding. There is here, that is to say, a mediated link. Many of those giving in this way are also outside the range of those actually invited to the wedding. While, as is obvious to all, invitations call out presents in a way that few ignore, it is common to find that a third or more of those received come from people displaying an interest in the wedding but not invited to it.

Table 2 **Donors at four weddings**

	A: N	%	B: N	%	C: N	%	D: N	%
Family and kin	9	21	32	42	32	30	30	19
Couple's associates	13	31	12	16	25	23	57	37
Parents' associates	12	28	26	34	49	46	58	37
Others	8	19	7	9	1	1	11	7
Totals	42	99	77	101	107	100	156	100

Table 3 **Guests at the four weddings**

	A	B	C	D
Full reception	23	81	49	117
Evening reception only	24	0	36	44
Totals	47	81	85	161

Such mediated relationships are at one extreme. The donors are clearly separate and independent of the parties marrying. At the other extreme are their own parents and immediate families. Unless those marrying have been financially and domestically independent for some time, which was unusual amongst the marriers studied in Glasgow, for the families wedding presents are a part of a wider pattern of support being offered to one of their members in the process of setting up a home of their own. Presents are in the most direct sense contributions to what is needed for this. The ties involved here are intra-group, multiplex and of the most unchallengeable kind known. Presents are given in the context of such relationships but the relationships in no way depend upon them; they bear no symbolic burden of claiming or representing relationships (cf. Hyde 1983). The utilitarian perspective has a natural base here. Presents of money feature strongly at this familial centre, though they may also come from others. Long-standing friends of parents, with whom the child marrying has grown up almost as 'one of the family', feature amongst money-givers too and are in a partly analogous position, but there are of course others who are differently placed. For them, the excuses for giving money discussed above may be relevant.

It is in the range of relationships between the two extremes, amongst uncles, aunts and cousins and the couple's own various associates, that the personal perspective makes most sense. Here gifts can reasonably be seen as standing for a relationship, as part of what maintains pre-existing relationships and expands them from relationships with individuals to relationships with and between the couples whom marriage constitutes as proper units of interaction. In the wider family, and particularly when its members have scattered across the country or – as one can hardly avoid noting in Glasgow – across the world, participation in one another's weddings in this way may indeed be one of the main things which keeps relationships alive.

The show of presents

Ways in which wedding presents represent more than a private transaction between donor and recipient and in which they have different significances for different people have begun to emerge in the first section. They are commonly given a collective existence by being displayed in a show of presents. This is the name for a distinctive and firmly patterned event. As a term it is so well established that it is frequently treated as a single word, highlighted by the common use of 'show-of-presents', rather than 'shows of presents', as the plural form.

Generally mothers hold 'show of presents' for daughters getting married. They hold them at their own homes as events entirely separate from the wedding itself. They are usually held around the weekend preceding the wedding and particularly on Sunday afternoons when people with jobs and those living at a distance can more easily come. People are not invited for a particular time: open house is held between set hours and often on more than one day. Attenders are the womenfolk amongst the givers of presents.

The event itself has two parts to it. a hospitality side and the showing of the presents themselves. The two are kept spatially separate. The presents are not just available but are displayed. They are unpacked, assembled if necessary, and set out with the cards which have come with them. This is generally in the bride's bedroom, which is often upstairs and not infrequently shared with a sister. There the presents are set out as effectively as possible on all available surfaces, of which the largest is likely to be the bed or beds. So crucial are beds, indeed, that it is often felt impossible to clear them for the night between successive days of showing: the usual occupants of the beds must sleep on floors or elsewhere.

With the presents set out and the visitors arriving they are, a few at a time, shown round the display. Generally the bride does most of this. She goes through the whole stock of presents each time, noting whom they are from and trying to comment appreciatively on them.

DM. What was everybody's reaction to the presents?

Jean. 'Oh my! Isn't that lovely!' [she laughs] 'Look at that, Oh, beautiful, beautiful,' That's the usual. 'Oh, she's done well' – that was the ubiquitous expression that was there all the time, you know: 'She's done well.'[T46]

It is a recognised duty of bridesmaids to help with this showing but often the bride does it all. Even she, who has seen all the presents arrive, regards it as something of an ordeal and certainly the hardest part of the wedding. Afterwards she may be proud of the achievement:

> I didnae forget anybody. Nobody was offended. I got it off pat eventually, 'cause I knew who everything was from and what order I had it in – memorised it all.'[T19]

But mistakes do get made, particularly when bridesmaids take a turn.

As regards the hospitality, the bride's mother is clearly in charge. The commonest pattern is to offer visitors a drink, probably alcoholic, when they arrive. They are then taken off to see the presents, returning for tea, sandwiches and cakes, with home-baking prominent. For this and for the general servicing of the event the bride's mother has considerable support. An excess of food tends to be prepared, with aunts, the groom's mother and neighbours all contributing and often helping out in the kitchen as well. Talking, eating and drinking are the style of the party, rather than anything more active. When she is not taking people round, the bride is expected to talk to her guests, but the expectation is that people will not linger long after they have been shown round. There would not be the seats or the sheer space otherwise. But when newcomers cease to arrive there may be some settling in:

James's mother. If you go at night to a show of presents and you're the last there, there's a crowd and you have a party. Like that friend of

> ours, Julie Doyle's show of presents – you [Helen and Catherine, her two unmarried daughters] were with us – we went there to the Sunday night and ... . They have a bar actually, in the house, and then everyone got another drink, and we had a singsong. We sang all the hymns that was to be sung at the wedding, and some different songs. It was a party really. It finished up a party.
>
> Helen. That was better than the wedding! [she laughs]
> Mother. It was really good. It all depends on the company.[T106]

In this pattern of marrying, the presents are therefore set apart and displayed as objects of collective celebration. At the time this certainly overrides their utilitarian significance. They are also firmly associated with women, both as prime givers and receivers.

Neither part meets with universal approval and there are other causes of discontent too. One at the time of the research was alcohol, either in itself bidding to change the nature of the event or for the way its provision necessarily raised costs to an extent which some found threatening. An unemployed bride in the east of Glasgow seemed to face a particularly alcoholic local culture:

> I'm getting my buroo money – you know you get it every fortnight. And my sister's man, he's getting the drink out the cash and carry for the show of presents – £15 I'm giving him for drink. I think it's really terrible now. You used to go and you'd get a drink and a cup of tea, and you did enjoy yourself, but now they just think they're coming for eight good drinks. See, when I was working – I'd only just started working; I was only sixteen – and it was a show of presents up Blantyre, and we'd get about two drinks and then somebody says 'Everybody put money in', and we'd get a kitty, and they'd go out and get a carry-out in. Plus you had what you wanted to drink. But now they just think they're coming for a good bevy ..., free drink. They're going to get their full at the wedding. I don't know. I would rather put the money to better use but it's kinda expected at your show of presents.[T1]

Some brides, in particular, felt so strongly about the show of presents that they wanted to avoid it altogether. A few women would refuse to attend even as guests. Mothers too, aware like everyone else of the work involved, though they were far less likely than their daughters to disapprove on principle, might sometimes require little persuasion to abandon thoughts of a show. Others were adamantly in favour. This was indeed one of the aspects of wedding arrangement over which conflict was commonest. Most mothers probably would have echoed the idea that 'it's only manners to have one, to let everyone see what you have got as a kind of thank-you to them'.[T8] But some had more formulated reasons:

Catriona's mother. It has definite advantages and very definite disadvantages. You can meet people that you are never going to meet before the wedding otherwise. They will then have to meet for the first time at the wedding – close relations of the bridegroom. That's a definite advantage. You can entertain people who you are not entertaining at the wedding. That to me are the two most important reasons – the two most important reasons that I had the show of presents for. The disadvantages are that people come to be nosey – and you just have to accept that some people are nosey. [...] They just openly compare, which is a bit ..., which is a bit ignominious, isn't it? But it didn't happen with us ... to any great extent. It might have happened covertly.[T40]

Women may also feel uncomfortable about the exclusively female nature of the event even though they have held one. They will then often try to prove that their own show was different. Usually this turns out to be the kind of exception which proves the rule. Most fathers and bridegrooms even are packed off elsewhere for the duration of shows.

Just as, in Glasgow at least, the rejection of lists is normal without being inevitable, so the female show of presents is a standard part of getting married without being universal. Those who reject it seem often to be expressing not just a balance of advantage tilted against it, but alternative values based on a different view of the process of getting married. Marriage, it may be assumed, is an essentially private affair for the couple concerned. On this view presents represent, with varying emphases, personal contributions to their private schemes, and with this goes distaste for an event which makes the giving and receiving public and even competitive. The articulate bride quoted in the first section for her 'personal' perception of presents expressed, in the same passage, strong feelings on the matter:

Barbara.   I'm more than grateful to people for their gifts and I'll write to everyone, and I'll thank them, but I don't think my appreciating has to be shown by having a room full of stuff on display, you know. The appreciation of anyone's gift is for them to get a thank-you letter at the time, and then come to this house and see that we have put their gift into use – being in use – not to see it wrapped up in its plastic parcel on top of a pillow in a bedroom somewhere. Forget it![T42]

To display these personal things, let alone to set them in a context which might imply comparison, can even be felt to be a betrayal of the relationships which they express and certainly to be in bad taste.

Resistance to shows occurs, therefore, on the basis of 'personal' interpretations of presents, but such interpretations are difficult to sustain in face of
practices of giving and reciving over which brides have limited control. A
fuller view of this experience is now possible. One side of the matter is
obligation. Obligations to invite lead to obligations to respond with a
present, a typical Maussian sequence of gift-exchange. Even amongst those
not invited to the wedding there are often obligations between workmates
and colleagues. Direct workmates give, and are expected to give, individual
presents, whilst more distant associates will contribute to a 'sheet' put round,
a collection from which gifts or a present of money will be provided. In some
offices and factories this can involve as many as several hundred people and
even a show of presents at work. This will not prevent close workmates also
attending the domestic show.

Obligation does not of course account for everything. As presents begin to
come in it often becomes apparent that they are being received from people
whom the couple hardly know,

> even like, a neighbour of James's mum and dad, her mother who
> stays up in Clydebank or something. Well, I've never set eyes on
> her. And a lot of people from up that road there, that just know ...,
> that know James's mum and dad – I don't know at all and I
> daresay James doesn't know half of them.[T52]

These are the mediated presents discussed above. Where they involve business or professional colleagues of parents, sometimes they include some of the
most spectacular offerings of all. Why 'people you'd hardly know' should be
so keen to associate themselves in this way with the wedding is not clear to the
parties concerned. A bride who had drawn attention to the phenomenon had
nothing to offer by way of explanation; her husband-to-be thought that
'maybe they're just happy for you'.[T17]

By now we can do a little better and understand at the same time the
importance of the show of presents. It is the bride who is chiefly associated
with the presents. She it is who is primarily regarded as doing well out of
them. In Glasgow at least it is not in an altogether personal capacity. At the
most general level people are, it appears, using the opportunity of giving a
present almost impersonally to pay tribute to marriage itself. More directly,
presents are being received in terms of a couple's place within networks of
family, kin and friends, and often in work organisations too. It is these links
which she is displaying in showing people round her presents, and especially
the positions of the two families from which she and her husband-to-be come.

There is therefore a powerful interest behind the determination of so many
mothers to hold shows of presents and for the family support and input – even
on occasion to the extent of redecorating the house – so willingly given. A fine
collection of presents which a daughter or daughter-in-law can show herself

off in displaying is, most directly for the parents, an achievement all the more valuable in that, while it provides a direct return for expenditure on the wedding, it cannot be simply commanded or bought. From the point of view of the guests the show asserts a collective side to the wedding. If the bride has done well it is they, the present-givers, who have enabled her to do so. It is for what she represents that the bride is, justifiably and for all participants, the star of the show.

Taking out

From their show of presents girls are often dressed up and taken out to be paraded around the streets, and much the same thing may happen at or from work. There is no unanimity as to whether this has a name, and if so whether it is 'bottling', a term documented from the late nineteenth century,[6] or just, more descriptively, dressing up or taking out.

One contributor described events in which she had participated before her own marriage in the 1920s. Her memory of the period was all the sharper for the fact that neither she herself at her own wedding nor subsequently her own children had done anything of the kind. She was indeed one of those with the not uncommon idea that the practice had disappeared.

Mrs M. They used to take them out and run them around the streets – hammering things, er ..., you know, chamber pots, you know! And filled with salt and a candle. I never knew what the salt was for, and the candle.[7] Well, that was never done in ..., mine were too ..., mine were never out ...

SC. Were they too respectable for that?

Mrs M. Yes, You know, they were kinda reserved – that's the word for it. [...]

SC. But do you remember before you were married yourself going out with other girls who were going to be married?

Mrs M. That's when I've seen it. I've seen them all dressing her up and giving her a long train, you know – old curtains, you know, draped ... dressed up ... and her face all done up wi' rouge and stuff. And then everybody come out to see, you know, what the racket was. They made such a racket. [...] Oh it was fun! We used to love to join in it, and they threw rice over her, you know, and ... och aye! it was really funny.

SC. They kissed men in those days?

Mrs M. They flung coppers – you know, the old money.[8] It was pennies. They flung pennies and the girls all gathered up the pennies, and they'd a right wee drink at the end of it, at the end of bringing

the girl home, and they dragged her for miles, painted up her face.
SC.   They threw the money, not put it in the pot?
Mrs M.   Aye. People would say, 'Well, that's for luck.' They threw money
            for luck. In these days it was associated ..., it was the same as
            throwing pennies out the taxis. I think that's never went out [i.e.
            in the form of scrambles: see Chapter 7 below] (cf. Kay 1980).[T74]

At the time of the research, the early 1980s, the recognisable descendant of
such events still flourished. A girl who is to be married gets specially dressed
with help and encouragement from other women. Unlike comparable
practices reported from England (e.g. Westwood 1984, pp. 112–19), it is a
matter of dressing up, rather than of dressing as anything in particular.
Multicoloured crêpe paper and balloons nowadays feature strongly, and an
oversized hat made with the same material is common. The girl is also
provided with a child's plastic potty containing salt, a baby doll, perhaps a
dummy and a few wedding trinkets. The party arm themselves with noise-
making equipment in the form of pans and pan lids. They go out and the
singing and crashing begin.

Laura.   They shout this at the top of their voice, and everybody comes to
            look, at their windaes. 'There's so-and-so getting married!' 'Oh
            look who she's marrying!'
June's mother. But it's a funny thing when you hear it ... . It's no so long ago
            we heard it there, bangs and ... .
June.   Everybody runs. You see everybody at all the windaes.
Mother (imitating). 'Oh, that's so-and-so getting married!' 'Oh, there
            they've got her out!' Everybody likes to see.[T61]

Songs are sung and there is one in particular which is usually mentioned first:

            Hard up! Kick the can! ... ... has got her man.
            If you want to know his name, his name is ... .

'Hard up!' was in the past a standard children's taunt, designed to extract
expected contributions from adults, particularly in the form of wedding
scrambles. As was seen above, this probably had a more direct connection
with the context in the past than it has now. Indeed, occasionally in discussing
songs, 'Hands up' was substituted for 'Hard up', reflecting the lack of
significance the expression now has for those who go round shouting it and its
variants. Today, money is to be collected into the pot in return for kissing the
bride.

The second component, 'Kick the can!', has receded slightly less far from
consciousness, though few would immediately identify its significance. In fact
it is a game widely known in the recent past, famous for delighting children
and infuriating adults within earshot by its noise. The appropriateness of the

idea to the occasion is clear. The Opies (1969, pp. 164–5) give an excellent account of it. Indeed, they cite the 'Hard up' rhyme in connection with it, though this was certainly never its primary use in Glasgow.[9] Other songs are less specific. Well known children's songs – 'The big ship sails on the illy, ally, o' – mingle with anything connected with weddings, new or old and sometimes adapted to the occasion: 'Daisy, Daisy, give me your answer do', 'Turn, turn, kiss the bride', 'She's getting married in the morning'.

Mother.   There aren't very many.
Helen.   We always run out. We just start and go round again.[T106]

As far as the potty is concerned, it is to be carried but also:

Mother.   They used to make you jump over it in the street.
June.   That's right! You put it in the street and jump over it three times.
           And you have to sit on it, and they all laugh at you! [she laughs,
           and they go on to talk about a nervous girl who came out in a rash
           at the prospect].[T61]

The starting point may be work or home. A form that was commoner in the past, but was still occurring at the time of the research, took place when a girl was leaving her work on the last day before getting married. It was then workmates who would dress her up and take her home in that state. This was likely only when girls' homes were fairly close to their place of work, as was more frequent in working-class areas of the city before the major programmes of rehousing in the mid-century scattered people into its peripheries. Nevertheless, local traditions might still build up in factories, and practical-joking and horseplay appear. Hospitals and superstores are also inclined to develop their own more boisterous traditions.[10] If a girl is not to be taken home after work, similar things may happen at the dinner-break. Whatever else may be involved, touring round exchanging kisses for money is now a characteristic feature.[11]

In offices the horseplay element is unlikely and there the tone can remain genteel. A girl is likely to arrive in the morning to find her desk decorated with streamers, balloons, even flowers, and a decorated costume ready for her to wear. There may even be a show of the presents received at work, with refreshment offered to those who come to see it, or at least sweets brought in by the bride to be passed round for all those who contributed to her sheet. A large office with staff of both sexes will provide scope for being taken around there, kissing the men and getting money from them even without going outside. From city-centre offices however, a girl may be taken out into the streets visiting lunchtime pubs, there to find the men from whom to extract the money.

From home, as has already been noted, taking out is likely to follow a show of presents. It is most likely to follow an evening session to which workmates and friends come, but it may still happen if the girl has already been dressed up at work or is going to be. The older generation may even instigate it. Aunts and mothers may help to prepare costumes and accoutrements and encourage the young ones to go out regardless of the cost in kitchen utensils the worse for wear on their return.

Carol (a recent victim herself).   Jean Adams had a sore foot – she had strained her Achilles tendon playing hockey. So she was limping along, dragging me down, shouting 'Get that man!' And Joyce would run over and grab this man and drag him back over. You know, it was an absolute conspiracy ..., and Janice and Aileen at the back there saying: 'I'm embarrassed! How common!'[T36]

The search for men is the main determinant of where the expedition goes. If there are pubs nearby, the party will go on foot through the streets to them, but if they live in one of the large peripheral schemes without pubs they may well board a bus and ride to a centre where pubs are to be found. Allowing free travel in such circumstances was at the time of the research well established in the city. An alternative and alarming strategy was to block a main road by standing in it. The girls would force drivers to stop, and get them out of their cars to kiss and pay.

Pubs are certainly the most popular hunting ground, but they are not necessarily ideal.

Carol.   The first pub ..., when we went into the Horseshoe, the men ran into the toilet. It was the funniest thing you've ever seen. They'd only got two of them left at the bar. And the rest, they just heard the pots and they went [swoosh] into the gents' toilet. Jean was standing at the door going 'Are you men or mice? Get out of there!' But they didn't come out.[T36]

If the bridegroom happened to be present, he would certainly avoid the party. Men in offices too can find a sudden urge overtaking them as the characteristic sound is heard.

But sometimes there are other hazards:

Mary.   So we went down to the Clifton Arms Hotel and first of all we went round the sort of quieter bit where the older people sit, the older couples and things. We went round them, and all the old men were 'Oh! Come here, hen!' and all this, and 'Oh, best of luck!' and all the rest, you know, putting the money in the potty. We went through there. So then I thought, we'll no go into the Stables Bar, 'cause that's where all the young ones are. But suddenly one of them must have said, 'What's this door here?', and they looked and ...: 'Oh, come on in!' And the jukebox was going. Oh, I met everybody that I knew that night. I'm saying, 'Oh, hello there!' 'Oh, it's Mary!' And I'm going: 'Oh no!' But we went round the whole bar. Then we met up with three English chaps and they hadn't a clue what was happening. They were giving the money but going 'and what ..., what is this?', you know. I was telling them: 'Traditional Scottish Bride,' you know, 'for good luck!'[T62]

Some girls are dressed up and taken round more than once in the days leading up to their weddings, but others avoid it altogether, even if they have shows of presents. In the first place there is, unlike the show of presents, a definite class difference here. Older people commonly associate taking out with 'factory girls'; girls who work in libraries or offices or hospital laboratories may be expected to be above such things.

Mr Hillis. Mind you, you'll only get that in working-class folk. I mean, middle class or upper class, you'd never get that – because they'd be looking down their nose at that sort of thing, you know. They would think that was terrible! I mean, there's nothing in a bit of light-hearted fun, nothing whatsoever. It doesnae matter if you're a millionaire or ..., a wee bit of light-hearted fun does you good, you know. And I think that people who object to it are awfu' sort of narrow-minded.[T48]

And there are indeed, and always have been since they were settled, resolutely middle-class areas of the city in which girls are not dressed up and taken out at all. It is possible to live in such an area and never come across any such happening. There are also other parts of the city with so few families with children of marrying age that it is possible, living in one of these, never to see it and to believe it to be an old custom which has now died out.

People who are bothered about their status, who wish to be other than working class, are therefore likely to be happy to avoid being taken out – they will at least think twice about it. There is, however, no neat coincidence with class as measured by any other criterion. Many in Glasgow are pleased to identify themselves as working-class even if by socio-economic criteria they have little claim to be so regarded; others are simply not bothered. The decline in the number of factory jobs has meant that the daughters of those who in their youth were 'factory girls' were bound by the time of the research to be largely office girls if they had jobs at all. It was probably this basic change which had taken the practice so firmly into the office world. It had diffused across a wide range within the society, becoming in consequence less highly charged with status implications than it was even a generation before.

Enthusiasm for the practice varies. Amongst those who do get dressed up the commonest stance is protest, but protest which their friends know is not

to be taken too seriously. Often girls expect to be embarrassed – one
participant thought the whole purpose was to embarrass the girl. A good deal
of embarrassment certainly occurs, but most girls would be disappointed
were people not to insist on taking them out.

June.	And they start taking you out in the street and dancing you about. It's a bit of a worry!
Mother.	It's an old tradition, isn't it?
J.	But it wouldnae be the same if they didnae do that to you. I mean, much as you're going to be mortified, but I mean, ... [if it had not been done] I think you'd have been annoyed too. It's a part of your life. It's never going to happen again. I mean, if you marry again, they'll no do that, because it's only the first time that they do all these sort of daft things.[T61]

And from a recently married woman whose friends did not dress her up:

> Oh no! My friends don't have that in them. My bridesmaid said
> 'Let's go out!' and everybody went 'Er-mm ...', but they never
> made it. It would have been different if I'd been working.[T6]

But others are genuinely alarmed at the prospect. They will not necessarily
escape it, but they may do so or at least reach some compromise. Objection is
most likely to be taken to the idea of kissing men, probably drunken men, in
pubs. Older people with whom the matter was discussed were almost always
disapprovingly preoccupied with the modern practice of girls going into pubs
at all, and even amongst the young, very many girls still had reservations
about it. Going out but keeping away from pubs was therefore a possible
compromise, though this might be seen as leaving behind a rather empty
form, with men, money and kisses all largely lost.

Such a rich development of popular ritual practice is bound to excite
questioning from time to time. People may ask themselves or each other, or
are asked by an inquisitive stranger, why particular customs are performed or
what the meaning of some item may be. One person may be puzzled by the
salt: why should salt be taken around? Others may subsume the salt, being
struck by the potty with its contents including the baby doll and the salt: what
can be the reason for that? For yet another it may be collecting money into the
potty, or the giving of money for kisses, with the potty more or less disregarded. Even an unusually comprehensive attempt at symbolic interpretation by one bride-to-be did not get far:

SC.	Why?
Jan.	Fertility and good luck. The salt's ..., the salt and the money are prosperity, and the baby's to symbolise ..., the doll's to symbolise

babies, and the candle's to symb.... Oh, I don't know.
SC.   Why the potty?
J.   I suppose it's handy to carry it all about in. [She laughs.] I don't
          know. I really don't know, but that's the way it's always been.[T8]

Or the focus may be on dressing up, taking out and noise-making, or simply on some conception of a whole 'thing' as a single custom: the puzzled English lads were told, it will be recalled, that it was a 'Traditional Scottish Bride', 'for good luck'. When it comes to looking for meaning and reason, the fundamental problem is, as with all ritual, that they may be located at any one or more of several levels. It is clear here too that what exactly requires explaining is in principle and often in practice as much of a puzzle for the people concerned as it is for any would-be analyst.

This is to touch on the basic issue of the anthropology of ritual. In the context of this chapter however, I mean to note further only that participants' efforts at attributing meaning were observed to bring into play the two most general frames of explanation familiar to anthropologists, the synchronic and the diachronic. The young face the practices as they have, quite recently, found them in existence. They tend to try making sense of them as they stand. This is the stance of the classic functional anthropologist. Those who are older and have noticed change may, on the other hand, invoke a sense that things are not in the longer perspective just what they seem.

The contrast was neatly caught in a further part of a conversation already quoted above. It began with one of the younger generation noticing the baby's potty, the baby doll, perhaps the dummy which her mother had earlier mentioned, and jumping to the same conclusion as Julie above.

Helen.   I presume it has something to do with a baby.

In classic anthropological terms, drawing on much the same cultural base, this may look at first sight obvious too: getting married, having babies and fertility, together make up a familiar package. Though the implications were not here followed up, her father then delivered the diachronic challenge:

Father.   I suppose that's introducing a bogus bit into it, because it's not
          called a potty, is it? It's called a chanty, no?
Helen.   It's called a potty.
Father.   Well, that's a polite name. It's still called a chanty.
Helen.   I'm not as old as you.[T106]

The potty, that is to say, is not quite what it seems.

The plastic potty is, it is in fact clear, a recent innovation, a functional replacement for the adult chamber pots – 'chanties' in local parlance – which are no longer available. These older articles are documented in wedding parades from the West of Scotland well back into the nineteenth century, and from elsewhere in Scotland too (Napier 1879, p. 47; Rorie 1934). To note this is not to say that the link with babies which the potty now allows people to make is in any sense unreal. It is, however, one which arrived with the substitution, and the substitution itself may well initially have had little or nothing to do with this meaning. The likelihood that the doll of recent times replaces an earlier everyday object, the candle, will also have been noted. Chamber pots with salt and a candle, and perhaps, as in the nineteenth century instance recorded, not even carried by the bride herself, would have set a very different challenge to the exegetical imagination. As to possible precedents being set for the future, for one participant a bowl was substituted for the potty; another was padded up as a pregnant bride; and a third had the baby's dummy stuffed into her own mouth and an apple, described as Adam's apple, suspended round her neck.[T36, 38 & 62]

Stags and hens

The equivalent for men to the dressing up and taking home of girls from their work was, and still is to the extent that there are men employed in traditional working-class settings, a good deal rougher. Local traditions certainly varied and there might be variation over time following a cyclical pattern of development and suppression, but the outlines seem remarkably constant. The young man getting married would be seized and messed up in some way, perhaps using dirty substances found around the particular works, perhaps soaked, perhaps stripped of part of his clothing, or some combination of these. He would then be mounted on or shoved into some trolley, or barrow, or bogie used for transport around the works and taken away somewhere, often into the outside world. There he would be left tied up in such a way that he could hardly escape without being rescued.

There was not, however, at least in the 1980s, any complete separation of male and female activities.

Helen.   We take them out. You get these barrows you get, that messengers carry bottles on, [...] tie an ordinary chair on to it, and you tie a guy on to the chair, put a hat on his head and they ...

SC.   Are girls doing it to the guys?

H.   Girls **and** guys do this to the guys, if it's a guy that getting married. They take him out and chain him up in the street.

SC.   But guys don't do it to girls?

H.   No, it's just the girls. The guys just get conned for money [laughter]. We take them and usually leave them somewhere for a while.[T106]

While girls might take part in the boy's event and perhaps introduce more of a dressing up element into it, male apprentices might on occasion get more actively involved than merely the kiss-and-pay role in the girl's. A rougher ride and sometimes even the standard indignities inflicted on males might then face her, such as has been reported from England (Westwood 1984, pp. 112–19).[12] Males in offices normally escaped indignities of this kind but there were occasional signs of the logic of sexual equality being applied there too, but in the other direction. One participant related the dressing up of a male colleague who was then persuaded to go around the office kissing the women there. He himself was thankful to avoid this at least.

What he did not avoid was the application to himself of the alternative male pattern. He was persuaded to go with male colleagues for a drink at lunchtime on his last day at work. In consequence he had to be hidden from management – in the union room – 'blitzed' for the rest of the day. He was so ill that he was unable even to start drinking at his stag night the following evening. Drinking to excess, which normally has its main focus in events called 'stag nights', is inclined, that is to say, to escape into other occasions too.

The idea of the stag night is certainly separate however. The 'last fling' as a single person associating primarily with others of their own sex is an important part of it. The man about to be married goes out with other men, on their initiative more often than his own, to indulge himself to an extent and perhaps in ways which, as a married man, he would in future be expected to forswear. To most male imaginations it seems clear that drinking to excess must feature in this. The way events turn out is likely to depend partly on whether the company is a group of 'lads' accustomed to taking their amusement together – fellow members of a football team for instance – or whether it is a heterogeneous mixture of the males who are performing central roles in the wedding itself. Both, and uneasy combinations, are possible.

Getting the groom drunk is a usual first stage, particularly where the lads are well represented. Spirits are liberally bought and, for a hardened drinker, drinks are mixed ever more wildly. Since the rest of the company is likely to be following him at least some way down the same road, neither the capacity nor the imagination for anything much beyond such drinking is often available, though there may be a certain amount of horseplay including attempts at removing the groom's trousers. A more heterogeneous party may well, on the other hand, be embarrassed by the whole event and hold themselves back. In either case therefore, a good deal less is inclined to happen on such occasions than is suggested by the many well-known stories – the plastering of the medical student, or the naked and ticketless wedding-morning groom on the train to Carlisle – which circulate.

There are enough famous exceptions to maintain the myth of the heroic stag night though. One participant in the research, a bridegroom himself in the wedding outfitting business, found himself at shop-closing on a Friday evening in a wedding dress. His experience has a peculiar interest for the present study: it shows in particularly dramatic form the way the various events in the complex pattern of marriage celebration interact and spark off one another. From this arises a conspicuous part of the scope for originality, creativity and hence change which are plain in all this unofficial ritual activity.

The Monday following, the man himself displayed the dress to his fiancée and DM, and explained what had happened:

Anthony.   As you can see, my dummy chest is there as well. Also we had balloons stuck down here because I was a pregnant bride, and, em, signs on the back saying 'Better late than never!', you know, and the veil over my head and, em, ... Oh, you name it – everything – the tiara and the wig from the dummy in the window. It had everything, you know. Em ...

DM.   So you put on this costume – without a struggle I hope?

Mary.   Made to measure.

A.   Well look, when you've got six male men round about you, and, eh, they are all looking in a pretty persuasive way, I don't think there's much point in arguing about it. So, em, I had to, eh – how could you say? – just get myself into it: [...] 'I don't mind traipsing about with this on'. They're all there – it's as much a neck for them as it is for me, you know. So, em ...

DM.   Hopefully nobody'll recognise you.

A.   Well, I had my wig on, my tiara and everything on. They were all ... . And the best man had this sort of goggles, his moustache and his dummy nose and his glasses and everything on. And if he took that off he was to get a pint of water thrown all over him – if he took it off all night. Well, he got ..., he got some water thrown over him [he laughs]. And the rest of them were all ushers at the wedding, so they had their suits on with the, eh – what d'you call it? – the buttonholes. And I'd the father of the bride on one arm and the best man on the other and all this kind of thing.[T62]

He was paraded around the centre of Glasgow collecting money for charity, in a parody at once of the taking out of girls and of the wedding-day bride herself. They visited pubs, a railway station where they waylaid arrivals off a train, and more pubs. His stag night ended more traditionally however. An eventful six or so hours later he found himself naked and, as his fiancée put it, 'meroculous' in the middle of a wet and windy city-centre night.

Yet it was, by a strange alchemy, a famous occasion:

Anthony.   When I think back on it it was ..., it was a bloody good night, you know. It was ..., it was a brilliant night, you know – what I can remember of it. But what I can't doesn't matter, 'cause it wasn't my fault. And if I didn't have that, I wouldn't have felt I had a good stag night. [...] If they'd told me they were going to do that, I would have been actually petrified. I wouldn't have enjoyed it. But all happening such a surprise, and it was such a brilliant laugh. I mean, it was great. [...] You need a good send-off, you know. I don't think a stripper would have, em, aroused me so much as this lot did that night, you know, because, em, really it was ..., it was amazing.[T62]

Something which participants will agree constitutes a 'hen night' is of less regular occurrence than certified stag nights. To an extent the man's stag night is seen locally as the male equivalent to the female taking out. It seems therefore only to have been in fairly recent times that a demand for a more exactly equivalent female event has emerged. Both come into the local scene from a wider, pan-British context and are not in any sense local growths. Leonard's (1980, pp. 147–52) account of stag and hen 'parties', the southern equivalent of the 'night' here, in Swansea in the 1960s applies well in most ways to the Glasgow scene in the 1980s.[13] Hen nights in practice lacked the determined male emphasis on excess, though the outcome on occasion might not be very different.

Tracy had asked DM if she was going to come to her hen night. It was to be held on the Friday night a week before the wedding in the local pub in which she, her fiancée, Gordon, and their friends, female and male, were used to drinking. They had told DM on an earlier occasion that they were in a pub at least four nights a week and spent a tenner a time on average: 'you get used to your wee circle of friends in the pub.' She had said she would be there at 7.00 and she actually arrived soon after. Eight other women including DM gradually joined the party, the last not arriving till about 9.00. Tracy had a new dress for the occasion and most of the girls were fairly dressed up. All could be described as friends but some had other connections too: there was her brother's wife, a cousin, a girl with whom she had herself worked – she was now unemployed – and the wives/girlfriends of two of her bus-driver fiancé's colleagues. All but one were married and three of them had children. Two were, however, not actually living with their husbands. Most were, like the bride, in their early or mid twenties, but one was definitely older, married with an eldest child of fourteen.

As people arrived, Tracy insisted on buying them a drink. After that they each put £5 into a kitty. Tracy said that at Gordon's stag night in the back room of the same pub the previous Friday there had been £120 in the kitty, and only £3 left at the end of the evening. On this occasion everyone drank different drinks,

Bacardi and Coke, gin and Coke, Malibu and lemonade, whisky and soda, gin and tonic, cider and Babycham, and so on. One started the evening on tomato juice. By closing time everyone was fairly well on. In view of the occasion they were allowed to stay a bit later. When they did finally have to leave, some found the means, as often happens on such occasions, to carry on the party elsewhere.

One of the girls had brought Tracy a present and the barman also had one for her, a set of four crystal sherry glasses. Tracy had joked with him when they first arrived: 'I thought these things had to be held in the back room' – which was indeed the rule for men's stag nights. In fact they settled round a table in one corner of the main bar. The other customers paid no particular attention to them, but the barman gave them special treatment by bringing over their drinks. In a sally of his own, he suggested that she should have had her night on the Wednesday: 'the place was really busy then – you'd have paid off your mortgage.' She, that is to say, had been likening the occasion to a stag night, he to a taking-out at which she would have been getting money for kisses rather than spending it on drinks.

The conversation, DM thought, was mostly just what would have been expected from any group of women on any social occasion. There was a fair bit of hilarity and joking, but not about anything in particular. They talked about their children, who's an angel, who's a terror; they talked about their husbands and the annoying things they did; they retailed gossip, much about a recent scandal at the bus garage at which several of their menfolk worked; they talked about hairdressers, driving and learning to drive, about holidays. In general they exchanged information about each others' lives, mostly in separate conversations between individual members of the party. Tracy talked about the show of presents she had had on the Wednesday and told everybody about her new house and their problems with it.

Attention to the reason for their gathering was, however, creeping up on them. It became gradually more insistent as the night wore on. There were many comments, particularly from Tracy herself, about it being her last night, and one of the girls began, and others quickly joined in, teasing her about what they had in store for her. She responded with a demand for six more drinks. When the last, late-arriving member appeared, she was asked to tell dirty jokes. She did not oblige. Around closing time, with the other customers leaving, things began to get rather more hectic. One girl produced a blue wedding garter, which was promptly put round Tracy's head, bursting in the process. Another was tearing up a carrier bag and trying to put Tracy's feet in it. Everyone was still sitting down, laughing, with Tracy trying to hide. A tray came over from the bar and to its banging they sang 'Hard up, Kick the can'. The barman encouraged the singing: 'you don't get a late licence unless you sing.' So they also sang 'I'm getting married in the morning', and for some reason – probably, commented DM, because somebody knew the words – Ringo Starr's 'She's sixteen, she's beautiful, and she's mine'. They also sang 'All for Marie's wedding' suitably changed to 'All for Tracy's wedding'.

Towards midnight the party seemed to be over. The one other unmarried girl's boyfriend came to pick her up, and people, including DM, began to leave. The main lights were by now off. Others stayed on though. One girl who had been teasing Tracy by letting the zip down on her dress whipped off her bra and gave it to the barman. Tracy was also at one time up dancing with him. Another girl had a fight with her boyfriend when he arrived to collect her and that reduced Tracy to tears. Eventually those who were left trooped back to her home nearby with a carry-out, to continue the party there. One sang songs, Tracy herself tried to pour whisky into her mother, and her father made a brave attempt to sleep through it all. They went on till three in the morning. It was claimed that when she was showing them out she had difficulty finding the door handle. She and her friends agreed that she had never been so drunk. All in all, it was regarded as a good laugh and an appropriate last fling'.[N28, N30, T28, T64]

Such an event was about the nearest a hen night would come to an exact equivalence to the stag night, even to the extent of endorsing the 'last fling' idea. It is difficult to decide in either case whether this is a realistic notion, whether the event really is the kind of thing which will no longer be possible for the married person. On the one hand the very common participation of married people in single-sex drinking groups and in stag and hen nights – one young man yet to face it commented: 'It's no yoursel' that's having the final fling; everybody else is having it for you'[T44] – suggest that it is mere pretence. It is rescued from total implausibility only by the fact that, as with every rite of passage, no bride or groom will ever be the focus of the same event again. Only in that logically generated sense is it something which is being in reality left behind for ever. As a cultural construction it is thus enabled to represent the single life, and even possibly its freedoms, in contrast to the responsibilities of married life.

Since until rather recently the male freedom to drink and to socialise outside the home was far greater than the female, the earlier and more insistent development of the stag night is hardly surprising. Even the hen night described above still differed from a stag night likely to be held amongst the menfolk belonging to these women in the weakness of any sense that the company **should** be getting the bride/groom drunk and that something **should** be done to her. But the outcome here was, as has been seen, very similar. Convergence between the freedoms in these respects of males and females does appear in recent years to have been leading to convergence in the ritual practices which appeal to them. Nevertheless, at the time of the research diverging tendencies did still remain. For women, an outing for a meal or to a pub with a group of friends, involving a good deal of hilarity but not much more, or even a 'night in the house' with drinking and talking and singing, was the usual style. For men a more definite and singular outcome was at least in mind and not infrequently achieved.

Finally it needs to be observed that the situation described here did not please everybody. Some could not happily accept the sexual segregation on which the pre-wedding celebrations discussed in this chapter were based, even when it was in practice being challenged at many points. It still implied for them a gender difference which they did not want to acknowledge. One response occasionally found was to attempt to obliterate the difference by insisting that it was actually a stag night a girl was having. This might be attempted with an outing separate from one's partner, either with a female group or, more ambitiously, with a mixed group in which males were preponderant. As long, however, as male and female drinking patterns and capacities, learnt or inherent, differ, this latter could prove hazardous. A commoner response, which we saw even in the case of the show of presents, was to reject and attempt to avoid such customs altogether:

Margaret. I think the **whole** point of this **whole** proceedings – the whole proceedings – is that **we**'re getting married; which is, you know, ... it was the biggest ... . What you are really saying is that you want to be with this person, and here's all these **silly** things where everybody's ... . You know ... . You know, it's all the **female** things to do, and all the **male** things to do. That really annoys me. It really does. I find these things awkward just now. They pose a real ... . They're really awkward because they're not the kind of situations we're used to.[T91]

Chapter 6

Wedding Day 1: the ceremony

The wedding day is the high-point of celebration in to which months of preparation and anticipation have often gone. It is the moment at which a marriage is considered finally achieved, and in many ways it is a single moment. The events of the day move around, they take place in different registers, but they are interwoven and make for the most part a single sequence in the experience of those who stay with them throughout. When it comes to analysing them, however, they are too many and too complex to be given immediately the unity of presentation they truly require. Here three separate chapters will be used. In the first, the performances of the wedding services briefly considered in Chapter 1 will be presented.[1] An examination of the events which frame the service and lead on from it follows. In the third chapter the major sequence of largely secular celebration which completes the day is discussed.

Services in the Church of Scotland

Church of Scotland wedding services vary widely in style and in the words spoken. The autonomy of the minister allows each to create his or her own form, a more or less personal and idiosyncratic response to the heritage outlined in Chapter 1. The scope for innovation is in practice constrained, however, by the simplicity and directness of the progression to be followed. All that is required is a statement on the Christian meaning of marriage, 'the vows', the putting on of rings, a pronouncement of marriage by the minister, and a blessing. The components are therefore few and they are performed in words which, though rarely identical, are combinations, permutations and transformations of the common sources on which all are drawing. Two hymns, at beginning and end, are also standard. There is little movement between entry and exit beyond standing up and sitting down. Accounts of two services in the same church in the same year, both based on Church of Scotland orders but developed by different ministers, will show both the scope for divergence in spirit and style and the nature of underlying regularities.

One of the services[N9] was based on the first of the two orders offered by the official *Book of Common Order 1979*. Some of the central items from it, such as the vows, were followed very exactly – there is often the feeling that legal validity may turn on getting these right – but most of the surrounding sections had been carefully rewritten to communicate views of marriage which the minister wanted to put over. They expanded upon and diverged from the topics of the established text and were expressed for the most part in the minister's own forthright language. The tone was conversational; words taken directly from the printed service were in no way differentiated from those added or varied. A sense of spontaneity, of response to the individuals present and to the moment in which things were happening for them, was aimed for and, it seemed, in considerable measure achieved.

After leading the bride and her party to the front of the church and turning to face them, the minister began with the opening words of the service from the book: 'Unless the Lord builds the house, its builders will have toiled in vain ...'. She continued:

> We are gathered here today to share this very happy moment with Angus and Carol. We praise God, for he is the source of all loving kindness and it is mutual love and affection that brings our friends here today for this very joyful start to a new episode in their lives. We praise God in song. You will find the first hymn in your order of service: 'The King of Love my Shepherd is'.

Tones, relationships and theme were immediately set. The minister here identifies with the congregation, together sharing the event with friends being married. The event is immediately related to God and the connection with love which is to be the central organising concept throughout established. The hymn offers an immediate way in which all present can participate actively in getting the event under way. Here, as very commonly, the words reinforce the theme of love. The congregation were then told to sit.

Minister.   What we do today is done to mark a very important occasion in the lives of our friends and in the lives of our community and our families.

She then set out a credo on Christian marriage, in three parts.

> We believe that marriage is ordained by God. We believe [this] within the reformed tradition, because Jesus was present once at a wedding in Cana and it was there that he worked his first miracle. We derive from that episode in our Lord's life the indication that God is indeed involved in marriage and blesses marriage with his

> continuing loving presence. We believe that the power of the risen
> Christ is there in the marriage of a man and a woman.

From this assertion of belief in God's involvement with marriage, marked
with an awareness that there are other Christian traditions too, she went on
to procreation, sex and the family.

> We believe also that marriage is provided by God as part of his
> loving purpose for the procreation of our race. We believe that
> God is a creator God and that he creates out of love, and that it is
> only in love that people should be created. And so he ordained
> that it is love that brings a man and a woman to leave the family
> wherein they were brought up, and begin a new family with each
> other. That is the setting for the physical enjoyment of love which
> we believe, blessed by God, brings forth children, and when that is
> not God's gift for us, nevertheless he enriches our presence with
> the enjoyment of children who may be [?not our own]. Marriage
> is meant to create a family unit in which children grow and learn
> to love one another and by that they come one day to understand
> what a loving God means, because thay have parents who love
> them dearly.

Marriage as a spiritual and sometimes difficult journey was the third part of
the credo, before turning to the wedding itself.

> It is therefore very serious what we are doing today, and we do not
> come here ... – as I know very well you haven't done – we don't
> come here lightly. This isn't something that is just a pretty picture
> for us. As Christian people this is the highlight of our lives:
> promises made before God himself to one another in love. When
> the vows that you will exchange are kept in all loving kindness,
> then we, your family and your friends, 'reap benefits also, because
> through your married life and the joy that will come from it, we
> shall derive encouragement and hope. And so, although this day is
> very important for both of you, it is important also for us, because
> we are looking forward to days of happy sharing to continue after
> this great day.

The almost conversational tones, the strong sense of talking directly to the
couple and to each person in the congregation, were sustained throughout.
When forced into formality, as immediately after the passage just quoted by
the requirement to ask whether there was any reason why the couple could
not marry, the minister used little jokes to involve, or re-involve, the congregation and to lighten the tone. In that case she commented after a pause:
'Awfully glad nobody spoke,' and there was laughter. 'We'd have all had to

put our clothes back in mothballs,' and there was more laughter.

'Let us pray' signalled a different range of speech forms, now addressed directly to God.

> Almighty Father, we praise your glorious name, for out of your overwhelming love you created this world, and it is good.
>
> Out of your overwhelming compassion you created mankind, male and female, that they might live in loving harmony, and it is good.
>
> We praise your holy name, for down through the generations you have always been faithful to your people, shedding your love all over the world.
>
> We give you thanks this day that Angus and Carol have responded to your loving gifts to them, in loving worship to you. You have further blessed them by bringing them to this day full of loving kindness for one another.
>
> Beloved Father, we praise your glorious name, for your protection and guardianship over Angus and Carol.
>
> We pray earnestly now that the love you have given them will grow stronger as the days go by, and that this covenant of marriage made before you and their friends might be a continuing source of strength and joy for them.
>
> We earnestly pray, Father, that you will grant them depth of love, that the vows which they will exchange be kept faithfully and lovingly all the days of their life.
>
> Bless them with your presence now and always, for Jesus' sake. Amen.

All the sections here were, in a general sense, prayer, but they ranged across four rather separate forms, praise, thanks, request and exhortation. 'Praise' is here a somewhat formalised rehearsing of another's merits, of a kind which takes place regularly in some societies in relation to the powerful, but in this is limited almost entirely to God. 'Thanks' is a specialised form of praise which is in contrast very widespread, often as an almost unthinking social form. It is generally seen as called for by the gift which has been given. In daily life this is almost invariably an appropriate account of interchanges involving thanks. However, as a social form it has implications which can be used rather differently. In praising or merely acknowledging the giver, thanks assert that a gift has been given, that there is therefore a link between giver and recipient. It enforces this implication whether or not any such link was intended. As a form it allows an initiative to be taken by someone wishing to define them-selves as a recipient. It is this potential which makes the common social form so peculiarly relevant in prayer. 'Request' stands more simply for prayer in the narrower sense, asking for something. 'Exhortation', lastly, is a more positive, confident form of request, moving towards command. It features strongly in Christian prayer, calling on God for action, often as here in the non-specific, generally benevolent form of 'blessing'. Blessing is so much part of the Christian conception of God that exhortation to provide it cannot be thought of as liable to rebuff or in any way impertinent. The form carries, however, an implication of closeness to God which is liable to variable interpretation. At the end of a sequence in which the minister has been speaking explicitly on behalf of all present, the exhortation to bless can most readily be seen as expressing a closeness between the congregation as a whole and God. This would be an appropriate interpretation in the reformed tradition of the Church of Scotland. A similar form differently framed can however individuate the speaker, as one with a special capacity to secure God's blessing or even with a power to deliver it on God's behalf. Such a power is in practice, as will be seen, easily assumed, whether collectively by a congregation or by the celebrant individually. The interplay between form and doctrine and perception is necessarily subtle.

Following the prayer all stood.

> As a seal to the vows[2] you are about to make, will you give each other the right hand.

First Angus and then Carol were to repeat after the minister, a phrase at a time, the vows as in the 1979 Book:

> I, A......now take you, B......, to be my wife/husband. In the presence of God and before these witnesses I promise to be a loving, faithful and loyal husband/wife to you, until God shall separate us by death.

The words actually spoken did not make a great impression. Angus, talking a month later about the way they had said them 'about three words at a time', produced not what he had actually said but an earlier version: 'I, Angus, take thee, Carol, to be my lawful wedded wife.' But the moment had certainly been special.

SC.   Did the words strike home?
A.   Yes, they do. It's all terribly fatal.
C.   Ah ha, because she's looking at you ...
A.   And you thought, 'Oh ho! This is it! There's no way out now. All these people have heard you just say – that's it – the words. It

> seemed all of a sudden, then, very important, because that's you. You've had it. You can't run away any more after that.
>
> C.   [...] You tend to forget there are people behind you. It's all you.
> A.   Very powerful words.[T36]

As the minister put it in discussion,

> for the reality of this marriage you have to have that moment when you speak to the essence of the people, the two there. And at that moment they are ready. You know, there's a moment ... sometimes they fuss with their dresses and they're worried about whether they've got the rings, but there's a moment of concentration, and that is the vows, all round about them.

Another minister would instruct the couple to look at each other with all the love and sincerity they felt as they repeated the vows.

Rings followed, and rather more was made of them than in the Book. The minister first asked for 'the' ring from the best man. She held one up, saying: 'This ring is the token of the covenant into which you have entered.' This is close to the Book, but explanation was then added:

> 'Covenant' means an agreement, and your agreement is to live in unconditional love with one another, strengthened always by God's merciful hand. I remind you that when you look at the ring you should know also that it is symbolic of the kind of love God gives to us. There is no end to it and it's for ever present with you.[3] It is on this understanding that [– and here she was getting back to the final words of the passage in the Book –] these rings are given and received.

Putting the rings on was the subject of more good humour: 'We're having a little bit of difficulty here [laughter]; more difficulty here [laughter]; there we are!' There is generally no 'I thee wed' here in the Church of Scotland.

The ancient 'to have and to hold' words, present in Scotland in pre-Reformation times but carried down into modern times chiefly by the Anglican Church, followed – they may on occasion be incorporated into the vows themselves – and led into the pronouncement of marriage by the minister.[4] All of this followed the Book exactly. With the couple kneeling and the minister resting her hands on their heads, a blessing in one of the two forms offered by the book was then sung. 'We bless them', the minister observed on another occasion, and this 'goes back to the time of Moses'.

In context this is a striking episode, a fairly recent innovation but beginning to be quite widely known if still only occasionally practised. Kneeling is uncommon in the Church of Scotland, as is singing of anything other than hymns, but a sung blessing of this kind has been established for some time, though never of course mandatory, for baptisms. Few of those marrying are in a position to register that link, though for parents it can on occasion produce a real and emotional echo, but it makes in any case a distinctive and effective conclusion to the central marrying episode. As the minister had explained, 'the ritual element is important'; but 'they know this is happening to them, and in that sense it is not just a ritual'. And the congregation of family and friends of the couple are finally incorporated into it: 'We bless them'.

Another of the minister's own set pieces followed. She delivered a whispered instruction to the groom to kiss the bride, before turning away to pick up a book, ostensibly a Bible for the readings to follow. Angus raised Carol's veil which had been covering her face to this point, and kissed her. The minister could then turn back with the jocular comment: 'It's terrible the things that go on behind the minister's back these ...!' This was all a planned and in effect well-rehearsed performance. Another ripple was produced, renewing the feeling of down-to-earth friendliness in the gathering which the more formal and overtly ritual action of the preceding episode has temporarily suspended.

A probationer, a trainee minister who was at the time attached to this church, was then introduced, 'to read from holy scripture for us, because as Christians we always find in the word of God our guide and our help'. It was familiar verses from I Corinthians, xiii, on love. It confirmed the theme already established, as it does in very many contemporary marriage services. The minister talked directly to the couple about their vows, their marriage, faithfulness, and above all love. She could speak to this particular couple as Christians:[5] 'You have access through prayer and worship to the source of all love, the source that renews us day by day in our ability to love one another, and that is our God, who is complete and total love himself.' As is common in such addresses, the difficulties to be faced in marriage were a preoccupation: 'We all must make adjustments if we are to live in a civilised community, and marriage is a community of two, and that makes it even more difficult, not easier.' 'As Christian people you know very well that love is never anything wishy washy. Oh, Christians enjoy the romantic side of love too, but Christians know that love is firm and strong in its resolve to face all difficulties and all problems.' She ended:

> I know that perhaps you feel today is the most loving day that you have ever experienced together,[6] but those of your friends and family who have been married much longer will tell you that there are even richer depths in the quality of love that human beings can share, and we pray for that for you both now.

> Beloved Father in heaven, we ask for your blessing, your blessing on Angus and Carol as they embark on their new life together.

You have held them in your care all their lives and we commend them to your care for the rest of their days. We pray, Father, that you will for ever be near each one of them, binding them together in mutual love and affection. If it is your wish, Father, we pray that you might grant them the blessing of children, to enrich and deepen their love. We pray that their home might be a place where your spirit dwells, that they together might show rich hospitality and kindness to those who come to their home.

We give you thanks this day, for their parents and for the families from which they have come. Bind them also together in mutual love and affection this day and always, that they might give your support and help to Angus and Carol.

The prayer did not finish at this point but it was beginning to change direction. The service had so far been directed towards the newly marrying couple; now a further purpose for it, as a reminder and renewal for the already married, emerged:

We remember now those who have exchanged marriage vows many years ago. Renew your love in their hearts, that, refreshed and encouraged, they might make an even deeper commitment to their married life together, and by so doing enrich the community in which we find ourselves, making it a place more loving.
Father, you are for ever near those who love you and we pray to you now, out of that love: 'Our Father, ...' [The Lord's Prayer said with the congregation joining in].

The second and final hymn, 'Love Divine, all loves excelling', was sung. Carol was struck by the fact that she was able to sing it, and she noticed Angus singing too. On its completion the minister announced: 'The new Mr and Mrs Drummond will now leave for the vestry, and the parents of the bride will come out ...'. The wedding party formed up and the minister led them out to the vestry in an only slightly ragged procession.

The second wedding[N77] in the same church some months later was conducted by a distinguished but recently retired minister known to the bride's family. This one was based on the 1940 Book but was full of minor divergences, paraphrases, additions and subtractions. No book was actually referred to during the service, even as a prompt. Not even what were said to be biblical readings were actually read. The older tradition in the Church of Scotland is to absorb readings into the flow of instruction rather than marking them off as separate entities. Here this was taken to an extreme: well-known wedding passages, from Ephesians v, from the Corinthians passage used in the service above – the 'hymn to love' as the minister here termed it – and from St John's Gospel xv, were paraphrased to such an extent as to be recognisable only with difficulty.[7] There was no further address to the couple.

A prayer, relatively lengthy and mainly in the exhortation mode, followed immediately on the 'chosen passages from scripture'.

> O God, our loving and heavenly Father, in the quietness of this time and the holiness of this place, do thou give thy blessing to these thy children.
> Thou hast given them youth with its hopes and love with its dreams. May these come abundantly true, through their trust in each other and their confidence in thine unfailing goodness. Teach them how great is the joy which comes from sharing, how deep the love which grows with giving.
> Sanctify this covenant of love, these promises rich in forward-looking trust and joy.
> Make them loving companions and true help-meets of each other, secure in a devotion which will deepen with the passing years.
> [...]
> Strengthen the bonds of family life in your Christian fellowship, that we with thy servants may ever look to him in whom all the families of the world are blessed, even Jesus Christ our Lord.
> To him and to thee, Father, and the Holy Spirit, One God, be ascribed all glory, thanksgiving and praise, both now and for ever. Amen.

There was no Lord's Prayer but only the second and final hymn, again 'Love Divine, all loves excelling', in which the congregation could join. The service ended with a blessing in a form which suggests that it is the minister who is imparting it:

> The blessing of God Almighty, Father, Son and Holy Spirit rest on and abide with you and with all whom you love, this day and always.

Neither the prayer nor the blessing in this final section of the service derived from either of the Church of Scotland books.

These two examples suggest the range of difference which can be found. Besides being briefer and tending to be expressed in an older style of liturgical language, the second altogether lacked the personal and pastoral orientation of the first.[8] Instead of immediately naming the couple at the first opportunity, they were referred to obliquely: 'these two now standing before us' – 'this man and this woman' is another still more formal possibility – 'these thy children'. It was only in the vows that their names were spoken. On the minister's side too, there was no point at which he clearly identified himself as speaking in his own voice by using the personal pronoun 'I'. The lack of an address, together with the tenor of the last prayer, meant that there was no place for the consideration of marriage as something personally demanding and often difficult which has become a major preoccupation of many ministers and others professionally concerned with it in recent times. There was no attempt to address the already married or to make the service a renewal for them. With this restraint went the absence of any clear intention to involve the congregation beyond the singing of hymns. Though there was also a sung blessing on this occasion this was, as subsequently emerged, because the mother of the bride had had it printed as part of the Order of Service and insisted upon it: it had been sung when the bride herself as a baby had been baptised twenty-three years before. The minister suspected, wrongly as it turned out, that the congregation would not be able to sing it. The active participation of the couple themselves in the service was limited too, the vows being taken in the more passive form which requires them only to respond: 'I do'. These brief though important words, the joining of their right hands and the silent putting on of rings become, here and commonly, their only active contributions to the event. This was thus an example of the currently minimal style of Church of Scotland marriage service. Its total duration from entry to going off to 'sign the register', and including hymns, was twenty minutes exactly.

The spirit of these two services, and most of the words actually spoken in them, were therefore very different though they clearly derive from the same tradition. They are made up mostly of the same kinds of component and many of the ideas are echoes of one another. They have in common their simple progression from first hymn to second and last. The simplicity and brevity is striking when compared with the Catholic nuptial mass next to be examined. In addition, here neither minister was reading a service available to the congregation. The latter's only guide, should they be interested in one, was the order-of-service leaflet usually provided for guests, if only by photo-copying one from a previous wedding. Even, however, when these are smartly printed with elaborate motifs embossed on their covers they rarely contain anything beyond the titles of the entry and exit music, the words of the hymns and perhaps the blessing if this is to be sung too. Church of Scotland services therefore remain predominantly performances by the celebrant, and there is relatively little scope for the development of more complex interactions between the various participants.

The Catholic Nuptial Mass

Whereas in the Church of Scotland, texts provide a starting point and guide for individual ministers' celebrations of marriage, in the Scottish Catholic Church there is a text to be followed and a complex and elaborate pattern prescribed. The pattern has three main sections, 'Liturgy of the Word',

'Liturgy of Marriage' and 'Liturgy of the Eucharist'. These are framed by an 'Entrance Rite' and a 'Concluding Rite'. A rich mixture of ritual speaking and acting builds up to, confirms and supports the couple's marrying of one another at the centre of the entire sequence. In prayer, praise, invocation and reading from the Bible, aspects of Christian doctrine are repeatedly recited and referred to, and Christian imagery expressed and evoked. Most of the forms have an ancestry going back deep into Christian and even pre-Christian history. Parts are to be spoken by the priest alone, parts are to be spoken in unison by all present, parts are to be spoken reciprocally by priest and people, parts are to be spoken solo or reciprocally by other individuals, and there are parts which may be sung, again individually or collectively.

But even here performances, the concern of this chapter, are by no means fully accounted for by the text. As was noted in the earlier chapter, choice is stressed even in the text itself and explicit provision for it is made. Alternatives are offered at many points. Already in the Entrance Rite there are three major choice points, one of them itself offering three contrasting forms for a Penitential Rite. Of the third form of that, it is noted that this is only one of a number of optional texts. There are choices within choices. There are also unscripted or only partially scripted sections. The major items here are the 'Homily' or sermon in the Liturgy of the Word and the 'General Intercessions or Prayer of the Faithful' in the Liturgy of Marriage. The latter follows immediately on the exchange of rings and is to be related to the couple and the circumstances of the particular occasion. For this prayer the Priest's book offers two 'examples', to be used in whole or in part or something else 'previously composed' may be substituted for it.

There is therefore a detailed and elaborate but intentionally adjustable text, to be performed by several voices, but even this does not exhaust the words spoken. A rubric early in the Entrance Rite allows the priest 'very briefly' to introduce the Mass, and in practice a verbal framing of events may begin even before this. There is commonly a welcome to the congregation in which the priest explains how he means to conduct the service. This is particularly likely where, as in the inevitably common 'mixed' marriages, non-Catholics are conspicuously involved, but it may for any wedding become the main or only point at which the priest addresses couple and congregation, replacing the homily altogether.

The ways in which performance and text may differ can be explored with an example, though it will be neither necessary nor practicable here to set out the sequence of a particular service in the detail required for the Church of Scotland above. As in that section, it is not a 'typical' performance which will be examined. The typical in either Church might well be a service for the religiously uninterested, and such occasions tend to provide more or less impoverished versions for analysis. It is services conducted for and amongst church people which best reveal and highlight issues and possibilities; performance in mixed marriages will be considered subsequently. In the case to be examined here, Margaret and James, the couple concerned, were both active Catholics, interested in Church matters and knowledgeable about them, and they both came from families similarly involved. The event took place, as is usual, in the bride's own parish church and in the New Town from which she came. She did not, however, normally attend this church and it was not one of its own priests who officiated, though the parish priest kept an eye on events. A priest from another parish whom the groom had known personally for some years acted in his place. This helped a couple who were keen to have a hand in planning their service, as officially encouraged, actually to achieve it.

With the couple standing facing the priest at the front of the church, this service began with a succinct establishing statement:

Priest.   May I welcome you all most sincerely this afternoon, to this wedding service? As James and Margaret pledge their love for one another, they do so in the presence of God. So let's start the mass by singing our opening hymn: 'We are one in the Spirit, we are one in the Lord'.[N73]

The presence of those attending is immediately recognised, the event defined centrally as a pledging of love between two named individuals – the names continued to be used repeatedly throughout the service, their order roughly alternating – and the hymn used to assert the unity of all participating in the event in the presence of God.

Subsequently, where the rubric permits the brief introduction, a more elaborate, two-minute gloss on the occasion as pledge of love appeared.

... in the sacrament of marriage, what they are doing in effect is quite simply acknowledging that their love for one another is but a very small share of the infinite love that God has for each of them. And so, by its very nature, what they are doing today is prayerful. Love is prayer and God is love. [...] And in that, each and every one of us is sharing. And it makes our presence then a share in the prayerfulness of the sacrament of marriage ... .[N73]

The homily later developed the same themes but at three or four times the length. As will be seen below, the particularising of the event in terms of the couple at its centre was an important part of this, the 'personalising' which was so strong a contemporary theme, but this was never allowed to detract from the elevated conceptual and doctrinal messages indicated by the brief quotation above. The problems to be expected in the course of married life, that other great contemporary preoccupation, were not ignored but were subordinated, as were the particular couple, to the message:

... their life together in the future is going to be supported by that spirit of loving prayerfulness. And it means that whenever the crosses and the difficulties come their way in married life, then they know from the very outset, because of their preparation, how they are going to overcome the difficulties and hardships together. Because as they start off in the spirit of love, which is prayer, so also it is through love and prayer that they will be able to cope with all the problems and difficulties that are part and parcel of life together.[N73]

This impersonal personalising, this striking use of couple and occasion to address primarily the congregation, was all the more noticeable here where the priest's personal knowledge of those marrying was considerable. He had known the groom from his school days and at one period subsequently they had even gone away together on climbing trips. He was not therefore, as may sometimes seem to be the case, glossing over an absence of personal knowledge; like the examples in our first section, he was adopting a carefully thought out and in many ways individual style, despite textual constraints. Another priest, who paid great attention to the preparation of those he was to marry, made the point explicitly that, by the time of the wedding, the couple had had their talking to; it was then the congregation's turn.

Each priest has his own ways of handling such events. They vary in the extent to which they think it necessary and proper to alter the tone and content according to their sense of the particular couple and congregation. As far as direct addresses from the priest are concerned, our instance was unusual in its succession of three, each an elaboration on its predecessor. In contrast to this, ignoring the text's requirement for a homily in favour only of a somewhat extended welcome and explanation at the beginning seemed a particularly common strategy. This might be combined with a more-or-less reliable series of indications of progress through the service and the pages of the Nuptial Mass booklet where they would be found. Even the style of this was variable. Anything between the crisp and efficient, firmly marked off from the text itself by changes of voice, and the chatty and informal, blending with the text, was to be found:

Now, if you've got the booklets, they're to help you follow the ceremony. We don't say every word. We skip little pieces here and there. We start on page nine – oh no, it's not: page five.
Now we'll stand for the next little one. It's on page ten.
'Let us proclaim the mystery of faith' – just the first one [since the text offers a choice of four].[N38]

Returning to our main example, the framing and bridging aspect of the priest's own distinctive contribution is there very clear. The homily ended by making a link to the Liturgy of Marriage to follow:

> So we come now to the very beautiful time when Margaret and
> James express their love for one another in the sacrament of
> marriage. [...] And as we listen to Margaret and James exchange
> these vows, then the very fact of listening and feeling with them
> and for them is itself a prayer.
> At this time now, we move to the exchange of vows. Can I ask you
> all to remain seated, to listen and to pay attention to this time of
> great feeling and emotion, happiness and joy?
> I would now like James and Margaret to come forward on to the
> altar [i.e. into the area normally reserved for the priest and
> servers], ...[N73]

The interchanges of the vows followed without further commentary, but
moving on to the rings received another interpretive link:

> We have now witnessed this beautiful and very moving exchange
> of vows. Now, as a symbol and as a sign of their pledge and of
> their love, they will exchange rings.[N73]

They did, James following up his ring to Margaret with 'this gold and silver' –
in fact here a Churchill commemorative crown piece which he had been
keeping – 'tokens of all my worldly goods'. Margaret, following the text and
unlike one boldly feminist bride encountered,[9] did not reciprocate. The priest
completed the episode with

> Let me be the first to congratulate the new Mr and Mrs Maclaren,
> who have pledged their love. We're going to sing about that now:
> 'God is love'.[N73]

The same style of commenting and moving the action along continued
through the rest of the Mass. There was clearly a sense that the words of the
text, printed and spoken, were not in themselves adequate to the occasion. A
separate task needed to be done, a task of communicating with the congregation and ensuring their involvement in the event. The priest therefore had a
dual role, not only performer of the ritual but also as a kind of master of
ceremonies.

On this occasion he clearly wished to play a third role too, a back-stage role
as person and friend as well as priest. This added yet another dimension to the
spoken side of the total performance. His very first words with bride and
groom before him at the front of the church, spoken *sotto voce* but using the
public-address system to make them audible to all, were: 'She's really
smashing, isn't she?'. This produced a ripple of response around the congregation. Only after that did he change voice and role for the official priestly
welcome recorded above. Before the service he had in fact come into the
sacristy where the bridegroom was standing and asked him whether he was

nervous. James had replied, as he later reported it, "No, I'm fine". 'So he [the priest] shut the door and stood there throwing his hands up in the air, saying "I'll need to rework the sermon!"'[T94] And when the sermon was reached he had indeed reworked it. He began with another *sotto voce* remark, to the effect that Margaret was dreading what he was going to say. He then changed to his public voice and manner, saying that James when spoken to in the sacristy had been 'as calm as can be'; it was 'the poor best man' who was suffering.

> But I'm sure, as the first notes of the 'Ave Maria' [to which the bride and her father entered] were played, the exterior calm of James was deceptive. And as Margaret came down the aisle the nerves were to be seen on her face. And as the two of them came together at the front of the church, and took one another's arms, Margaret's head was shaking. And yet, within seconds, holding one another by the arm, peace came over them. And that is love.[N73]

He was firmly on track again and had made the jump from the personal to the markedly impersonal and highly abstract discourse on love and prayer and marriage which we have already noted.

In fact other things were going on. The bride afterwards thought it had been not love but arriving safely at the front of the church which had calmed her. Certainly, from the moment when the couple reached him he was talking to them privately, calming them and encouraging them: 'Just enjoy it now!', and later 'All these people are here, but just you concentrate on what you are saying,' and later again: 'Are you happy now?'.

Even therefore when words alone are considered, the authoritative text is far from a complete specification of all that may go on. What it does is to establish boundaries between kinds of words which, without it, scarcely exist in the Church of Scotland service. It brackets off those that are printed and in doing so risks appearing to disqualify them from the function they might otherwise perform as communication amongst those present. The couple here, looking back on the service and prompted by photographs of its stages, suggested this strongly when they spoke jokingly of a key part of the service:

Margaret. I think this is the point where [the priest] was reading out the ... . What's the bit before you actually say the vows? You know, where it says: 'Are you ... ?' 'Do you ... ?' 'Are you ready to freely give yourself?' And you say 'I am,' and 'I do,' and 'I will,' and all this kind of thing. [She said this laughing].
James (joining in in the same joking vein). And 'I **should** ... .' 'I might!'[T94]

And if even such words are displaced from communication – on which so much emphasis was placed in the first example of the preceding section – so even more are the special kinds of priestly speaking identified as prayers, praise, blessings, etc. As soon therefore as there is an interest in such communication, as is certainly felt strongly in the contemporary Catholic Church, new kinds of speaking are felt to be called for and the total event grows rapidly more complex and multi-dimensional.

Words, which have been discussed so far, are relatively easily specified, though the manner of their speaking is less so. Special intonations and even voices are commonly though by no means always used in ritual speaking whether or not there is a written text. This is not something which is easily communicated, either in the form of an instruction or in analysis, but it clearly recognises and signals to others the specialness of the speaking in question. Non-verbal actions, with few exceptions, lack even the degree of clear notation which is available for words. In Catholic liturgy the making of the sign of a cross is represented by a pictogram inserted into verbal texts. A notation makes clear who is to speak which words, and there are a number of simple instructions of a repetitive nature, such as 'stand', 'sit', 'kneel'. Otherwise the specification of action is more laborious ad inevitably somewhat open-ended. It is not surprising therefore to find it appearing very patchily in rubrics. There are only seven points in the entire service at which instruction is given. First, bride and groom are to hold each other's right hand as they make their vows. The most persistent attempt at specification is the second and it involves the movements of the ring or rings. They or it should be given by the best man or server to the priest to be blessed.[10] The husband is then to put the ring on to the fourth finger of the wife's left hand and the wife now commonly reciprocates. And the husband hands (gold and) silver to his wife, the ancient practice which still finds a place in the Scottish liturgy. The third and fourth points for which action is specified are the offertory procession and the sign of peace, to both of which we return below, and the fifth is general instructions in connection with communion. If a solemn blessing is to be pronounced, a sixth instructs the priest to extend both hands over couple and congregation together. Lastly, 'All depart, to the accompaniment, if desired, of a hymn or suitably joyful music.'

These rubrics undoubtedly serve to draw attention to the actions concerned, but they are a mixed bunch and conspicuously incomplete. The procedure for handling the ring, for instance, though apparently specified in detail, altogether omits another piece of ancient action still generally observed. The ring is taken to each finger along the hand in turn, as 'In the name of the Father, and of the Son, and of the Holy Spirit' is recited, before it is finally put on to the correct finger at 'Amen'.

The Sign of Peace is likewise interesting. It is again an ancient practice but not one connected specifically with marrying. Term and practice have been enthusiastically revived in recent times, not only in the Catholic Church. The actions involved are handshakes or kisses between participants, with each pair choosing what is appropriate to themselves. What might otherwise be simply a friendly greeting is given a special gloss by being required and identified as giving or exchanging 'the sign of peace' or Pax. In the context of the wedding it readily takes on a special appropriateness and may begin to develop as a rite with a distinct patterning. This would not be new; in its pre-Reformation form a pattern was specified: 'the bride and bridegroom shall rise from prayer, and the bridegroom shall receive the Pax from the priest, and shall present it to the bride, kissing her, and none other, neither he nor she. But the clerk receiving the Pax directly from the presbyter shall present it to the others according to the usual custom' (McGregor 1905: 40-1). Today bride and groom will give each other the sign of peace, usually though not invariably in kissing – linking also with the theme we met in more eccentric form before as kissing behind the minister's back – but here their respective parents may come forward to join with them and with each other in the exchange. It will likewise spread around the congregation, a ritualised form of the greetings which are such a prominent part of wedding days.

A third example illustrates a more general point, namely than any set of instructions for procedures as complex and extensive as those with which we have to deal here necessarily operates against the background of a mass of understandings, the specification of which on any given occasion would be a vast and laborious undertaking. In the nuptial mass the prime example is certainly the entire Liturgy of the Eucharist. The movements and actions here are taken for granted, as deeply familiar in minute detail to the priest and in considerable detail, more than adequate for their own participation, to congregations. There is, correspondingly, no way in which this central section of the mass can be spelled out here.

It begins however with an episode, the offertory procession, which will illustrate the point adequately. It is at the same time germane to the wedding theme in the way it may again be developed for this special context. This procession has, as was noted, its own rubric, but this says merely: 'The bride and bridegroom should themselves take part in the offertory procession, presenting the gifts.' What an offertory procession is or what is meant by 'gifts' here is not explained. The latter are in fact bread, wine and water to be used in the celebration of the Eucharist, carried in special containers and presented to the priest as symbolic offerings on the part of the congregation. The action would normally be interpreted as making a complex symbolic link between the congregation and the central action of the mass. How it is to be handled is not specified however, and for good reason. Possibilities vary with circumstances and the personnel available. Our instance provided a setting in which a procession from back to front of the church would be called for. It did not seem feasible to require bride and groom – the bride in any case feeling precarious in her voluminous dress and veil – themselves to go first from the front to the back of the church in order to process forward again. There were, however, active Catholics in the families on both sides of this marriage so, with a little persuasion, it was possible to find aunts and uncles who would make up an appropriately balanced procession. These would therefore bring the gifts forward. The bride and groom could then be involved, without moving away from the altar steps, by receiving the gifts from their relatives and passing them on to the priest at the altar. This is what occurred, a possible solution, practicable on this particular occasion, and at the same time producing a ritual enhancement of the underlying symbolic idea.

The kinds of non-verbal action we have been looking at so far can be regarded as roughly equivalent to the verbal part of the service set out in text. As in that case there are necessarily further and even less specified dimensions. Even at its heart, various kinds of enabling action are needed, and the offertory procession is enlightening in this respect too. It is enabling the priest to celebrate the eucharist but, being identified by rubric it becomes an official part of the action of the mass. It is necessarily preceded, however, by a gathering and equipping of the participants to allow the procession to take place. This requires a form and order to it but is not, at least at present, more than enabling action. The raising of the bride's veil is a similarly necessary action which, by having neither rubric nor set timing nor any particular procedure attached to it remains at a purely enabling level. Such events are necessarily a part of the total action but they are not picked out in any of the ways which can then be understood as making them a potentially meaningful part of the ritual. But they might be.

Services for mixed marriages

Differences of family identity based on historic religious oppositions can prevent people having a wedding service at all. The risk of furore and recriminations within families may deter couples from exposing themselves to it. This is, however, now unusual in the kind of 'mixed marriage' common in the West of Scotland, that between Catholics and Protestants. By the 1980s there was rarely sufficient animus to be found on either side to cause more than an occasional individual refusal to attend.

Differences of belief on the part of the couple themselves, and active religious commitment, are still less likely to prevent a wedding being held in church. It is normal to choose the Church of one or other partner, though a Free Church and Catholic couple marrying in a Church of Scotland were included in the study. As was seen in Chapter 3, whatever is intended, friendly acquiescence is most likely to be encountered. Though the forms of one Church are bound to provide the basis for the service, various kinds of accommodation including participation by a minister or priest from the other Church are possible. In the Catholic Church, marriage to someone who has not been baptised as a Christian will prevent a full Nuptial Mass being celebrated, but this may sometimes be preferred in other cases too. It can be felt either that the full complexity of the service would be unwelcome to those used to something shorter and simpler, or that communion withheld from some of those present would be divisive. In practice however this may be an unnecessary worry. In the first place, there is often no clear religious division between the sides attending a mixed wedding. Those who come forward to take communion may therefore emerge from either side; and in the second, particularly where communion is in one kind only – the traditional Catholic practice – it can be administered so simply and quickly that it is scarcely apparent even that one partner has received it, the other not.

Mixed marriages, that is to say, while they may stimulate celebrants into more explaining and even a greater than usual friendliness towards congregations, usually make little difference to the procedures outlined in the preceding two sections. A mixed marriage is for the most part only a special case of the general problems for celebrants of variable interest in religion and knowledge of practices. The tone and the fullness of a service are usually most affected by the celebrant's sense of whether it will be religiously meaningful to the couple, which often goes with his or her personal knowledge of the couple, and of whether the families will contain sufficient people with the experience to sustain an active participation. Personalising and the kind of ritual innovation which has been touched on above and will be considered further in the last section of this chapter, are most likely to be found where such factors are positive.

Music

No firm line can be drawn between speech and music in ritual contexts. Speech itself can form the kind of acoustic patterns which may be described as musical, and this is particularly so when a special style of delivery marks it off from mundane forms of speaking as 'ritual' or 'poetic'. Where, as often in the Church of Scotland, special speaking is avoided, a relatively sharp distinction between speech and music therefore exists, with the latter largely restricted to the special, self-contained songs called 'hymns'. Elsewhere, however, the two may shade into one another through various more or less musical kinds of declamation, and there may be parts of texts which can be simply said or more complexly vocalised as desired. Even when such relatively discrete sung items as hymns are introduced they generally continue the themes and sentiments of the spoken texts.

There are continuities between the spoken and the sung therefore, but the singing of words inevitably affects the significance they may have (Merriam 1964, pp. 188 foll.; Bloch 1974; Jules-Rosette 1975; Frith 1987). Stress and timing contribute directly to the meaning of phrases and these, like repetition, are often imposed by the music. Words are put into an extra frame of meaning, the non-verbal acoustic patterns to which they are being made to contribute. An interplay is set up between this musical meaning and meanings that the words by themselves could be seen as having. This may be experienced as enriching both, but the words are in a sense necessarily devalued. The singer is not only performing a text for which she or he is not responsible but it is a text of which meaningful words are only one component. Singing uses words therefore, but involvement with their significance becomes largely optional. In practice, the scope offered by hymns for participation in a collective activity is likely to be more important than any contribution they make through the ideas and sentiments they express. When participation is not achieved they become therefore a liability rather than a contribution.

At a more straightforwardly ethnographic level, music forms a valued element in observed wedding services, with no very firm distinctions to be drawn between churches. As was noted in Chapter 4, even those with no knowledge of the textual side of services, or indeed interest in it, are often able to identify with and may be pleased to have a hand in choosing the music. Two pieces of purely instrumental music are firmly identified with weddings and are immediately identifiable as entry and exit music by many who would not be able to say anything else about them. For many couples they are as much a part of the procedure of marrying as the veil and the dress and going down the aisle. The entry music can have considerable impact. As one bride commented, when she heard 'Here comes the bride' her heart missed a few beats: 'As soon as they started playing that music, that was the worst time in my life. After that I settled.'[T6] There is usually somewhat more music at a wedding than just the entry and exit pieces and the hymns chosen by the couple. The organist will often play her or his own choice of more or less religious and/or popular classical pieces before the bride arrives, after the couple have gone out and in the period while documents are being signed,[11] unless some family friend or a cantor has been explicitly arranged to play or sing then to provide an interlude.

Those who want to make more of the musical side have greater scope in Catholic services unless they are being married in such exceptional Church of Scotland establishments as Glasgow Cathedral or Paisley Abbey which have choral traditions and professional organists. This is both because of the larger number of opportunities for music offered by the more complex procedure and because of the greater range of music familiar in Catholic services. Of the services considered in detail in this chapter, one of the Church of Scotland brides would have liked to make more of the music but was unable to, whereas the Catholic couple actually did. For their wedding, 'Ave Maria' was sung as a solo by a cantor as an alternative at the bride's entrance, there were five congregational hymns, further solos at the Sign of Peace and the time of Communion, and the classic Mendelssohn 'Wedding March' for going out.

This was to seize almost every possible opportunity. It was done here not simply out of a love for music in general or for the elaboration of the service, but out of a sense of the appropriateness of particular pieces to particular moments and of their meaningfulness for parents as well as for the couple themselves. 'Panis Angelicus', a Latin communion hymn which had been sung at the bride's parents' wedding, and 'Sweet Heart of Jesus', the groom's father's avowedly old-fashioned choice, could readily be accommodated, as well as such modern hymns as 'We are one in the Spirit, we are one in the Lord'.

Music, therefore, is certainly an embellishment for the occasion but it is more than this. It is a key area for choice, participation and, perhaps more often than in any other aspect, for the inclusion in what is essentially an externally provided episode, of items which will be meaningful to participants. It should be noted, however, that the bride who took a leading part in the organising of the elaborate schedule of music listed above, in the event 'felt as if [she] didn't hear the music' she had set up (cf. Ottenberg 1989). Like much else to do with weddings, it turned out to be essentially for other people.

Innovation

Concern with change and innovation in ritual, a major theme underlying this study as a whole, has surfaced from time to time in preceding sections. In particular, the almost paradoxical contrasts between Church of Scotland and Catholic practices in this respect have been noted: official encouragement to adapt and to personalise in an authoritative regime may give rise to faster and more apparent innovation than the ministerial freedom of the Church of Scotland, though neither display anything like the rigidity and resistance to change over long periods which often appear, particularly from within the Church of England, to be in the nature of ritual. This section examines one particularly striking piece of ritual innovation encountered, as an example of the way in which quite new ritual practices may over time become established.

In our Catholic instance, in the middle of the mass, after the Nuptial Blesssing and before communion, the priest announced:

> Now James and Margaret are going to be holding and lighting a candle together. At the christening, lighting the candle is very symbolic. It is symbolic of faith in the resurrection, and it is a symbol that Christ must be for us a guiding light. So James and Margaret asked to light a candle, symbolising the coming together of their candles of baptism, something that they will unite together in, as together they ask Christ to be for them a guiding

light in their marriage.[N73]

An altar boy was called forward with one of the altar candles. The priest held an already partially burnt red candle. James, with Margaret assisting as far as keeping her dress away from the wax would allow, took a taper and lit the red candle from the one from the altar.

No words were spoken; this ritual was purely action, but it came complete with a developed and complex symbolic interpretation offered in explanation of something which would be new to all present. This was a masterly statement of the complexity of reference which can be achieved by a single, simple action. Like the sung blessing in the Church of Scotland, it linked the occasion of marriage back to baptism, but it did not then rely only on individual memories and emotion for its impact; it established in this earlier lighting of candles references to basic Christian faith and to images – the guiding light – deep in Christian literature and consciousness. Indeed, for the practising Catholic it referred to more than needed to be said explicitly. As the priest later explained,

> within the Catholic Church [candles] have always been a symbol, but I think they are taking on an even greater significance because, relating the candles to baptism ..., at the sacrament of baptism the candle that is presented to the godparents and the parents on behalf of the newly baptised child, the light for that candle is taken from what's called the Pascal Candle, or the Easter Candle. And that relates them to the Easter vigil service when there's a time when the whole church is in complete darkness, and that darkness symbolises sin – and the result of sin, death. And that Easter Candle is lit – the lighting of the one candle at the back of the church – and it gives a light to the whole church, and it's the symbol of Christ's rising from the dead. And then the candle is brought in procession down the church, and everyone in the church has a candle, and a light is taken, with tapers, and passed round all the candles, so that all the candles are eventually lit from the Pascal Candle. And eventually, from a darkened church, suddenly with the light of candles it's really brilliant.

> And it symbolises first of all Christ's rising from the dead, but as each person takes a light it's the symbol for them that Christ is to be, not only the centre of faith, but the guiding light overcoming sin for the person, and ultimately overcoming death.

The candle-lighting had therefore the characteristic potential of religious symbols to draw into any occasion on which it is used a halo of significance from other occasions of its use. Every lighting has its own immediate contextual significance but it is at the same time a token of all other lightings and, indirectly and increasingly diffusely, of all their contextual meanings. Here, as a new use, it was being made explicitly to tap into this web of significance, reaching as it does in this case into the heart of the system of Christian thought and values. In the brief exposition in the service, from reminding all present of the existence of this fan of Christian significance of candles and their lighting, the priest went on to a personal meaning for this couple of this lighting. They had wanted to symbolise their own coming together in this way which would carry with it the charge of significance into which the ritual was intended to link.

The ritual which emerged in such polished form on the day had an instructive history behind it. It was undoubtedly innovative; the priest had never done or even seen anything like it before. But it was constructed out of elements to hand, with an eye to practicalities and through the application of symbolic thinking. It had its starting point in an Engaged Encounter weekend the couple had attended. There, in a model of explicit symbolic action, a candle – the same red candle which was to appear in the marriage service – had been lit to symbolise the light of Christ in their relationship. Somebody said at the time, 'Some couples keep them and use them at their wedding.' As Margaret told the story

> So that's what we thought of, lighting a candle as a symbol of the light of Christ in our marriage. And then [the bridesmaid] told me about some wedding she'd been at where they'd had the candle: 'What they actually did at the one we were at was they lit two candles and ...' – what did they do? Something like, lit the candles at the beginning and had the vows, and later on blew out the two candles, or lit from the two candles just one candle, which signified the two becoming one.[T94]

The first thought, that is to say, had been to take over into the marriage service a piece of ritual encountered, like the sung blessing, elsewhere. This had then encountered other ritual experimentation going on and from this source another symbolic idea became attached, one particularly appropriate to ideas already in play in the marriage service, the idea of two becoming one. It was then discussed with the priest. He was encouraging but more aware of practicalities. With two candles – actually there would be three – it would be just too complicated. There would be 'all this wax going about'. The priest kept saying to them, as they later explained it:

> 'I think you've got to be practical. Think about your dress.' So we decided we'd just have the one candle. And he said, 'Light the candle' – with the two of us holding the taper – 'then I'll give a wee spiel about ..., about what the candle signifies, and so on.'[T94]

But at the same time as he was simplifying the action, the priest was taking the next step by developing the symbolic meaning. He made the link to baptism by way of the baptismal candle. With an acute awareness of the full range of current liturgical practice – and, it should be said, a particularly strong personal interest in symbolism as a traditional teaching device of the Church – he was immediately struck by the way in which the range of symbolic reference could broaden out, in a manner which had not occurred to the couple themselves. The action came therefore to be simplified but its intentional meaningfulness increased. The priest's explanation on the day surprised the couple since it included the baptismal link of which they had not previously been aware. The priest himself was unaware until it was pointed out to him exactly what he had himself contributed. He was, however, pleased with it and used it again subsequently with other couples to whom he proposed it.

This instance shows the way in which new ritual[12] may in present circumstances be established. Most of those present are unlikely to have sufficient interest in the religious side of marrying to pay attention or indeed even to notice them. To some who do they will not appeal; in others they may even excite hostility. But occasionally priests and also others who may be thinking forward to their own or their children's weddings may, as has been seen, take up ideas they come across, move them around between contexts and remodel them. Even in a supposedly secular age, the dialogue between liturgy and life continues and has its implications for both.

Chapter 7

Wedding Day 2: framing the ceremony

The pattern

It is often said that the wedding is a day. Indeed the patterned sequence of events special to marriage, of which the service is one complex episode, does in Scotland often run more or less continuously throughout a long day. A mass of enabling actions have to be undertaken, weeks and even months ahead, before it can take place. Some of them, as has been observed, take on characteristics for which the term 'ritual' is appropriate, but most are to be done as and when the opportunity offers, without any special forms or any sense that they are in themselves required by the kind of abstract force so variously identified in systems of thought as God, the ancestors, *dharma*, society, custom, etc.[1]

When it comes to the day itself, however, the balance between preparation and what has to be done as an end in itself quickly shifts. Getting into and out of the ceremony is, for all concerned but particularly for the bride, a matter of being faced with an increasingly intricate regulation of events. These are often highly meaningful to participants but are separate from the service itself in their lack of reference to the patterns of religious thought which shape it. Indeed they may be applied in much the same way to a civil ceremony if this is not being used as a means of escaping the very framing of the event which they represent.

The couple are assumed, in the standard shaping of subsequent events, to be starting out apart. In the research, with most of those marrying living at their parental homes and within easy travelling distance of the ceremony, this was not something likely to be remarked upon. The couple would be travelling to the church or registry office direct from the homes which had been theirs up to that point. Even for such couples, however, to spend apart the time immediately before the wedding was to be required to make an unmissable statement of separateness. At such an important and for many a nerve-racking moment in their lives, they were being denied each other's support and encouragement, exactly what in the marriage service they would promise henceforth to provide for one another. People already living together might also, even without any concern to hide the nature of their previous arrangements, return if possible to their families for the preceding night, or at least keep apart on the day. The great majority of those marrying would, that is to say, represent in their actions the separate lives assumed as the starting point in the ritual.

Separated in this way, the pressures are undoubtedly greatest on the bride. She has heard incessantly that it is 'her day'. She cannot escape the fact that she will be the first focus of attention, and not for herself as she may feel herself really to be, but as the beautiful bride. With what balance of challenge and threat, of excitement and dread, this will face the particular bride will depend on her own personality and on the immediate circumstances.

Margaret's experience can stand for the practicalities of the lead in to the wedding.

M.   I couldn't sleep the night before. I woke up next morning and my eyes were really puffy, you know, just from lack of sleep. And I was really annoyed at this. And then I spent about half an hour at breakfast time with slices of cucumber over my eyes. And then when I got to the hardresser's ... . I remember wearing my sunglasses in the car driving in, because I thought I looked so terrible. I didn't want to put on any make-up because I knew I was going back later on to get ready. Normally I wouldn't go anywhere without some kind of make-up on. And at the hairdresser's, to get my hair done I took off the dark glasses, and the hairdresser said to me, he said, 'My God! What were **you** doing last night?' [She laughs]. And then the other guy came up and **he** said, 'Good grief! You look terrible! Have you been up all night?' So that really bothered me that day, and I went home again and sat for about half an hour again with cucumber slices over my eyes, which is supposed to take the puffiness away. I don't know if it worked. You see, before the wedding ... . One or two of my cousins before their weddings took a sleeping pill to sleep the night before, and I thought I wouldn't do that. 'I'll just try and relax and just calm down.' And the night before, after the rehearsal, Anne [the bridesmaid] and I – Anne was staying the night – we walked down to the off-licence – in fact it was the Lounge. And Anne got a bottle of Martini and a bottle of lemonade, and I thought, if I get a wee drink that'll make me sleep. But it didn't. I hadn't anticipated being so hyped up. And I kept thinking, I'm going to look terrible in the morning. And the more I thought that, the less I could sleep. And eventually I got a few hours' sleep. [...] That

	really bothered me. I always regretted it afterwards. I just wished I had had a sleeping pill.
SC.	I'm sure everyone told you how lovely you looked.
M.	Oh yes – everyone says that anyway [she laughs].
SC.	But it was true, [...] And I suppose James had a good night's sleep.
James.	Aye, aye. I was a bit late getting to bed. We had a wee do .... Fine!
M.	So predictable, isn't it?[T112]

For brides, hairdressing and make-up, and for both parties getting themselves spruced up and into their appropriate costumes can take up a good deal of the day. Brides are inclined to feel they need all the time allowed by afternoon, even late afternoon, weddings.

For most people the means of getting to the church are merely a matter of convenience. They will be bearing in mind their outfits and the fact that they will be going straight on afterwards to a reception at which there will be drinking and from which they will need to return home many hours later. Distances, cars available and how many chauffeured cars and buses have been hired to make what journeys for the occasion will affect individual planning. At the centre, however, which is at this stage the bride's home, choice is transformed into one of the more rigid of wedding requirements.

The bride and her father, or whoever is 'giving her away', will be the last to leave and they will keep to themselves the grandest of the hired cars. Their departure is something which neighbours are likely to turn out to see. They will wish the bride well, say how lovely she is looking, and probably throw confetti. Before this other members of the family will have gone, the bride's mother the last of them. She goes, often with the bridesmaids, in another hired car which will sometimes also be ferrying other people in a series of journeys to the church. Bride and father ride therefore in some splendour; the car is grand and clearly labelled for all to see with a V of white ribbon over the bonnet. They sit together in the back, a white sheet covering the seat beneath them and, usually, an arrangement of flowers decorating the shelf behind their heads. But the display here is not at this stage for anyone in particular; the wedding car will be noticed by many strangers on its journey but there are generally few who know its occupants. At the first sign of their arrival, even on a fine day when people are reluctant to go into the church, guests are inclined to scuttle inside to take up their places for the next stage.

By then the guests have often had their first encounter with the photographer. He, or more rarely she, may have been commissioned to take pictures of them as they arrive, may indeed have been keen to do this in the hope of selling copies of the resulting photographs later in the day. Occasionally he may instead have been to the bride's home to take pictures before she left or even to video her departure and the journey to the church. More often, however, it is on arrival that her first photo-session of the day takes place. It is often a major one. The bride, it is sometimes said, should be late arriving; in reality, the celebrant and those within do wait, but it is often for the photographer to release her that they are waiting.

The celebrant may be at the door to meet the bride or standing at the front of the church where bridegroom and best man will also be waiting. Eventually, in her distinctive dress, usually veiled and to recognisable entry music, she comes in on the right arm of the man who has come with her. Her arrival sets the event discussed in the previous chapter into motion.

Once the service is completed, the marriage schedule is signed. This is another standard moment for a photograph. The procession out of the church then leaves the celebrant behind. It is likely to be halted in its tracks for a moment while another official photograph is taken. The major photographic session or series of sessions of the day then begins. The couple, the bridal party and close family members in almost every possible permutation and combination will be posed either outside the church or at some picturesque spot the photographer takes them to or at the place where the reception is to be held, or even at all of them. At some stage of this the couple will lead the departure from the church, the bridegroom replacing her father in the car in which the bride earlier arrived. He will often throw a scramble as they leave (see below). The rest of the party will follow, distributed much more flexibly in whatever transport is available, some of the senior men also throwing scrambles as they move off. At the place of the reception all will wait once again for the professional photography to be completed, for the couple to be released and for the final stage to begin.

Photography

Margaret. I was kind of toying with the idea of saying to my mum and dad to cancel the photographer. But again it's one of these ...: **everybody** has a photographer at the wedding. You know, what will we **do** at the time you're supposed to be having ...? I mean, there's time, the time we get to the reception ..., there's time out, put aside, for getting photographs taken. What will we **do** with the time if we don't have a photographer?[T91 2]

By the 1980s wedding photography had as fixed a place in the procedures of getting married as the ceremony in church or the reception and only slightly less fixed than the wedding cake to be cut. It was the photographer who, having intervened before the church service and buzzed around it in a manner not infrequently to upset the celebrant, then took over the couple and their supporters between the service and reception for one or more sessions which often rivalled or even exceeded the service in length.

This position had been established and was being maintained in the face of the efflorescence of amateur photography not out of any simple interest in a record of the wedding, though many couples did feel this strongly. The roots of wedding photography go back almost to the beginnings of photography itself in the mid nineteenth century. Its first manifestation was single or double portraits for which the couple would visit a studio. As soon as open-air photography became practicable, group photographs in gardens or other convenient spots near where the wedding was being celebrated were added to the repertoire. Wedding parties were amongst the most obvious subjects for such photographs. It was only after the First World War that any advance on these two early-established possibilities began. Then, perhaps under the impact of increasing amateur photography, the couple leaving the church established itself as a new possibility. It was then not until the 1960s that wedding photography took off again, with photographs in the church itself and the gradual arrival of colour (Lansdell 1983, pp. 5–7).

From that time, drawn on by commercial advantage, by the presence of the photographer on site and by ever more sophisticated and manipulable equipment and film, the wedding came to be seen as offering a series of – in the language of the 1980s – photo-opportunities. A progression of posed photographs suggested by the stages through which weddings such as those under discussion[3] move was the result. The varying personnel, circumstances and physical surroundings of individual weddings would allow scope for the photographer with a quick eye, quicker wits and a skill in handling people to obtain ever-interesting variations on more or less standard themes.[4] The ability to martial people was seen in the profession as far more important for a wedding photographer than mere technical skills; the performance of leading photographers at work was as impressive as the results they achieved, though this was not always appreciated by the subjects at the time. The occasional couple would, in the special situation of the wedding, shine as models. Since most of those involved would be looking their best, the occasion would in any case be propitious for portraits which their subjects would be pleased to see and might even wish to buy.

By the early 1980s the series was expected to include:

1 The bride getting out of the car on arrival at the church.
2 Bride and father before going 'down the aisle'.
3 'Signing the register'.
4 The couple heading the procession out of the church.
5 A profusion of portraits at the church and/or elsewhere, perhaps of the bride alone but generally stressing the couple, and the couple as the centre of wider groupings, the bridal party, the families of each and the combined family constituted by the marriage. Group photographs including the guests as well were rarely attempted and then only for small parties; photographs of

the guests in couples or in the sets in which they arrived were seen as a more practicable way of recording the attendance as a whole.

6 Bride and groom with the wedding car.

7 'The cutting of the cake.'

All these were posed shots, though the procession out might have to be seized as well as practicable and some photographers would try to catch the odd moment of spontaneity too. It was not the actual signing of the marriage documents any more than it was the actual cutting of the cake which was photographed by the professional, but a posed representation, in the one case of what had already taken place, in the other of what was to come. Sometimes the series might be expanded with more posed shots, perhaps a whole session with the bride at home before she left for the ceremony, or perhaps being given lucky horseshoes or other objects by small children of the family immediately after the ceremony. Some photographers might offer special effects too, 'misties', double exposures or montages, typically involving champagne glasses. These were not widely popular and it was in any case necessary to arrange for most of them beforehand if they were to happen. At the end of the main session most photographers would ask whether there were any other shots the couple or the bride's mother wanted taking, or whether anybody important had been left out.

There might also be a 'garter shot', in practice often a series of variant 'garter shots'. This was well known, regarded with enthusiasm by many brides and some photographers, but avoided by others. Where it was included, it introduced the one note of levity into the series. The bride would be posed with her dress lifted to display a wedding garter round her upper leg.[5] Whether or not they anticipated such a photograph, many brides would be wearing such a thing, a pretty, decorated circlet of no practical use but often blue and representing the 'something blue' required at a wedding by the rhyme: 'something old, something new, something borrowed, something blue'. The groom and perhaps other males of the party would be posed round about in attitudes suggesting eager interest in the sight, and the taking of the photographs would – with luck, for anything can go wrong – be attended by a good deal of merriment.

In contrast, if the layout of the church and the attitude of the celebrant allowed it, there might also be unposed photographs of the ceremony itself, of the bride and groom standing before the minister or priest and of the rings being put on. On occasion a photographer might even lead the couple back into the church after the service, with or even without the knowledge of the celebrant, for posed shots either to represent the ceremony itself or perhaps just to substitute for shots taken outside. One firm termed this their 'winter wedding'. A certain tension between celebrants and photographers was common. The former might worry as to what the latter might try to get up to and feel challenged on their own ground; the latter saw celebrants as tending to stand unreasonably on their dignity, often to be inconsistent and sometimes totally unreasonable. The same firm just mentioned, with eight photographers, kept notes on particular celebrants and venues but even then made a point of asking every time what might or might not be done within the church building. 'You've got to keep these guys happy', as the owner of the firm said.

The first product of all this endeavour would be a set of proof colour prints of all the photographs which had been taken. Photographers would be hired at fixed prices to attend, take photographs and provide first the proofs and then an album or albums of selected and properly finished enlargements for the couple and often for their parents. If orders for extra prints could be secured, profits might be improved. One strategy for achieving more orders was to take the proofs back in the evening to the reception itself. Though there were necessarily costs involved in doing this, some photographers would be able to process their films immediately and have the prints back, if they and the clients wanted it, before the end of the evening. Going to look at the photographs would then become an extra entertainment for the guests.

The albums, in a range of elaborate and distinctively wedding bindings, usually contained twenty, sometimes thirty, enlargements. These could be chosen freely but would be likely to follow more or less the pattern of stages outlined above. The stages and the various combinations would generally produce about twenty separate possibilities; an album with more was likely to contain variants of some of the basic set rather than including any of the pictures of the guests. In one not unusual set of thirty, bride and groom were together in twenty-three, by themselves or in various combinations with others. Of the remaining seven, the groom was in two, the bride in five. Only one was not posed. Albums therefore provided a focused and highly edited image. They might well be all that survived to the future of the huge effort of organising, dressing and presentation put into creating the evanescent moments of the wedding.[6]

In, through and out

The first section outlined the general sequence of events before and around the service. In this section patterns of location and movement at the tightly controlled centre of the sequence are considered in more detail. These are aspects which are clearly ritual in senses which anthropologists will recognise as such, at least when they are away from the familiar context of their own culture. They are potentially meaningful but not in terms of the specifically religious ideas which inform the service itself.

At a wedding without ushers, those attending distribute themselves in the church as they arrive. It is clear in the way that this happens even without direction that there is here a generally accepted plan: the bride's family and friends are on the left of the central aisle if there is one, in any case in the left half of the church looking forwards, the groom's on the right. Those closest to bride or groom will be nearest the front – some may modestly position themselves too far back and be encouraged subsequently to move forwards – and any non-guests present, those who have not been invited to the reception but have merely dropped in to see the wedding, will sit towards the back. They may be joined there by guests who, for practical reasons such as young children, may need to make a quick getaway. Where people locate themselves has meaning therefore in terms of relationship and standing. For the entry of the groom and best man and of the celebrant there is no fixed pattern. When the service seems about to happen, the former are brought in or find their way from wherever they have been waiting to the front right-hand side of the seating, the groom nearer the centre. The celebrant may be waiting at the front of the church or at the entrance at the back to welcome the bride and her father when they arrive or, more probably, after the photographer has finished with them.

All is therefore set up and awaits only the entry of the bride for the service to begin. Unobtrusive music is played. When the entry is imminent, groom and best man stand side by side facing forwards if they are not already in that position, and, the signal given (though this is sometimes tricky when lines of sight for the organist are obscured), the bride and her father, followed by the bridesmaid(s) and sometimes led by the celebrant, proceed slowly down the aisle to loud and distinctive music. As a moment prepared and awaited, and as the first sight for almost everyone of this particular woman as a bride in the full culturally prescribed meaning of the term, this is for all concerned one of the most impressive moments of a wedding.

On arrival at the front of the church, the bride normally separates from her father and joins the groom, positioning herself on his left. Their attendants generally stand to their left and right respectively. The Church of Scotland service, as has been seen, involves little movement thereafter. All stay in their initial places, with only the joining of right hands for the vows, a possible kiss, sometimes a kneeling for blessing, and probably the putting back of the bride's veil at some variable and not necessarily even foreseen point. The Catholic service involves more movement, as has been seen, usually including the taking of the couple 'on to the altar' at least for the mass. In both Churches the couple and their attendants and families usually leave to sign the necessary documents. In this more private and informal situation there will be a chance for kisses and congratulations.

With this episode completed, an exit procession forms up and moves through the church and out in a way which excites comparison with the entry procession. Where there is no central aisle, the route out is likely to take the opposite aisle to the way in. The procession's focus is again the bride and it moves to similarly distinctive music. The established favourites, two nine-teenth-century marches, are officially a 'bridal march' and a 'wedding march' but to many people they are never entirely distinguishable. The changes supposed to have been made by the intervening service are registered in comparison between the two processions. The celebrant is left behind. It is now bride and groom who lead, the bride now generally on the arm of her new husband, but his left in contrast to the right arm of her father on which she arrived. Whereas her veil usually covered her face then, it is now raised back over her head, contributing to the bolder, more confident and happy aspect she now presents. Behind the couple come the leading people of the two sides who entered separately but are now going out in mixed pairs. They are, in so far as there are people of appropriate sexes and relationships available, joined in couples which echo the couple at their head. The rest of the congregation may then join in and follow at will, except when, as sometimes happens, the photographer halts the procession at the door for a series of photographs of the couple. The procession may than be imprisoned behind them, deprived of the opportunity to wield their own cameras and with nobody thinking to show them an alternative route out.

Scrambles

At significant departures, perhaps from home but particularly from the church after the wedding service, two things are thrown. One is confetti, tiny shapes of prettily coloured paper which those around, particularly women and children, throw over the bride before the wedding and bride and groom after it. Though the idea is sometimes found that the confetti was 'originally' rice and its throwing has something to do with fertility, the most that can be realistically said is that it is a way in which people, whether invited as guests or not, can participate in the event and perhaps add to the jollity of the occasion. It may, in youthful high spirits, also be thrown around more widely and stuffed into pockets and bags with a view to embarrassing the newly-weds when they subsequently try to return to normality in the outside world. But the confetti is directed mainly at the bride. Being coloured, like the flowers she carries but unlike rice, it contrasts with the white dress and veil on which it may land. It would doubtless be possible to construct meanings on this basis but no tendency to do so was ever encountered. Those in charge of churches or registry offices are inclined to regard confetti as so much litter and to try to forbid it on their premisses.

Handfuls of low-value coins are the other things thrown, this time on to the ground. Similar practices are widespread in Scotland though the names they go under differ. The universal Glasgow term, 'scramble', seems to express the idea that the coins are thrown to be pursued, which indeed they are, mainly by children who have nothing otherwise to do with the wedding. It is the bridegroom and other leading men, only occasionally women, who 'throw scrambles'. Circumstances and reactions vary, and some see differences either as connected with class or with change.

Colin.   I don't know if you noticed the scramble in the video. Did you notice the scramble at [his bride's] house? I always say that is a different scramble from a Possil Park scramble. [Possil Park is a working-class housing scheme in the north of the city in which he had grown up.] The Bishopbriggs scramble is just a few kids and they pick the money up. A Possil Park scramble is hundreds of people, and they're all on top of each other [he laughs], fighting and pulling at the coins. [...] You've never seen them in your life before, and they somehow get wind of this scramble ... . There's a wedding, and they'll come. 'There's a wedding!' We used to do it.[T105]

At some weddings indeed, small change rains out of the windows of the cars and even of coaches which have been hired for the guests. Often however, drivers try to intervene, aware of the danger to young life, not to mention the threat from flying coins to their own immaculate paintwork. They try to relieve their passengers of the coins they would otherwise throw, and scatter them on a nearby patch of grass or some other convenient surface well away from road and vehicles. The children follow.

No particular explanation is offered for scrambles but they are maintained by enthusiasm on either or both sides. Whether many children are present or not will depend on the area and the time of day, whether the schools are on holiday, nearby, at work or just coming out. If children have gathered, they will not let the wedding party get away without their expectations being made very plain: 'It's time to throw out your money, missus' was one command overheard. The prospect of scrambles is also used to keep children in some order whilst guests are coming out and photography is under way. Drivers can be heard threatening recalcitrant children that if they don't do as they are told, the groom will be asked not to throw a scramble. The central men have however usually armed themselves with small change, five or ten pounds-worth even. They may then be determined to throw it out as a necessary part of the event even if there are few or no children around and certainly no pressure on them to do so. One groom was noticed throwing money out for friends of his whom he saw coming out of a pub as he passed in the wedding car. Some may merely remember afterwards that they forgot to throw the scramble.

Interpretation

The preceding sections outlined the patterns to which people are expected to conform which are almost minutely prescribed in the framing of the service.

Conforming generally attracts no attention to the particular performance, raises no question as to what the performers mean by it. They do not usually mean anything by it; it is just what one does in getting married. Failure to conform, on the other hand, risks making oneself conspicuous and raises questions: is one just ignorant or confused, or is one making a point? Sitting with one's family at a wedding is conforming; sitting on the other side, though no example of this was ever observed, would risk being read as a rejection of membership in the family, just as sitting far back may be read as disclaiming any closeness of relationship with the person marrying. By implication here, the normally unmarked practice is attributed meaning both by those who do choose to flout it and by those who, correctly or not, attribute that intention to them. Interpretation of practices is not, that is to say, an esoteric pursuit; it is, in this form at least, a part of the pursuits of everyday life. As such, it provides a grounding for the strategies of interpretation which may sometimes be developed, which are more complex and even esoteric.

Interpretation, the attribution of meaning to actions, including the patterns which are usually acted upon unreflectingly as normal or natural, is itself a common human interest. Interpretations may be more or less 'obvious'. Where anyone who considers the matter is likely to jump to the same conclusion, it is as obvious as the link made at a wedding between physical proximity in seating and closeness of relationship. This is a link which is mediated by the use of the term 'close', but even this is not quite so simple a link as it may at first sight seem. There are other kinds of closeness such as friendship and in age and sex which might also be used to locate people and hence be represented in a pattern of seating. It is the context which rules these other possibilities out. The stress on the family throughout the wedding makes the relevant principle immediately apparent and meaningful to all.

Little less inevitable is the perception of the arrangement of seating into two 'sides' which are destined to meet and mix in the wedding, and of the procession out at the end of the service as the first representation of its achievement. There is a systematic logic here which emerges repeatedly in the ways people talk about weddings and the values they apply to them: a good wedding is one at which the sides mix. The weddings of each succeeding generation assume, in the way that the sides for them are defined, that mixes were achieved in the parental generation, and from the point of view of those marrying, the mix has indeed been achieved. All members of both their parents' sides have always been their own kin. To others attending, however, each new wedding is a chance to meet or meet again not only people on the other side but, and often more importantly, to meet members of what present circumstances define as their own side. These may well include people with whom they have never actually mixed at other times. We have here therefore a characteristic ritual situation, a mix of undeniable logic and recalcitrant human relationships which it temporarily overrides (Bloch 1980).

The right–left distinction, in contrast, has no such obvious meaning beyond the convenience of having a rule of some kind, like driving on the right or on the left. No instance of anyone worried by the rule was recorded. Many indeed are hardly aware of any rule here and do not notice therefore when it is not being followed. A source of confusion is the ease with which right and left are reversed: an observer's view of the matter corresponds to the actors' only when they are facing in the same direction. But at weddings the right–left orientation is generally maintained. The event is set up in this way initially and it is often reinforced by explicit guidance from ushers and from the main controllers, the celebrants, photographers and managers who watch out for subsequent reversals. It was in this context that the only implied interpretation was observed: an elderly priest said to the groom as the exit procession formed up: 'Remember the sword arm.' He was appealing to an image of the gentleman, sword in right hand, defending the lady hanging on his left arm. Whether there is any real historical basis for the orientation here or not – every practice must of course have a history – the practicalities of drawing a sword with someone hanging on one's left arm are unclear. But the idea of the husband as protector of his new wife had some appeal to an earlier and perhaps more chivalrous generation. To the present, it is more likely, if they encounter it at all, to seem comic rather than enlightening.

Ingenuity is sufficient even here to generate a meaning if it is, as by an eager anthropologist, really desired. The phenomenon of handedness and the possibility of attaching different significances and values to each of the hands as a bodily basis for binary opposition have received a good deal of attention in anthropology (e.g. Hertz 1909; Needham 1973). Though right–left distinctions could not by any stretch of the anthropological imagination be identified as a theme in British culture, there are indeed contexts in which the right has a certain priority. Right hands are shaken and, as has been seen, it is right hands which are joined at a crucial moment in the marriage service. The military always march and dress 'by the right' and, as in dancing, step off on the right foot. Perhaps more apposite, to place someone immediately to one's right, at table or in any formal arrangement of people, may be to honour them. Such dredging for analogies[7] might found a case for attributing a superiority to right over left, though this is not exactly what the last example implies. It might be reinforced by an appeal to supposedly general structural oppositions, with a magic formula cited:

husband / wife : right / left : dominant / subordinate.

The orientation of bride and groom could then be seen as a symbolic statement of the superiority of the husband. As such the rule might be meaningfully flouted.

One cannot say that this would be simply wrong. It is the nature of interpretation to expand in this way, making meaningful what may initially have been no more than accidental. All that can be said is that it is not an interpretation which was observed as being made. It is not either, it may be asserted with some confidence, one which is likely to be taken up in the future on the basis of reasoning which would seem plausible within the culture.

With the ways in which people move with one another and hold one another it is different. In getting into and out of the service this is, as has been seen, for the bride and those closely associated with her, carefully regulated. Here, though meaning is not generally read, a case which is more plausible within the culture can be made, and divergences which are more than sheer accident are to be observed. There is a set of culturally permissible and identifiable ways in which a woman and a man can walk together. They may, like anyone else, simply walk side by side; they may walk hand in hand, or with the woman on the man's arm, or with arms around waists or, in the present liberated age, anywhere between shoulder and buttocks. This is an interesting set in which the poses are symmetrical with the exception of what has been referred to as 'being on the man's arm'. The same pose may be called 'arm in arm', which disguises it. Two arrangements have unambiguous readings, 'obvious' in the sense noted above: both hand-in-hand and arms-round-waists will be read and experienced as statements of mutual commitment, establishing the two concerned as a couple. Arm-in-arm is only a little less immediately readable but with a meaning which may be identified as 'support'. It cannot be read as asserting that the people concerned are a couple since it is a proper pose even for those such as fathers and daughters or aunts and nephews, or two women, none of whom would constitute couples in the usual sense, but it certainly suggests some kind of attachment. Support may range from the directly practical, helping someone to move safely on a surface difficult for them, to the moral and emotional. What it always has is the clearly asymmetrical significance of identifying supporter and supported.

Such a meaning is highly appropriate to the first occasion on which the hold appears in the wedding. Though individual brides react very differently, there is a cultural expectation quite often borne out by experience that at the moment of her grand entry the bride will require support. The bride overwhelmed and hanging tearfully on her father's arm is by no means unknown. Particularly if this is contrasted with the groom's unregulated entry, it is easily read here as an assertion of a relationship of support between father and daughter, forming the starting point for the events to follow. 'Giving away', in practice merely parting at the end of this walk, can therefore be read as a symbolic terminating of this relationship. Since a general practice is involved here – a script is being followed – such a reading does not necessarily correspond to the circumstances of the individuals concerned. Both on this occasion and more generally, a daughter may in fact be supporting her father or at least be entirely self-supporting. Their parting may be similarly without any wider significance than it is given by any reading made of it. It may well be entirely confined within the logic of the occasion itself.

It is when, at the end of the service, the bride walks out with the groom that matters become more interesting. The groom has not taken the exact place of the man who gave her away, for it is now the bride rather than the groom who is on the left. There is however the expectation that the bride will walk out on the arm of her new husband as she walked in on her father's. But whereas the 'support' interpretation is uncontentious where a father is concerned, it may well not be so in the case of a husband. More generally it offends the values of symmetry and equality to which most of those marrying at the time of the research subscribed and which were well represented, if not always wholly consistently, in contemporary marriage services. Hardly surprisingly, it was not a pose which many young people would spontaneously adopt. Most nevertheless were still acccepting it as the proper way for a married couple to leave the church; in only two observed cases did couples avoid it. One pair managed to link arms and hold hands simultaneously in a way which became symmetrical; the other moved side by side but without holding one another in any way.[N51]

What had happened was discussed with the former couple, with photographs of the event to hand:

SC.   You came down holding hands, with your arms out in front. Did that just happen? Did you think about it?

James.   Well, we did. Because you said you weren't – remember? – as we were coming out ...

Margaret. I said, 'What will we do?' And you said, 'Just take hands.' We just did. I think, what we might have normally done. I'm quite glad we did that, because we wouldn't normally have what? – held each other's arms kind of thing. But it's just the way it happened.

SC.   All the others were holding ...

M.   ... the formal way.

SC.   You could see that one as being the woman supported by the man.

M.   I'm really glad we didn't do it [laughing quite excitedly]. You can probably see it when we're coming out the vestry here [she points to a photograph]. There I'm doing it with my dad. Yes!

SC.   You couldn't hold your dad in this other kind of way.

M.   No, that's true. [Looking at the picture of them coming out] Ah ha, there! We're just holding hands there. That was the way we came out the ... . It wasn't premeditated. I think we were holding on really tightly as well.

J.   Mmmm.[T94]

Neither couple had in fact thought about the matter in advance or planned it. They were responding on the spur of the moment to a sense of inappropriateness about a standard practice which they might otherwise have been expected to follow. In a sense it was perhaps no more than chance, but it did have a clear grounding in the interests and attitudes of the two couples. They were the most obviously feminist of all those whose progress towards marriage was studied. They were, as the passage above shows, ready to recognise a meaning for the action when it was explicitly offered to them, but it had been on the basis of a meaning sensed rather than formulated that they had acted.

Chapter 8

Wedding Day 3: the reception

The reception is the event on which the bride's mother's attention has generally been fixed. She comes into her own at it and she often feels that it depends upon her. Some mothers will already have experienced the pressure of their position even in church, with the requirement that they should, without the support of a husband, come in and take their conspicuous place in the front. This may be lonely; it is bound to identify her clearly for all to see. What she is wearing is, she will know, second in interest for other women only to the outfit of the bride herself. Some even feel a dilemma here, whether to take their place as soon as they arrive, in what may well at this stage be a largely empty church, or to wait at the back till most of the guests have come in. But the moment is only a foretaste of the limelight to come.

Mrs Gilligan. I'm not very good at these kind of things. Some people are very good at it. [...] You have to accept that you're going to make mistakes. And one of my friends said before Sarah's wedding, 'Now look! Stop getting worried before it. Accept the fact that there will be mistakes and don't let them spoil it. Don't let the mistakes you make ruin the whole thing,' which is about the best advice I got. [...] Because mistakes were made, and you do things intuitively at the time, because you don't have time to do them with any degree of thought or consideration, and then you have to get on with it.

SC.　　　Mistakes in dealing with people?

Mrs G.　　That's what the whole thing's about. [...] You say the wrong thing. Obviously you don't mean ever to say the wrong thing. You hope that people understand that **you're** nervous and excited and all your friends ... . I mean, what other occasion in your life are all your friends gathered together round you? Never! It's a unique occasion. It certainly is for us anyway.[1] [...] I'm not too keen on being the centre of attraction. I like it when I'm organising it for other people. I prefer to be a little step back from the limelight. I mean I love people and I enjoy their company, but ...

SC.   But you were pretty close to the centre of attention.

Mrs G.   That's right! You are! Unfortunately you're responsible for everything that's going on, and I think the weight of responsibility really does weigh heavily. But I think the most important thing is, if you plan it and don't leave anything that **you** can think of to chance. There **are** things that have to be left to chance, that you haven't thought of, that crop up. But don't leave anything to chance. [...] The whole thing has got to dovetail. It can be pretty hectic that![T40]

Such a weight of responsibility may well be experienced but it does not have to be assumed. The bride's mother is culturally represented as the hostess, but the progress of the reception is controlled and directed first by the hotel or catering management. At the meal the celebrant is often present to take the lead, and later in the evening the band leader takes over. The best man is a general assistant and reserve, and in some respects both the bride, supported by her best maid, and her father will be concerning themselves with the proper running of the event.

How the opening events of the reception are held depends on the spaces available. The entire reception, including the official photography immediately preceding it, may be carried out within one hall; there may be several areas more or less secluded from one another between which sections of the party and different events as the occur can be moved; or in some settings, if lucky with the weather, it may be possible to begin outside and move indoors only to eat. Using the spaces available, the management normally keeps guests waiting more or less apart from the wedding party until the photographer has completed his routine and withdrawn. The manager then sets going either the formal receiving of the guests, generally called 'the line-up', or 'the cutting of the cake'. There are three possible sequences: line-up → provision of drinks → cake-cutting and toast → moving to table; or: provision of drinks → cake-cutting and toast → line-up → moving to table; or: line-up → provision of drinks → moving to table → cake-cutting and toast. A line-up after the meal was also seen on one occasion.

The line-up

All the guests greet, and congratulate as appropriate, all the members of the bridal party arranged in a line. This normally includes the best man, bridesmaids and sometimes even the celebrant if he or she[2] is present. A queue forms in no particular order and, particularly in hotels, names may be called out by the manager in attendance as each couple or individual approaches from the right of the first person in the line. The order in it is somewhat variable, but the bride's parents as hosts usually come first and couples stick together, though one hotel manager advocated mixing the parental couples so that they could introduce their own guests to one another.[3] Everyone passes down the line and greets everybody in it, even when, as is particularly the case with a late line-up, many have since leaving the church already greeted one another, done their congratulating, and even chatted together. Enthusiasm for the line-up is generally slight but it is unlikely to be dispensed with altogether unless numbers are very small. It may be experienced as an ordeal by brides and grooms who have inevitably to respond again and again to the same well-meant remarks, but it can be enjoyed, particularly where drinks have already been provided. It is then not being treated as a gate to be passed through as quickly as possible, with the prospect of the first drink drawing the line forwards. Kissing as an alternative to hand-shaking appeared often to have become the norm for greetings between women and people of opposite sex, though it still retained a special value, at least for some: a minister in the line on one such occasion, displaying an obvious interest in kissing all the younger women as they came by, was overheard asking jocularly why else anybody would imagine he attended wedding receptions.

The cake and toasts

The cutting is bound to strike the anthropologist – though not perhaps, through the screen of familiarity set up by his own culture, immediately – as a ritual action; it is required, importance is attached to it, and it does not accomplish the practical result for which it is named.

Nevertheless it is often over quickly and with little ceremony. Only occasionally is the cake placed conspicuously in relation to the tables at which the meal will be eaten. It may then be cut by the bride and groom in front of the already seated company, before they take their seats at the top table. Otherwise it is placed on one side somewhere and the couple cut it with no more than an informal clustering of the company around them. A floral setting is made for the cake by placing around it the bouquets which have up to this point been carried by bride and bridesmaids. Bride and groom hold a knife and together force it into the centre of the cake, the bottom tier if, as is usual, there are two or three. Occasionally, and not only in military weddings, someone insists on using a sword which has some particular significance for those involved. Achieving the cut is applauded; it may in truth not be easy. There is no question of cutting up the cake in the everyday sense of preparing slices for serving; it will subsequently be removed to be cut into portions by others behind the scenes. The cake is first cut in a special sense therefore, and the cutting is marked as one of the major events of the wedding in two ways: a representation of it is included, as has been seen, in the standard set of official photographs, and a toast immediately follows it, a toast which may indeed be thought redundant since it is subsequently to be repeated.

The toast has to be noticed in an anthropological context as one of the commonest pieces of British ritual. It is a procedure by means of which expressions of well-wishing are made collective and somehow effective. One member of a gathering 'proposes a toast', inviting the company to drink together to signify good wishes of some kind. Participants 'raise their glasses' in a gesture which exaggerates the usual motion of drinking, and echo the proposer's last phrase. Toasts are proposed to the happiness, health, success or whatever is desired for the intended beneficiary.[4]

Minister. Ladies and gentlemen, I give you this first formal toast to the health and happiness of today's lovely bride and groom, Mary and Anthony. God bless them!
Company. God bless them, [A sip and applause followed.][T80]

Unlike later toasts this first one is rarely made the occasion for a speech.[5]

The meal

The line-up sets the formal style of the event. A 'proper sit-down meal', a formal dinner in most respects except for its unusually early hour, has next to be provided. The lay-out, with a top table for the wedding party and tables for the guests, and plans for the seating at them, have all, as has been discussed in Chapter 4, been prepared in advance. The guests generally find their appointed places first. If the cake-cutting has already been accomplished, managements often like then to bring the wedding party in in two waves, with everybody standing and clapping: 'Please be upstanding for ...'. First come all except the bride and groom, and then 'the happy couple' themselves.

Jan. By this time we were really cringing, weren't we? We went up, and everybody applauded again. And then we sat down and he whipped a tea towel out of nowhere and fixed it round my waist: 'Oh thank you,' [in a little voice]. Patted it all around. I think it was so I didn't drop all my dinner [she laughs] in my lap [she laughs]. It was just the way he did it. He was dead professional, wasn't he?[T71]

The meal begins with grace, at least if the celebrant is present, and unrolls as previously planned. Provision was becoming more lavish at the time of the research: there were by then generally four courses, accompanied by wine. The meal was completed with coffee or tea and a small piece of wedding cake, followed quickly by a new service of drinks for the toasts to come. Managers who have had experience elsewhere – such as the Spanish manager who was assisting Jan above – were impressed by what they saw as a Scottish keenness on formality for such occasions; they themselves quickly became exponents of it and would sometimes insist on it even against an occasional customer's resistance.

So familiar is the notion of a ceremonial meal that it is easy to pass over its significance as a whole in favour of attention to details. The feast in European culture is the lavish provision of food and drink spread in a complex pattern over a considerable period and made the occasion of jovial social interaction. It varies in scale from banquets on great state and civic occasions down to relatively modest dinner-parties in people's own homes. Though food and the provision of food are universally meaningful, a distinctive institution with its own values and uses has to be identified here. It has developed in a context in which food is abundant and those to whom it is being supplied have no great need of it. The accent is therefore not, as in many other parts of the world, on the provider of the food, or even on eating food together with other particular people, but on being invited to participate in the event. Such events are usable, and often used, to mark occasions, as here the marriage, in ways which it is hoped will be memorable and impressive. Hosts in such an event are honoured and thanked, but guests are commonly thanked too, for their attendance. Reciprocation may be called for, but not urgently, for the event clearly depends on those who have attended and participated as well as on those who have provided the entertainment. In terms of exchange there is, that is to say, a degree of balance within the event itself, particularly when wedding presents and the contributions of others to the occasion are explicitly considered. As for the succession of similar events, it is emulation rather than reciprocation which is the main principle linking them, though guest lists may, as has been seen, be marginally affected by previous invitations given or withheld.

The meal as itself a marker should not therefore be ignored. It may occasionally have a special force for the central participants for whom its potential as a jovial social occasion is inhibited by the requirements of their ceremonial roles:

Brian.   When you talk about the meal, that was the time when .... I said before, I didn't think it was me getting married that day. It felt like anybody else's wedding. But that was the time when it sort of came home to me that it was me that was married. You were sitting at the top table. The starter was laid on the table. All the tables were set. Everybody was at their place, and I was busy talking to the best man. And Donna was poking me, and I said 'What is it?', and I looked round and all these faces were staring at

you. She says, 'They're waiting for you to start. They're not going
to start until the top table starts.' And it was really then, when you
looked round and everybody was looking at you, waiting for you
to start your starter, you realised it was your wedding that day.[T19]

The meal, however, and particularly the speeches, also mark a boundary
within the wedding as a whole between 'the formalities' and what is seen as
free and informal, the real celebration. To an extent the distinction is illusory,
for the wedding throughout its entire progress is a series of forms asking to be
acted out, but differences of emphasis do creep in. From tightly prescribed
roles under the control of celebrants, photographers and managers, allowing
little scope for individual contributions even by such central actors as bride
and groom, there is a shift to more loosely and even confusingly prescribed
roles. For these, individual capacities and inclinations have to be brought into
play, and in consequence they turn out variously. At the same time there is an
enlargement in the initially small set of people of whom any kind of active
participation is required. Scope for people, even ordinary guests, to take
initiatives of their own and to participate in their own preferred ways
increases.

Speeches

There is no way in which a typical set of speeches can be represented but those
at James and Margaret's wedding can usefully be quoted.[N73] Here it was not
the celebrant himself who opened but, as is explained in the text, another
priest known to the bride's family. Let us call him Father Christopher. He
stood up.

There were lots of things he might say – he'd just say 'Praise the Lord!' An
air of gentle, hesitant, Irish humour was immediately so strong that even this
opening raised a slight laugh. He referred to the abundance of alcoholic
refreshment – a profusion of 'champagne cocktails', a mixture of sparkling
white wine and brandy, had been served even before guests had reached the
table – and went immediately into a story of a medical professor demonstrating to his class. He had a little worm which he put into a saucer of water.
The worm wriggled out. He then took a saucer of alcohol, 'and it may have
been whisky or it may have been brandy, or poteen – some of you Scots will
not know what poteen is: it's what gives us the Irish accent. Well, it doesn't
matter what the alcohol was, the professor put the little worm into it, and it
curled up and died.' 'Oh's of mock pity sounded from around the room. 'So
what does that show?' the professor asked his class. Silence. Then from the
back a bright spark says, 'It shows that if you drink alcohol you'll never have
worms!'

He went on to remark on having survived the Raffertys [the bride's family:

laughter], and tonight the Maclarens [the groom's: more laughter]. 'I felt them all coming at me, one after another. Actually it reminded me of my own family.' He was the eldest of eleven – or was it thirteen, or fifteen? In any case there were appreciative noises at the number. 'But this is not a speech about me. I broke the first rule that we are taught: never speak to strange girls! And that is how I got involved with the Raffertys. It was at a charismatic meeting. Margaret was there, with her father and mother. And I spoke to her and that was it.[N73]

(Margaret. Father Christopher – he's lovely. He's a nice person.
James.   A lot of fun!
M.   His Irish accent as well. But he's a bit of a natural comedian,
             Christopher, as well.)[T94]

Father C.   And now I know that Margaret's father is keen to say a word.

Peter stood up: 'Father Christopher, Sister Mary, ladies and gentlemen, ... but that's not the way to address you – you are all my brothers and sisters. Margaret Anne is my sister in Christ as well as my daughter, James is my brother in Christ as well as my son-in-law.' He continued for a few minutes in this vein, ending up: 'Wherever Christian people are gathered, there is Christ amongst them, and he is here today. But I am sermonising – I'm sorry.' He talked about how everybody there was their friend, and about the great amount of support they had had from people in arranging the event: how people had given their time, their thoughts, and even their money. He explained how he had rung up Father Christopher quite late last night to ask if he would stand in, as Father Morton couldn't come: he had been given another wedding to do that same afternoon in his own parish. (Father Christopher put in that it was **very** late and that he'd been **told** to do it, but such was the charm of his little-boy innocent manner and his smile that any sense of criticism was dissolved into humour.) Peter then came to his third topic, James and Margaret. He spoke of how Margaret's mother and he had watched their love for one another growing over the past year. This led into proposing the toast to them: everyone rose.

Margaret.   Anne [the bridesmaid] was crying during my dad's speech. I could
            see her. Anne cries – she cries quite easily, Anne. I could see the
            tears running down her hands and I thought, 'Oh!' And James's
            Aunt Mary [the Sister Mary Peter had mentioned] was crying
            too.[T94]

It had been a speech of great intensity and seriousness, powerful in the absolute conviction behind it, even if some of the party were not quite ready to go along with its Christian seriousness.

James's father. I think it was Ian – was it Ian who said, 'How do you follow that?'

His mother. That's right! And my brother Chris, he said, 'That was some speech.' He went up and congratulated Peter.

Sister, Helen. Dad was going to tell a joke about Rangers [of Rangers and Celtic, the leading and rival football clubs of Glasgow, Protestant and Catholic respectively]. Peter was up speaking about 'brothers and sisters in Christ' [laughing], but before Dad heard that he was going to tell a joke about the Rangers.

Mother & H. together. John Greig [the Captain at the time] was taking them out for a meal ...

Father. Oh yes.

Mother. He was going to tell a joke.

Father. It was a terrible joke. I was going to tell a joke.

SC. But you felt the tone was not quite right?

Father. Well, after Peter doing this, ...

Mother. He thought he couldn't say this.

Father. ... making this very deep speech ...

Mother. And it was from the heart.

Father. ... about being a Christian and that. One of the jokes I was going to tell ...: John Greig had the Rangers Club out for a meal, and the players were ordering **steak** and various other things ... – I can't remember the joke!

H. And he got the potatoes and that, and the waiter says to him:

Father. 'What about the vegetables?' 'They can order [for] themselves,' [laughter].

Mother. That was because Rangers were playing bad at the time [more laughter].

Father. I decided to put that out of my head entirely.[T106]

Father Christopher then called on Jámes. He stood up and began in a low voice:

> If you've seen my act before, you'll know it's a couple of jokes, a few mumbles, and that's about it. But that's not what I want to say now. I want to say more, but I don't know what it is in words. I asked people what I should say. They said I should thank you for coming and for your lovely presents, which I do. But that's not it. You are all my friends. If I don't know you personally, you are Margaret's friends. You have helped Margaret and I to grow up. You've carried me home ...' ['recently', put in somebody amidst laughter; 'you're quite a weight', added somebody else]. You are all our friends. And that's just what I want to say.

Margaret. The first thing I said to him when he sat down was: 'You didn't say, "On behalf of my wife and myself"!' [she laughs].[T94]

At the time I was thinking, 'James! He hasn't said that!' This is one of the things I've always liked at weddings, at the point in the speeches when the groom says, 'On behalf of my wife and myself.' I was waiting for it, but of course it didn't come. And I thought, 'James!'. In fact there's a photograph that John took, or Stephen, immediately after you sat down; and I'm turning to speak to you, and it looks as though I'm congratulating you on your speech, but I remember it was the point I was saying, 'You didn't say ...!'[T112]

These are indeed amongst the best known and certainly the most explicitly appreciated words of the entire marrying procedure. Humorous cheering and applause regularly greet them, as if, in the wake of vows and ring, the marriage is at this point finally achieved.

Margaret.   But thinking about it afterwards, I was thinking it was just as well. I think it was more ..., because **everybody** says ...

James.   It never occurred to me to say it. I was actually quite surprised: I thought I was last. I thought I'd be the last one to speak. And I was sitting ... . After Margaret's dad speaking – that was nice – and I was sitting next to Joseph and I was saying to him: 'You're next! You're next! Do you know what you are going to say?' [he laughs]. And the next thing, Father Christopher says: 'I'll ask,' you know, 'I'll ask the groom' [he laughs]. 'I'm not ready for this,' you know; I got the fright of my life. But Joseph, Joseph just sat and drank wine.[T94]

Then it was indeed Joseph's turn as the best man: 'Father Morton commented at the chapel on how nervous I was. It wasn't anything that was happening at the chapel, but this here.' He had also been asking people what he should say. 'About the bridesmaid and everything,' they had said. 'But what's the "everything"? I haven't even been at a wedding before!' He then read the greetings cards, about ten of them, some just the names, some with the messages as well. Each one was clapped. 'And lastly the telegram – they did get one, from America.'[6]

'So that's the worst over.' He then spoke about how unreal the first part of the service had seemed to him. It was only at the vows that he had realised that James was really away. He wouldn't be having to share a room with him any more, or put up with his snoring, with him borrowing his clothes, with his socks lying about everywhere. (There was appreciative audience participation throughout this recital.) 'I now just have to say to the people in the coach: "Remember, the door at the back opens outwards." ' There was laughter from one section of the audience and instructions to 'tell them about it'. So he went on to tell the story of an uncle who was a coach driver in America. He had had to brake suddenly and the door of a toilet at the back of the coach, which opened forwards, flew open. A fellow with his trousers down round his ankles rocketed up the bus.

Finally Joseph turned to Anne. He complimented her but, he said, he wasn't saying much because her boyfriend was there. The company stood again and toasted 'The bridesmaid!'. There was applause.

Father Christopher called on James' father. Afterwards he recalled:

> As a matter of fact, I was a bit put out about that, because being last in the line ..., once you've had Father Christopher, Peter, James, Joseph and it's got to me, then ... you're **struggling**. You can thank Peter and Mary for the reception, but you've got to say more than that. [...]

H.   He said something about the linoleum.
Father.   Aye.
Mother.   He just said he'd lost his linoleum.
Father.   'You wonder why I'm ..., you wonder why I'm standing like this,' [he was demonstrating hand on hip and elbow sticking out] because Joseph had been standing like this as well. And I'd said to Joseph, 'Where's your linoleum?' He didnae know what I was saying. I says, 'You wonder why I'm stand...'. I says, 'I've lost my linoleum.'T106

He also talked about cuff links: how Joseph had come in and asked to borrow his cuff links. He gave him them, only then realising that he was wearing a shirt which would need them too. So he himself had then to set off to borrow some. He spoke about having had an accident with his flower, a red carnation, which had come off. Casual informality was the tone through all this, as in most of the speeches, responded to with friendly banter and comment, as well as laughter and applause from the audience. Here a few people managed to see a double meaning in the loss of the flower, and this produced its own eddy of comment and laughter. More seriously, he thanked Peter and Mary and made appreciative remarks about the meal and in particular about the drinks outside before it. He assured Peter and Mary that they hadn't lost a daughter, they'd gained a son: 'No, Both families have gained, son or daughter'. And he gave the toast to Peter and Mary.

This example represents the mixture of formality and good-humoured informality, of seriousness and joking, of purpose and inconsequentiality which successful speech-making can display. The speeches represent a first stage in the transition from formality to celebration. The celebrant, if he is present, maintains a link backwards to the formality of the service and acts as master of ceremonies. With his experience of weddings and practice at public speaking, he can get this episode off to a fairly reliable start or at least ensure that some semblance of the expected pattern occurs. Some may themselves make lengthy speeches or intervene repeatedly. They but not necessarily others may see this as a matter of encouraging those who are to follow. The pattern to which such controllers usually subscribe requires speeches from the bride's father and the bridegroom, the best man to 'read the telegrams' and probably to speak too, and often also the groom's father and/or a family friend known as a good speaker. There is a formal rationale linking contributions through toasts: the bride's father is to propose a toast to the bride and groom, the groom to respond on behalf of his new wife and himself and propose a toast to the bridesmaid(s), with the best man replying on her or their behalf. Thanking people provides a further though open-ended rationale: the guests should be thanked for coming and for their presents, the hosts for putting on the party, the bride's father for supplying his daughter, or both sets of parents for their services to their respective children's upbringing, the celebrant for officiating, and anyone else who has done anything which it occurs to anybody to thank them for. A short speech may indeed go no further than responding, with more or less conviction, to the promptings of these rationales.

Weddings, however, are one of the very few occasions in life when a manis expected to get up and make a speech entirely because of who he is and regardless of any ability he may have to do so. For grooms there is no way out, for best men and brides' fathers rarely any, though occasionally celebrants will stand in for reluctant fathers or, more often, for men who have substituted for absent fathers at the service. Performances achieved, even on a single occasion, are bound therefore to be various. The rationales available stop short of prescribing all that is required and give abundant scope for confusion and misunderstanding, particularly for the nervous.

DM.   Did you [a recent bridegroom] make a speech?

Ben.   Not a speech as such, a few comments and thank-yous and that was it. I kept it short and reasonably sweet.

DM.   Did your Uncle Willy [who had given the bride away] make a speech?

Aileen. Oh, the wee soul! He'd had it all learnt and everything written down and he says to me, 'I've got it all ...', you know. And it actually came his turn, he just went to pieces. He was so nervous and he just ..., he said what he had to say really, but it wasn't the way he'd wanted to say it or ... . I don't think he said everything he'd wanted to say either. And everybody felt so sorry for him 'cause he was so nervous. And that was it. We never even got a speech from the best man. He read the telegrams – I think he was that nervous he forgot he was to make a speech.[T58]

Thanking people is fairly straightforward, though even this requires adapting to particular circumstances and may easily slip a mind under pressure. Young men – many grooms and their best men – have often had little or no experience of weddings before those at which they must perform central roles, and even for the senior generation, the desire for a prompter by one's side is the main reason why parental couples are sometimes not mixed at the top table. Anything more than a short and simple list is inclined to become, in the circumstances, tricky. Many find even the rationale of the toasts of limited help, having either never been clear about it or in the event getting it confused. Some may add to their confusion by referring to etiquette books, almost all of which set out an English pattern which has no celebrant present. They may prepare on the basis of one set of expectations and then on the day discover them irrelevant because the celebrant or occasionally the manager has other ideas. Bridesmaids prove a frequent stumbling block: doubts about who should be complimenting them – one celebrant was quite clear that it was inappropriate for the groom at this point to be praising women other than his bride – and what responding on their behalf could possibly entail may, one or both, create confusion. In any case this rationale does not cover all who are likely to speak. Above all, it gives no guidance as to the potentially large voluntary element for which wedding speeches offer the opportunity. As a result speeches range from the brief and gauche, from which the audience do their best to cover everybody's embarrassment by extracting at least a little unintentional humour, to the efficient and often intentionally humorous.

The examples in the sequence cited above show clearly the expectations of humour which surround wedding speeches and the way in which the audience are only too ready to collaborate in producing it. Even the well-known phrase which James surprised everybody by omitting may be spoken and is certainly received in a spirit of humorous appreciation. Both his failure and the fervour of his new father-in-law's speech took people aback partly for their denial of scope for humour, though even then in the latter the priest seized on the slightest of openings to interpose a touch of it. His own opening speech had offered a blend of jokes and reminiscence, sentimental or teasing, such as make up the content of most speeches when they go beyond the issuing of thanks and the proposing of toasts. Jokes are often set pieces linked to the occasion by some more or less apposite topic: food, drink, weddings, marriage and so on. But such jokes shade into humour connected to the key actors in the wedding, sometimes masquerading as advice for the newly-weds. Stories, the humour of which is at the bridegroom's expense, reaching back into his past life are one popular kind. They come often from the best man who is offering them, tongue-in-cheek, as a warning to the bride about the husband she has married.

Apart from the intention to be funny here, these stories, which rarely have much edge to them, can sometimes be seen as a way of welcoming the bride into the circle, whether if be the family or friends, which groom and best man have shared. Between groom and his new father-in-law, on the other hand, relationships, frequently appear to be not that simple. What they have to say about one another is often barbed, surprisingly so to a detached observer though apparently merely humorous to the company. Something of a 'joking relationship' appears to be present, a situation familiar to anthropologists in which a kind of closeness combines with a kind of distance, of friendship with hostility (Radcliffe-Brown 1952; Freedman 1977; Johnson 1978; cf. Karp 1987). Speeches seem to provide, amongst other things, a licensed occasion for the expression of this uneasy combination at the moment when all are bound to recognise the permanency of the relationship.

Whatever the bridegroom says or omits to say, a final striking characteristic of wedding speeches which deserves comment is the way in which men are required to speak on behalf of women as well as of themselves. As has already become clear, two of these women, the bride and her mother, are in most ways the central figures of the wedding, but despite this it is their men who become the spokespersons at this point. With the exception of a few brides, including Margaret, who recognised an anomaly here and talked of themselves speaking at the wedding, the pattern was, however, so familiar that it was rarely remarked on. In the event, no bride was ever observed speaking, nor was any case of a speech having been made by any other woman ever reported. Current practice was strongly supported by the way in which speech-making on such an occasion was viewed by most people. It was seen as an onerous burden, alarming in prospect and nerve-racking on the occasion itself. It was a responsibility from which the women, with all their other responsibilities, were ultimately, therefore, if they thought about it at all, always grateful to be spared. The established pattern is therefore supported by the sentiments generated by the event, as well as by precedent. As such it is resistant to revision despite the way it infringes values of sexual equality to which, in other contexts, an appreciable number of the young people marrying in the early 1980s would have subscribed.

The dancing

The dancing at Margaret and James's wedding began at a quarter to eight, with 'the first waltz' in usual style.

SC.   Was that an ordeal?
James.   No.
Margaret.   Not really.
J.   I had a dancing lesson the night before, off my dad. My dad
             showed me the waltz. He showed me and Joseph.
M.   Yes. James kept saying to me: 'One, two, three, ...'.
J.   What happened was, my dad showed me how to do the waltz, and

I was showing Joseph. We had it going great, and my mum
came in and we said: 'We've learnt how to waltz – Dad showed
us.' We started it. She says, 'Your father doesn't know how to
waltz.' So it had to be retaught.[T94]

Margaret and James were left dancing on their own quite happily for a bit;
then best man and bridesmaid joined in, Joseph hamming it up. He took
his red carnation off and held it in his teeth. They had been fooling around
with flowers in their mouths at the practice the night before. The parents
then joined in.

Dancing is a standard part of the wedding. Invariably it is started in a
way which makes a set ritual out of it. The running of the event will now
have been taken over by the band leader but he ensures that it continues
the theme of the procession out of the church and the seating at the meal.
Bride and groom are first called out on to the floor and must, surrounded
by most of the company, make at least an attempt at performing a dance
quite outside the range and even the previous experience of most young
people at the time. Bridesmaid and best man are then called on to join
them, and soon afterwards the parents followed by the rest of the
company. Such dances normally come in pairs, and a second waltz
immediately following the first is to be expected. For this an organising
band leader may call on the parents to swap partners in the interests of
mixing; if they have themselves already taken up this theme and mixed for
the first waltz, mild confusion ensues. The evening continues subsequently
much like any other dance, evening reception or club night. Band leaders
make efforts, more or less strenuous and meeting with more or less success,
to get people up and dancing. A common measure of success of the
wedding is how well they do so.[7]

At Margaret and James's wedding it was, quite typically, a three-piece
band, all men. The leader, on an electric piano, also announced, organised
and sang. A second man was on drums and the third played a saxophone.
They played vigorously with little break for an hour and a half, the
company producing energetic and jolly dancing throughout. There were
two main, interlinking rooms available, and drinking and chatting
continued in the other. One or two enthusiastic photographers amongst the
guests continued their activity too. It was a beautiful northern evening in
early summer, light until late. Guests could wander outside in the gardens
surrounding the house and down to the nearby shore of Loch Lomond.
After the first dances James and Margaret themselves went off for a quiet
walk, before returning refreshed to the energetic scene within.

Margaret. I did a cancan with your Helen at one point [she laughs], I don't
know if there's a photograph of that, but there was a ... . It
ended up with a big circle of us, a big circle of women it was,

and people were going in and out – people were getting pushed in and out – and it was a kind of cancan.

James.   I was there as well.

M.   Were you? Oh, I didn't see you.

J.   I was one of the first ones to be doing the cancan. I was ... [...]

M.   Mrs McDonald was running about the dance floor mixing people up. She would **dance** with someone, and then she'd take them up and she'd abandon them to someone else. She was mixing people up on the dance floor all the time.[T94]

J.   I think people were just happy to dance and have a drink, rather than get up and sing. It didn't have that kind of atmosphere about it.

M.   We spoke about it afterwards. We were quite surprised. [...] I think it was probably just as well in a sense. My dad would have had to sing, and your mum, and I think probably, you know, while they'd quite enjoy singing, I think it probably would have been ...

J.   Yes.

M.   You know, I think your mum had said beforehand that she didn't really want to sing at the wedding. She wanted just to be able to relax and enjoy herself. So maybe it was just as well really.[T108]

After the break the dancing resumed, as energetic as ever. The music was the usual mixture of 'golden oldies', with a few set-piece dances like the Slosh and the Birdie Song – 'good-fun, party music' as one bride's mother described them – and a few Scottish country dances towards the end.

Singing

Guests and even members of the wedding party are often expected to want to sing in the course of the evening.

DM.   So tell me, did you have singing in the interval?

Bride's mother. Yes, eh, we had one guy singing and I don't know what he sung but he was rubbish [she laughs].

DM.   Whose side did he come from?

B's M.   He was a friend of Ted's [the groom], ... and Moira [the bride], a friend of both of them actually – a couple, a married couple, but the guy – I think he'd a good drink in him – he got up. And then there was ..., Aunt Mary sung. She's a lovely singer. She sung ..., oh gosh! I can't remember what she sung. Then a friend of our's, Charlie Boyle. But there were four lads got up, friends of the best man – they were rubbish as well, [she laughs].[T30]

Performing is very much a part of working-class club and party culture. Many people have their party pieces and some may even learn numbers specially for particular occasions. At any wedding a few guests may be expected to be as good, in a variety of styles and degrees of seriousness, as the group or band employed to provide the music; the latter are rarely themselves full-time professional musicians. Guests may therefore sometimes perform competently and with the backing of the musicians. On such an occasion as a wedding, however, when many people will have had a good deal to drink, the talents which emerge are bound to be variable. Some performers are likely to be really bad, though for some of the audience that is all part of the fun. Those who are at home in this world may relish such singing and be ready, if with some show of reluctance, themselves to perform. There are even enthusiasts who ask the band whether there is to be singing and who may try to push the bride's father or the best man into organising a definite list of performers. They will often, if they are not going to have the band's backing, take over in the interval. Singing, then, is a distinct item on the programme, a possibility viewed positively or negatively but rarely with indifference, and never altogether predictable in its appearance.

Lorna. I didn't want any singing. Because we've been at weddings and that's the bit I always hate.
Colin. I don't mind it. I think it's OK.
L. Oh, I don't like when the wee drunk aunties get up.
C. That's part of a wedding!
L. I had said that: I said there were to be no singers, and there were a few people dying to sing, and the band announced it. You know, 'If anyone would like to sing, ...' [she demonstrates herself waving 'No!' at them].
C. I think that's part of ...
L. 'I said you were not to ask for singers.' [...]
C. I do enjoy the singers. I don't see anything wrong with that.[T105]

For many, feelings are mixed. Those who take a more serious attitude to music or are touchy about the cultural and class identities expressed by their relatives and friends may wish to avoid having such singing altogether. They may even – in prospect and perhaps retrospect, rather than in the well-warmed atmosphere of mid-reception – cringe at its possibility. There is some relationship between attitude to singers and social class, though it is undoubtedly more a matter of self-images and aspirations than any objectively measured class which in the wedding companies concerned is always likely to be somewhat mixed anyway. Outcomes are therefore often difficult to predict. Other activities in the interval – refreshments, including sometimes a slice of the wedding cake if it has not already been served, the return of the photographer with the proofs, or an automated disco which some bands may put on at this point – tend to crowd the singing out. It may simply break through later, but it is such factors, themselves more likely at the more middle-class wedding, which weight the scale against singing.

Variation

The pattern described here represents the broad middle of Glasgow society, a pattern with which almost all the indigenous population are familiar though they may, in any given wedding, diverge. Such divergence invariably pays tribute to what may be regarded as the cultural blueprint but is, in each case and whatever the motivation, more original.

Tracy and Gordon's wedding represented a strongly working-class variant, responding to the impossibility of affording all the standard expenses. They began at the Registry Office at three o'clock on a Friday afternoon, Tracy feeling almost out of place in a far more 'weddingy' dress, white but short, than anyone else around;[8] you could not, she felt, even tell which were the brides in the other parties. They managed without wedding cars, though her father did hire a minibus from a work-mate to take the party of close family members from the Registry Office to a Chinese restaurant for a wedding meal. They then went on to a local hall where about seventy guests were expected at 7.30. The cake – two tiers – was already set up and they had a mock cutting for a friend who was taking the photographs. The band arrived and got organised. They were locals who played for dances Tracy's mother went to and she had arranged them. There was a bar run by their own pub, the scene of their hen and stag nights reported above.

The guests arrived promptly and the band were ready to begin with the first waltz:

Tracy.   Gordon wasn't going to. He says, 'I'm no ..., I'm not dancing.' I said: 'Gordon, you have to.' But the guy in the band had said to my brother: 'Look, let them have a couple of shuffles and you get right up, 'cause it is embarrassing.' And they got right up right away, and then everyone else got up. But everybody got up and danced. The band was so good they made them get up and dance.

One of the guys that works beside Gordon is great at these things. He went round all the men and got ten pence off them. I was wondering what was going on. [...] He bought a half bottle of whisky and six cans of lager – or four cans of lager - and he got them up to the spot dance – is that what you call it?

DM.   Yes.

T.   It was planned so me and Gordon would win, but Gordon didn't ask me to dance – my uncle asked me first. So they were panicking. So there was only about two couples left on the floor, and he got me and [another girl] up on the stage. And they said, 'Right! First to show us a blue garter'. [She laughs.] Well, nobody else really had. So I won the half bottle and she got the cans of lager.

DM.   Who got up and sang?

T.   My uncle got up and, eh ..., who else? I can't even remember. A couple of people got up.

DM.   It wouldn't be a wedding without.

T.   No, it wouldn't be. It was good. It was really ... . And one of the guys out the garage [where the groom worked] – I don't know if I told you about Gordon's stag night [...] – one of the guys from the garage came along to the [pub] with his bus coat on, and a peg leg, and did that 'Jake the Peg'. Well, he done it at the wedding and it was fantastic. He's got it all down to a T [...], and he's quite a shy guy – I wouldn't have thought he would have done it. And everybody thought this was marvellous, you know, him coming in and doing this. Then my dad came in all dressed up, just as I was leaving. [...] My dad's a very shy man, but when he's got a drink in him he dresses up. So I bought him a couple of fake noses and that waistcoat thing for his Christmas. I felt really pleased with that – he's always looking for things to dress up in.[T65]

So that became one of the wedding photographs too. A wedding which produced a father of the bride in a waistcoat with false stomach attached, and a funny nose, was something else again.

Jan and Shuggie, who have also been encountered several times already, were, in contrast, seeking more consciously to direct the occasion to conform to their own preferences. They had done their best, not altogether successfully, to shape their marriage service: the priest had crowned a series of delays and minor confusions by delivering a startlingly unanticipated reading which, to the amusement of friends of the highly vocal bride, featured a silent wife as a blessing for her husband. It was, however, the music for the reception of which they really wanted to take charge. They had a disco to give them a good quality of music and keep themselves out of the grip of wedding bands which they regarded as almost uniformly awful. But their most striking effort at innovation was to arrange for the disco to substitute a Bob Marley record, not even in waltz-time, for the first waltz.

Jan.   When he played the first record, he went, 'And we have the first waltz. It's a personal choice by the bride and groom.' As if ...

Shuggie.   As if ... 'it's been nothing to do with me!'

J.   'I take no responsibility for it.' And he put it on [she laughs].

S.   I could hear stifled cheers in the background: 'They did it!'

'They did it! They were nae kiddin' ', because we'd told a few people we were going to do that.[T71]

But after that there were the usual pairs on the floor and the range of music for all tastes. Everybody danced, and drank abundantly. Nobody sang. It was deemed a thorough vindication of the disco's capacity to do a proper wedding, about which many in their circle had previously been sceptical.

Favours and the bride's responsibilities

'Favours' are in the first place decorations from the cake. They are more or less elaborate little confections, commercially produced from artificial flowers or heather and ribbons, and often matching the colour of the brides-maids' dresses. Their function is not only to decorate the cake but to be distributed once the cake has been cut to some or all of the ladies present. Since more are commonly needed for this purpose than the cake will accom-modate, extras are bought and then brought along separately for distribu-tion. They constitute the current manifestation of a line of decorative objects similarly labelled which have been given out at weddings in Britain at various times and places at least since the seventeenth century.[9] Other floral decorations from the reception, and even the bouquets, are often treated as favours too.

At Margaret's reception she and her bridesmaid spent a long time distribu-ting little lilac favours to all the ladies.

Margaret. The favours were just a sheer pain in the neck. That silly tray! Trying to think who you were giving what to and whether you'd left anybody out. I gave the table decorations out as well. I tried to give the table decorations to all the aunts. It just got beyond it, it really did. I can't remember ...

SC.   And what about the vase and the flowers from the top of the cake?

M.   Maybe I gave them to Theresa and Catherine [two maiden aunts], because I'm sure I gave them something special. They always get something special off their nieces' and nephews' cakes. My gran used to get it. They get it now [since their mother's death].[T111]

Her own bouquet went to her mother; James's mother had the bridesmaid's.

At this wedding therefore, the bride was busy and, as is usual, she and the groom spent the evening largely apart. There is always some expectation that the couple will each get around and talk to the guests. The groom will occasionally be trying to buy drinks for those who have joined the party only after the meal, but more often it is he for whom others are constantly keen to buy. This may, according to his appetites, result in a trail of abandoned drinks as he moves around the hall. Brides sometimes find on the contrary that they are getting nothing to drink at all. They may also dance much less than they had expected. Neither Margaret nor James were by any means overwhelmed though, or unable to enjoy themselves, but the demands of socialising, together with the need to distribute favours, may sometimes generate uncomfortable pressure for the bride. A mother's preoccupation with doing things properly is one exacerbating factor. The presence of numbers of guests who have known the bride as a child but are not in regular contact with her, who perhaps have come from some distance to the wedding and who need urgently to speak with her before she and they leave, is another likely source of extra pressure. In such circumstances the event may occasionally overwhelm her.

Bride's mother. Too many things had to be done all at once. People had to be received who were coming in **late**. She had to do wee things like giving out favours, **and** talk to people who were grabbing her. It was all just too much for her. You saw her losing her cool completely. [The groom] said to [her sister, the bridesmaid]: 'You take her away upstairs to the wee room, comb her hair, take her veil off, and I'll talk to folk. And when she comes down ..., you come down on your own and do the rest of the favours.'[10] She'd done all the main people anyway. [...] So that was fine. Sarah came down and finished that off, and when Catriona came back down it was all done and she just got on with the rest of the business. It's hard work! Very hard work![T40]

Going away

Margaret. Going away was amazing, wasn't it? – getting into the taxi. Because you looked back and **everybody** was out on those steps, and they were down the side of the steps like this: [she shows a crescent shape.] And they were singing 'They are jolly good fellows', I think. And they were singing 'Cheerio'. It was amazing going away in the car and looking back, wasn't it?

J.   Yes.

M.   Because there were all these people waving.[T94]

Some time during the evening and often as late as it was here – it was almost eleven before Margaret and James even went off to change – the final required episode takes place. The bride has normally kept on throughout the evening the dress which labels her clearly as such, and the groom has usually not changed either.[11] Though they became husband and wife at the service and their new relationship and its implications for others have been rehearsed at various points since, from the time they set out from their homes in their appropriate outfits they have been bride and groom. These identities they now relinquish in changing out of their wedding clothes into smart but essentially ordinary outfits prepared for going away in. The bride has had her day; custom now ceases to give her priority as she becomes the second party in an ordinary married couple, husband and wife, Mr and Mrs.

The change of dress can be seen as itself ritual, but the moment is otherwise one which excites attention rather than requiring particular procedures of any kind. The woman might well like to go round saying goodbye, at least to get some immediate value from a going-away outfit into which a good deal of effort and expense have often been put. This may sometimes be possible but her new husband, and she on his behalf, are often greatly alarmed at this point as to what may happen to them.

Carol.   One of my half-cousins, he's a farmer. At his wedding ..., you know, it was like the Young Farmers' Convention at his wedding, and ..., oh, they were tossing him in the air, and he was almost at the ceiling and ... head hitting the floor, and ... . Great fun! [said sarcastically.] All these daft big farmers. And Mary saying, 'Oh, don't! Don't! You'll kill him!' That's the sort of thing that happens.

At Maureen and David's [at which she had been the bridesmaid], people got saying, 'Remember what we did to so-and-so', 'Remember what ...'. And Maureen said, 'Oh, no!' So they went out the fire exit. But the taxi driver was running after them: 'Wait! I'm the taxi driver.' He had knocked the door[12] [of the hotel room they were changing in] and said 'Taxi!'. We were standing in the room, and David's going: 'Shh! It's not the taxi' – it turned out it was the taxi. And we waited until we heard the footsteps going away and then they ran out the room – I was left with the key to lock the room – dashing for the fire escape.[T36]

At Carol's own going-away, though they were apprehensive, nothing happened to her new husband. Three other couples in the study were not so lucky. In one case it was a simple matter of tossing, but in the other two the action was more pointed. As they were about to leave, the woman was distracted and the man forcibly removed to the toilets. One, who had been absolutely sure that he would not get away without some trouble, found ice cubes being put down the front of his trousers; the other, known as a smart dresser, had clothes removed and messages in lipstick written all over his best suit and fancy shirt.

More unusual was Shuggie's fate. He and Jan had the not unreasonable idea that showing no sign of going until very late would keep him fairly safe.

Jan.   We were going to stay right to the very end – well, maybe five minutes before – and then just vanish.

SC.   So it wasn't when you said you were going that you were attacked?

Shuggie.   No. They had started playing things, you know, party records.

J.   It was a kind of a party record, where two people go in the middle and everybody kind of ... dances round the two people in the middle, and they do a wee dance. Then another two. And we managed to get thrown into the middle, and they went: [cheers] because it was us, and attacked us, didn't they? Because a few other people had been in, just kind of done wee dancey bits. But when it got to us, they decided it was time to have ...

S.   Well, actually they had to drag me from the bar. Because I was standing at the bar at the time. I wasn't even dancing. I was just, you know, having a quiet chat to one of my pals that I'd hardly spoken to all night. And the next minute I was ..., Moira dragged me into the circle. I got thrown into the middle. And that was it. After that I was fair game.

As he had said earlier in the conversation,

      They tried to take my clothes off at the end of the night as well.

J.   It was only the aunties that did that.

S.   Jan's auntie went for me.

J.   It was my wee, teeny auntie. My wee spinstery, placidy auntie suddenly turned into a raving lunatic and tried to remove his clothes. I went, 'Auntie Isla, stop it!' 'You've got a wonderful man there' [imitating her in a silly voice: she laughs]. [...]

S.   One or two of my pals were ...

J.   And my Auntie Isla, and my Auntie Kirsty, and my Auntie Lizzie.

S.   Your Aunt Lizzie wasn't ...

J.   Yes, she was kind of saying, 'Go on, Isla!' [a silly voice again], or something like that [she laughs]. 'Go on yourself!' [silly voice and a strong Glasgow accent this time].

S.   The ones I found myself aware of were your Auntie Isla and Sandy.

J.   Sandy would have done that anyway. Sandy's like that – Raymond making up for the fact that he couldn't go up for the stag night by tearing all your clothes off at the wedding.[T71]

The timing of this attack, its manner, but above all the way in which it was not confined to one sex were what was unusual here. It was not altogether accidental: this was the bride who had had her own stag night and had been as close as anyone to making a speech at the meal.[13] It looked at the time as if it might be a pointer to a future in which the gender differentiation which was so clear a motif in established wedding forms might begin to break down.

Energies may also be directed to decorating the car the couple are going away in if it is available and can be found; in Glasgow however, a taxi summoned at the time is more likely to be used. Even this does not necessarily get away altogether unscathed:

Carol.   No rowdy characters there, just a lot of confetti, and a lot of cheering and banging on the taxi. I said to the man: 'Why are we sitting here? Why don't you drive away?' Because he was going sort of 'What's happening here?' 'Get away! Come on, quick!' Because everybody just kept opening the doors and throwing more confetti in. [Representing herself, in a high-pitched voice:] 'I'm awful sorry about this! I'm awful sorry about this!' [The driver answering, with resignation:] 'It's alright.' So we gave him a large tip.[T36]

Confetti also features strongly if somebody gets at the couple's cases or, worse, at the room in which they will be spending the night. It has the supreme advantage for those who use it of advertising quite unequivocally that the couple to whose persons and property it clings are newly married. Advertising the couple's status and drawing hardly-veiled attention to the sexual activity expected to follow are the twin themes of most of these final pranks. Most couples are keen to avoid them if at all possible. Elaborate precautions are taken to keep cases out of the way and to preserve secrecy over their plans for after the wedding. This latter is sometimes still thought of as a matter of the groom surprising the bride, but it has the much more direct purpose of attempting to avoid interference. Hotels holding receptions usually prefer their couples to go elsewhere for the night because of the trouble and even damage that can result if their presence in the bridal suite is discovered. Invariably couples leave as if going elsewhere. The taxi will if necessary take them round the block and back to another entrance.

Despite this, it is difficult to avoid taking someone into one's confidence and assiduous tricksters often win through. Their exploits provide material for one of the main varieties of wedding stories. Doing things to beds is a common theme, but some are more original:

Mary.   He says to me ..., he goes ..., he says, 'Mary, there's a wee case up in the bedroom', he says, 'and it's for something ..., it's got something for you to wear in it, and something for Anthony to wear in it.' And I thought, 'Och, it's probably a wee nighty or something. I don't really need it but that's ... oh, that's nice!' He's got me a wee nighty, you know. So we saw the case [...] all tied up with white ribbon and everything. I thought 'oh, that's awful nice ...'.

Anthony. So I went to open them up and, eh, it was rather embarrassing, wasn't it? And, eh, ..., it was, eh, ..., he'd a whole pile of Durexes [condoms] in it. And he'd blown them – wait till you hear – he'd blown them up and put Buttons [packets of chocolate drops] inside them.

M.   Buttons!

A.   He had put ..., what else?

M.   Mars Bars.

A.   A Mars Bar inside them.

M.   He knows he eats Mars Bars.

A.   He'd put some Irn Bru [a favourite Scottish soft drink] inside them. And they were sticking to the roof, and we're trying to get them down.

M.   Aye, he put that oxygen stuff in them or something.

A.   That's right. He'd got some ...

M.   And they all just popped out the case. It was funny.

A.   ... trying to get rid of them before the hotel staff appear![T80]

Afterwards

The couple's departure does not in itself mark the end of the reception. It is not a party just for them, and sometimes their going is hardly noticed. Those who leave early for some reason frequently discover, to their disappointment, that the best was after they had gone.

Aileen.   Apparently it livened up when we left, 'cause all the relatives were up singing, and my uncle who plays the drums was up playing the drums. And Ben's dad was singing, the best man was singing, and a cousin was singing. Oh, we missed all that. That's quite sad. [...] The band organised ..., it was things like ..., they played different pieces of music and you had to name the country it came from. So they were all up doing the flamenco and my cousin was charging the bull with my next-door neighbour's coat, and they were doing ballet dancing and everything. So I wish I hadn't missed it.[T58]

At the celebration for which Margaret and James's wedding was the pretext, as soon as the taxi was out of sight the guests went back in and the dancing resumed. But it was indeed late and quite soon the band leader was beginning the highly constant winding-up routine. The 'last waltz' led into 'Auld Lang Syne', with the parents in the middle. As the mother of another bride commented: 'Everybody gets up for that. In fact there was so many you couldn't even move round.' 'For He's a Jolly Good Fellow' followed. This was clearly directed mainly at Peter but he turned the compliment aside by singing energetically himself. There were three cheers for the hosts. The band leader made a little speech thanking everybody for being such good company

and saying how much they had enjoyed playing for them. There were three
cheers for the band.

Peter announced that anybody who needed transport should see him; the
coach which had brought the groom's party had returned. Goodbyes and
thankyous began. Margaret's mother was keeping out of the way but was
calm. She had, she said, been quite sad last week when it was very clear that
Margaret was leaving home, but not tonight. Peter was still running things.

For the groom's party there was a longish coach ride keeping them
together, and small impromptu parties continued at various homes.

James's mother. It was twenty minutes to one when we got home, all very
              happy [she laughs]. Oh, it was really a wonderful day!
SC.   You didn't have another party after that?
Helen & her mother together. We did!
Mother.   ... because I think I relaxed. They all started singing the whole
              road on the way back. When we came in here, two of James's
              friends, Paul and Dougie, were staying here, and they had brought
              a bottle of whisky. So we sat here and I relaxed then. Because
              being the mother of the groom you've got to sort of keep ..., watch
              what you are doing and see that you're keeping everything ahead
              of yourself. Whereas when I came in here I just relaxed, and I had
              a whisky, and we sang. We sang till half past two in the morning
              [she laughs].
Helen.   At least!
Mother.   Paul sat here. Catherine fell asleep, and Paul just keeled over, and
              all in their wedding regalia too.[T106]

Chapter 9

Familiar rites and anthropological interpretation

Earlier chapters have set out a parade of rites of marrying as they were recorded and studied in Glasgow in the early 1980s. The term has been used not as a means of forcing reality into a predefined set of categories but as a net for fishing in a cultural sea still oddly unfamiliar to anthropology. The haul has been rich and varied. Specimens have been described and assessed at least cursorily as they were removed in turn from the nets, but the point comes at which it is necessary to try to sum up the nature and significance of the catch. That is the task of this final chapter.

What the net was designed to take out of the sea was all the practices and procedures connected with marrying. The sense in which they might in any more exact or technical sense be called 'rites' was left over for subsequent consideration. Some specimens were found with the term already attached to them; its application, that is to say, was a part of the ethnography to be observed and recorded. This is true particularly in the Catholic Church. Elsewhere there has been much to which the anthropologist would be inclined to attach the term though the performers of the actions did not. A number of characteristics, often linked, made much of the action noted appear exceptional.

Some things, in the first place, have a right way of being done which is strikingly well known compared to any reason for doing them in that particular way. This presents itself as an internal rightness, dependent neither upon some causal logic of what is required to achieve a given effect nor on some external compulsion. Simple examples here would be the right-left orientations and the way couples hold on to one another in processions, both of which have been discussed in some detail. Right ways of doing things are of course common in the conduct of daily life, but in the context of marrying they have a particular salience. This is partly because, particularly for young people getting married but also often for their elders who have rarely if ever before been involved in arranging events of this kind, right ways constitute a specialised lore which has to be learnt in the course of preparations. It is also because of the way in which the lore becomes increasingly insistent. On the wedding day itself rule-bound actions come so thick and fast for the couple themselves, and even for the other members of the wedding party, that there is little scope for spontaneous activity or for following one's own inclinations.

Secondly, there are numerous sequences of action to be performed, often involving several people together and regarded as a single episode. The major sequences here, the marriage service and the reception, are of such scale and complexity that they are themselves seen as containing separate episodes within them, the sections which have been followed in giving accounts of them above. The Catholic service is indeed officially presented with two levels of internal segmentation: the sequence called 'Blessing and Exchange of the Ring or Rings' is, for instance, a part of the larger sequence termed 'Liturgy of Marriage', itself a section of the overall sequence of the Nuptial Mass. We have seen indeed that the service itself is then framed in such a way as to become part of a larger sequence still. Taking the bride out, or stag nights, are on the other hand relatively unitary events, with little internal complexity and not integrated in the same tight way into larger sequences.

Thirdly, much that goes on is a terminus of motivation. Setting up a bride explains and justifies sequences of action often running over many months beforehand, but no comparable further end explains or justifies the appearance of the bride in her distinctive outfit. In the name of making a marriage which could be achieved with four signatures in a Registry Office, a mass of events which are not necessary for their avowed end are put on, events which are essentially ends in themselves, self-justifying in their own intrinsic importance. Anything may of course be done for ulterior motives; the point here is that no motives, ulterior or otherwise, account for the detail of many of the procedures being adopted or for the importance which is being attached to them.

All these characteristics are matters of degree. Each appearing on its own may suggest the presence of something a little out of the ordinary but not such as to demand a common label, 'rite'. At the time and place studied, holding a party to celebrate an engagement or some other personal event had the terminal quality but no highly developed sense of a right way of doing things, nor the set sequences or programme of actions. There was a sequence to go through in obtaining and completing the marriage schedule, but it was firmly prescribed by authority and lacked lore on the right way to do things. There were right ways of doing many things, greeting someone or laying out a letter for instance, which did not have either the terminal quality or constitute a programme of actions. None of these would usefully have been termed a rite, but where two or more characteristics appear together, then something calling for a separate label seems to be emerging. There are common right ways to conduct and to eat meals. When the meal becomes an object in itself, deprived of any straightforward instrumental justification such as the provision of food for the hungry, then the term 'ritual' begins to make some sense. When in addition the meal, which already has a certain programme within it, becomes a part of the kind of large-scale sequence of the wedding reception, then a highly distinctive, cross-culturally recognisable phenomenon is clearly present (cf. Lewis 1980, p. 25).

The rites encountered fall into two rather sharply separated categories, the religious and the popular. The religious take place within spaces dedicated to religious activities and are conducted by specialised religious functionaries. They are heavily weighted with words, indeed predominantly verbal, and both their language and the ideas to which the words allude are parts of a distinctive Christian tradition. Popular rites on the other hand have no special location; they move around and happen in work places, on the streets, at home, in pubs and hotels. Though there are experts who advise and even exercise control over parts of them, overall there is no authority on the popular side comparable to the celebrant's on the religious. Above all, the balance of words and actions is quite different. In popular rites words are usually incidental; it is not what people say but what they do which usually counts. Such contrasts are not absolute even here, and there is nothing inevitable about the extent to which they are developed. They are an aspect of, or perhaps a product of, the segregated and specialised nature of religion in the society in question; it is after all the society which has given rise to the notion that there is such a thing as religion separate from everyday and other forms of life and thought (Asad 1983). A society lacking such a distinction – and it has undoubtedly been far less developed, if at all, in the majority of societies anthropologists have studied in other parts of the world – would inevitably display a more unified ritual field.

This final chapter reviews the ways of understanding the rites of marrying which have been studied, in their local socio-cultural context, against the cross-cultural experience of anthropology, and in relation to problems of interpretation.

Marrying in the social and cultural context of Glasgow

At the most general level, weddings are important in the collective imagination of the society. It is an imagining which has a clear focus in 'the bride', a fantasy figure generated by weddings which young women are offered the opportunity of embodying for a brief moment. 'The bride' flourished during the 1980s despite, it might seem paradoxically, the growth of doubts about marriage as an institution, and of unmarried domestic and sexual partnerships, and of single parenthood. The bride becomes a focus of associations and sentiments all the stronger and more poignant perhaps to the extent that they are, perhaps less then ever, to be taken for granted.

For the woman herself, being the bride, appropriately dressed and on her wedding day, is the moment when, within the circle of her family and friends, she is unquestionably the focus of attention on whom all wait. She is the star of her day, the day on which, in an ancient structuring of priorities, it is for an instant bride and groom – the bride and her bridegroom – before the twist of marriage makes it husband and wife. But it is what the bride represents for others which gives the role its widest significance. It submerges a woman's individual personality and makes her an instantly recognisable object, a source of interest, attraction and often emotion even to people who know her not at all. What exactly does she stand for? It is necessarily not easy to say. It is because such an object as the bride can stand for many things, with different ranges of them highlighted for different people in different circumstances at different times, that it can have such wide significance. It can stand for youth and beginnings and hope, for freshness and innocence, for successful growing up, for the passage of generations, for love and romance. It would be going further than the evidence can warrant to suggest that brides keep such sentiments alive, but they are certainly a major feature in the theatre of culture which currently enriches the sense of value and interest in life.

Kinship and families

Mrs Gilligan. Families – that's what weddings are all about. I mean, if you didn't have a family, I don't see that you would have the same kind of wedding. I wouldn't. Weddings are for families.[T40]

One of the most striking findings of this study is the vigour of the family, not just as a set of relationships between parents and children but as a more extensive and valued kindred. The speaker here had recently held weddings for both her two daughters. She was linking having a family with the kind of wedding presented in this study. She had in mind one which starts with a ceremony in mid afternoon, most often religious but sometimes in a registry office as had been one of hers, and which then goes into the elaborate and lengthy reception for a large number of guests with which we are now familiar. Such an event would be paid for principally by the bride's parents. Although the drink consumed after the meal would be bought by the guests themselves at a bar, the long list of other apparently necessary expenditures, which could be incurred at a variety of levels to extend all pockets, meant that for everyone the holding of such a wedding represented a substantial expenditure. At the prices of the early 1980s, upwards of £1000 would be spent;[1] for what was probably the most costly wedding actually studied, the bride's father estimated that it had cost him almost £6000 to get his daughter married. Weddings were clearly important to people.

They related to kinship, or 'family', in a number of ways. Close kin constituted the most essential guests to be invited and a responsibility for ensuring that they were was generally seen as resting with the couple's parents. Only rarely were events controlled exclusively or even principally by the couple themselves. The close kin invited, apart from the parents themselves, would include at least grandparents and their siblings if any, the parents' brothers and sisters – the uncles and aunts of the couple – and the latters' own siblings. First or sometimes more distant cousins might also be invited, but somewhere here a line would commonly be drawn. As has been seen, 'having a big family' loomed large in this Glasgow research.

It was kin too who were the ones who occasioned most concern. Before the wedding there was first the matter of invitations for them. On the bride's side, awareness of the style and scale of previous weddings in the family was then frequently important as an influence on planning. On the day itself it was the kin who required most attention. They might have to be included in group photographs; they had to be appropriately seated for the meal, in the light of their closeness to the principals at the top table and to their current relationships with one another; after the meal they might have to be danced with and bought drinks. In general it was the kin who had to be looked after. They therefore in practice loomed even larger at all stages of the preparations and of the day itself than the substantial proportion of the the guest list for which they usually accounted.

Mrs Gilligan's 'Weddings are for families' contained much truth therefore. Glasgow weddings were pre-eminently family events even if kin were rarely in a majority at them. For this kind of wedding, kin also had definite roles to play in the arrangements. These connected particularly with mixing of the sides, the bride's and the groom's, as a major theme. Mixing was an injunction on all guests; a common way in which the success of a wedding was asserted was to claim that everyone mixed well. In practice, however, it was primarily to the immediate families of bride and groom or, put another way, to the two sides of the newly constituted single family that the mixing applied.

The starting point was the separate seating for the two sides at the religious ceremony. They were then mixed in a series of symbolic expressions in which the parents, repeatedly exchanging their partners, were the chief performers. The procession out of the church, the 'official' group photographs – though these commonly included representations of the previous separation as well – the seating at the top table, and the formal beginning to the dancing all provided occasions for such exchange. Each time, the parents were required to echo the new partnership between their children. The best maid and the best man carried out the same schedule of engagements but in direct support of the couple rather than in fulfilment of this symbolic programme. Though they might often be close kin to bride and groom, sisters and brothers particularly, this was not mandatory; they were not, therefore, in principle recruited as representatives of any family and they did not therefore perform in any representative capacity or as part of the mixing of sides. Representation, though not mixing, was a consideration in the co-opting of other close kin to roles in the wedding, as ushers, as participants in the action of some Catholic services, and occasionally as speakers after the meal. Balance between the sides was then normally sought even though there was no symbolic interchange to be performed. At receptions where guests sang, this too was usually thought of in terms of family contributions.

Weddings are therefore shaped to a considerable extent by and in terms of kinship, both in direct relation to mixing and more generally. They also maintain it in two ways implicit in what has already been said. The gathering in of kin for the wedding itself is important, but this is only the high point of a much longer process and often a more widely ranging one. Almost every wedding has been preceded by a marked increase in communication, over a considerable period and starting as early as the engagement. One older bride commented: 'we want it to be a family wedding although we don't have many of a family – although it's growing in number. To our surprise we're hearing about cousins that we've never seen for donkeys ...'. Not only the news and the arrangements themselves, but the wedding presents and the shows of presents which often precede the wedding provide needs to communicate and a heightened level of mutual interest. Interaction is increased and the exchange of news promoted. The result is not invariably favourable; weddings which for one reason or another rupture relationships are not unknown. But for the most part there is little doubt that they have the effect of reactivating relationships otherwise liable to fade with the passage of time.

There are of course other family events which have similar effects, funerals, the much rarer golden weddings, to a lesser extent silver weddings and the birth and christening of children, but the impact of weddings is far greater. No other event attracts the same level of planning over the same extended timescale, let alone the excitement, emotion and optimism which commonly attach to it. It may even reconcile the previously estranged, as did one wedding studied, for brothers who had not spoken for seven or eight years. They had fallen out after the parents of the groom had not attended the brother's wife's funeral. They had, they said, been away on holiday at the time and had not even heard of her death until they returned. Making arrangements for the wedding provided in this case the opportunity for contact to be renewed, and the event itself allowed the reconciliation to be consumated. Funerals may have the same effects but they are in any case bound to be in the nature of emergencies. They can generate in busy and scattered families neither the attendance nor the amount of communication which a lengthy planning period allows.

The superiority in this regard of weddings is further accentuated by the way in which each is often placed within a stream of such occasions. The cousins within a generation, primarily the children of siblings, grow up and are gradually married in a succession of weddings over a period of years. Mrs Gilligan, already twice quoted, saw her two daughters' weddings as the first in a likely succession of ten which would gradually occur in the coming years. By means of each individually, and cumulatively, relationships in the wider family are reinforced at a key point in the onward movement of the generations, retarding the inevitable fragmentation which is inherent in this advance. Their occurrence is cyclical. For many there are periods in the cycle of family life at which weddings seem incessant, others during which they are so rare that people may seem to have stopped marrying one another alto-gether.

The second major way in which weddings maintain kinship is through the learning process which every such wedding constitutes for the younger generation. The processes of determining the guest list and of dealing with present-givers normally demand joint attention to kin by the couple and their parents. One recent bride denied that her extensive and detailed knowledge of her own 'twenty-three couples of family' came, except marginally, from this source. She put it down to the succession of weddings she and her new husband had been to before their own, two on her father's side, two on her mother's. But this experience was unusual and did not account for the conspicuous expertise she could also display on her husband's kin. This at least had, it was plain, mainly originated in the wedding planning. In general, couples are commonly led by the planning process into an increased knowledge of their respective families. The bride in particular often acquires a knowledge of her groom's kin which may well exceed his own. This is perhaps the most practically significant kind of 'mixing' in the end. By it the married couple are equipped with the knowledge of their joint families which they will pass on as a single set to the children they may produce. It becomes an integral part of family continuity. Where such weddings are not held the nature of the family is bound to be different.

Social class

In Glasgow there are not distinct cultural forms which can be labelled working-class and middle-class weddings (cf. Leonard 1980, pp. 256-7). The only clear distinction at this level is between the form which is common, in aspiration at least, across the full working-and-middle class range of those firmly rooted in the city, and the form of wedding which may be put on by members of the Anglo-Scottish upper class. The two disproportionate sections correspond, probably rather exactly, to those who think of education in terms of local schools, including those considered the best in Glasgow, which may be fee-paying, and those who think in terms of sending children away to English-style 'public schools'. People of the latter kind may be resident in and around Glasgow. They may send their children to Scottish public schools. They often give their weddings a Scottish dress with kilts and pipers, but the patterns they conform to are shared with members of their own class throughout Britain and grounded in the practices of a larger section of the population in the South of England.

For the bulk of the population, from unskilled workers living in council schemes and perhaps unemployed, to secure professionals occupying villas in the leafy fringes of the conurbation, the way to hold a wedding is the form presented here. There are those who have an image of the real working-class wedding of the past. This would, it is likely to be thought, have taken place in a hall, have had a steak-pie purvey and a barrel of beer providing free drink. It would have been more of a do-it-yourself celebration, without the managers or the formality of the present. Such a picture certainly has a strong element of the mythical about it, but what real weddings at particular times in the past were actually like has not been systematically investigated. In the present, however, those holding weddings do not differentiate separate images of the working-class wedding and how that should be conducted from images of the middle-class and how that should be. Many weddings in any case involve, even at their centre, people whose class positions and identities are far from uniform. Nevertheless, the weddings they achieve are affected in small ways by differences of value which are seen as class-related, as well as by the different financial resources at the disposal of those differently placed in the class system. Such differences are perceived mostly by the various professionals who have experience of many weddings and of the variety in weddings, rather than by lay people whose experience is likely to be too limited to stimulate any sense of patterned distinctions.

Making distinctions is not however an activity that most professionals relish. At least in any kind of public context, a sense that any distinctions made are liable to seem invidious and should be approached with caution is clear. It is other people who are snobs, 'those who think they're better than everybody', who want to be different to 'all the scruff', as one photographer put it. A band leader when first approached on the telephone produced a contrast between the genteel Saturday night wedding and Fridays when the punters could be expected to be swinging from the chandeliers, but when he was subsequently interviewed he had been thinking about what he should say and was taking a more cautious line. Whilst recognising differences to which he needed to respond, he stressed the middle ground. He contrasted the 'refined' to the 'rough and ready', the 'sophisticated' to the 'real rough working-men's type of audience'. If you thought it was 'the stockbroker belt' you were going to, you would select the band and their outfits accordingly; but 'if you have a working-class crowd, they're not long in sensing the Palm Court type [...], whereas for the true-blue Conservative type, it's no good sending along working men'. Some people do, that is to say, operate with a working-class vs. middle-class opposition, but often this merely masks what is clear in other cases, that it is extremes that are being envisaged, people who are distant from oneself. The stockbroker belt is set on one side, the least favoured parts of peripheral housing schemes on the other. No exhaustive division of the population within which one would be ready to place oneself is really being supposed.

With these cautions it is nevertheless possible to pick out differences between individual weddings which professionals see as relating to differences of value and over which the research experience tends to endorse their judgement. Flowers are one focus which has been noted. Enthusiasm for cut, fresh flowers and a keenness to provide them in some quantity for decorating the church, if they can be afforded, is a predominantly middle-class value. It goes with a tendency to scorn the artificial blooms and feathers with which working-class weddings may be lavishly decorated. Working-class enthusiasms are more likely to be directed to setting up large numbers of bridesmaids and other child attendants than to decorating the setting for the marriage.

Again, the tone of celebrations after the meal may differ, occasionally to the point of exciting the scorn of those whose values are different. Orderliness and restraint are likely to be middle-class values. In terms of them, a well-organized programme of dances for which the band play throughout the evening with a minimum of talk and without unscheduled events of any kind is the ideal. There should be scope for those who want just to chat with one another, implying some restraint in the volume of sound. Though the drink may be expected to flow freely, drunkenness should certainly be avoided. Whilst there are no values in play which are the opposite of any of these, a notably relaxed attitude to all of them may be taken. This then constitutes contrasting working-class values in application. The band may not be expected to keep so strictly to music for dancing. They may interact more with guests who themselves may be singing and otherwise performing in unpredictable ways. Though their performances are not necessarily, in anyone's eyes, good and may indeed be quite incompetent, they can still be enjoyed as a valued part of proceedings. Bands themselves may also set up little games or go in for patter in ways which depart from straight dancing. If people get excitable and have too much to drink, that is the mark of a wedding which has been successful and enjoyed. Though the evidence is too slight for any certainty, it seemed in the present study that the kind of assault on grooms attempting to leave their receptions which was discussed in the preceding chapter was more likely to occur in the context of the more restrained, 'middle-class' type of celebration than in the already more varied and eventful 'working-class' one.

Apart from differences of value, weddings are bound to work out differently according to the resources available for them, though this may be partially counteracted by differences in willingness to spend money on such events. With the exception of flowers, it is common to remark in wedding-related businesses that those who have the money are less lavish in spending it than those who do not. This means in practice that those concerned are often impressed by big orders from those they take not to be well off, and by less than generosity, as they see it, from those who seem to be. The anthropologist responded in some astonishment to thankyou cards priced at £18.60 for twenty by exclaiming that they were almost £1 a time. He was teased for this by the manager of the wedding-stationery shop selling them. That, he said, was a typical upper-class response and quite the wrong attitude. Nevertheless, such factors cannot be of more than marginal relevance. Those who have the money, even if it is only in the sense of being able to borrow it, are able to carry through the constantly accumulating expense of fulfilling the cultural norms established, whereas those who do not must compromise. Cutting back on the meal in one way or another, since this is the single most daunting item of expenditure, is the leading possibility. If this is seriously reduced the complex sequence of events associated with the meal begins to become impractical. There may be no particular desire to simplify or eliminate it, any more than there is in other cases a positive desire to carry it all through. But just as circumstances in the one case may bring the established sequence along with them, so in the other they may upset it.

The presence of a celebrant to preside is a further factor which may be relevant here. Particularly in relation to the Church of Scotland and almost regardless of whether people are religiously active or not, middle-class people are more likely to be able secure a minister's attendance than are working-class, even if this is only a matter of realising that the minister, and perhaps his wife, should be properly invited and in good time. It is possible, with relationships made tenuous by class as well as by religion, for working-class people to have the idea that ministers attend but to be unclear as to whether they really want them and/or how to go about getting them. Last-minute invitations, at a rehearsal perhaps, may well not be welcome to ministers, particularly since they, unlike priests, are likely to be people with their own spouses and families, domestic demands and arrangements. Without the celebrant the likelihood of the standard procedure being carried through successfully is so much the less.

Pre-wedding events are somewhat less uniform across the class spectrum. They are not of their nature as likely to gather participants of different class identities and positions since they are focused on one person only. Further, they often arise out of employment situations, themselves a key aspect of class. As was discussed in Chapter 5, the taking out of brides-to-be was historically based in the workplace – for 'factory girls' – and often it and events for men still are, though the range of workplaces involved has changed and broadened. Clear class connotations have accordingly weakened, though it remains true that taking-out itself is most familiar in such dominantly working-class areas as the large peripheral schemes and least in areas of privately-owned, high-cost housing in which it may be totally unknown to many people.

Religion

As regards what is often seen as the major divide in Glasgow, between Catholics and Protestants, differences in marrying are now confined to details of the religious services. The ground for a *rapprochement* had been prepared by the movement of weddings back into the churches of the reformed tradition in the first half of this century. They had, as was discussed in Chapter 1 above, previously been celebrated by ministers in private houses, manses, halls and hotels. There is still no specifying in Scots law of the premises in which marriage may be conducted. Catholic marriages had always normally been held in churches, though not necessarily in contemporary style before the altar. Catholics had however always had the possibility of a nuptial mass and where this was taken up, regulations about the times at which masses could be celebrated meant that such weddings had to be held in the morning. A distinctively Catholic pattern of wedding days resulted: an early wedding was followed by a breakfast for those who had attended the service. There would then be a break before an evening celebration, an excursion of some kind, perhaps to a theatre, or a reception and meal. After the Second Vatican Council, a relaxation on the times when mass could be said and on the rules for fasting before communion made afternoon masses a possibility. Far from celebrating group identity or for any other reason maintaining a separate Catholic form after this, the old pattern was rapidly abandoned. Catholic weddings are now distinguished from the Protestant in most people's eyes only in that they take longer.

Cross-cultural perspectives

Getting married is a concept before it ever becomes a fact. It is a concept which has frequently seemed to represent something unitary and inevitable. It has never of course been inevitable that everyone should get married; what has seemed inevitable is that whoever did so would be doing one and the same thing. It has often indeed been assumed that this same unitary concept would apply to the whole of humanity, even that 'having marriage' should be a touchstone of humanity. For a long time anthropology used such a concept, and with some success, as a more or less unexamined tool for recording the reality of other societies. There would always at least be marriage: the questions to be asked of one society after another were how they did it and above all what rules there were as to who could and should be marriage partners.[2] It was only gradually that the experience of stretching marriage 'as we know it' to try to encompass an increasing range of known variability began to undermine confidence in its utility for this purpose (Leach 1961; Rivière 1971; Keesing 1972; Schneider 1984).

It is a striking manifestation of the power of culture to induce blind spots that anything so many-sided and in some ways inconsistent as the marriage of the societies which produced anthropology in the nineteenth and early twentieth centuries could have seemed unitary to anybody. Marriage, it might have been perceived, was many things. As a term it pointed towards ideas and practices which the Christian Church, and various sub-traditions within Christianity, had been seeking to define, confine and attach values to for well over a millennium; it pointed to practices which civil authorities, sometimes in harmony with ecclesiastical and sometimes separately, had been trying intermittently to bring within the law and to regulate for still longer; it pointed to things which people of differing class and status in a range of traditions and circumstances lived out variously in their daily lives, as they always had done. With so complex a background, often with competing definitions and rules, it ought perhaps to be surprising that getting married should have seemed so simple and unequivocal. But it did and still for the most part does. In part perhaps this is merely the way language works. As soon as a term is made the subject of propositions which are accepted as meaningful and important – and 'marriage' is the subject of plenty of them – the reality of a something corresponding to that term seems constantly to be being asserted. But this is of course a false logic. Getting married is not a single end, the same thing wherever 'it' occurs but perhaps performed differently. Placing procedures for getting married cross-culturally cannot therefore be a matter of cataloguing different ways of doing the same thing. It has to be the far more complex enterprise of seeing what the procedures labelled – by whomsoever this has been done – as 'getting married' or 'the wedding' actually relate to.

The most striking aspect of the Scottish procedures studied here is, from a cross-cultural perspective, this very complexity and diversity of the ideas to which they relate. On to popular practice and understanding, which is all that procedures can and need refer to in more classically anthropological societies, here there are superimposed both legal requirements and the rich religious tradition. The three distinct parts of marriage procedures interact, both within the procedures themselves and in people's conceptions. Since, however, each has attached to it specialised personnel within established organisations they retain a formal separateness. This is a fundamental way in which the organisation of life through specialised institutions so characteristic of western industrial society feeds through into the procedures under study.

Of the legal side here there is little more to say. Though it is dominant in the sense of having behind it the power to declare its procedures not only necessary but sufficient, and offering therefore to replace other procedures with something simpler and far less costly, few first-marriers take the opportunity offered. Of those first-marriers who do choose to have a civil marriage, already a minority, most back it up with others of the procedures which have been discussed. The legal conception of marriage as merely an agreement between individuals, ratified by the state, which changes their legal status – i.e. the way in which certain laws apply to them and in which they are to be classified in official statistics – though inevitably effective does not do justice to, nor exhaust, the meanings which most people cause to be expressed by adding on to what is legally required other kinds of celebration.

Cross-culturally the second aspect which is most distinctive is the nature of the relationship which is defined – whether effectively or not is another issue – in the religious service, a second element in usual procedures. Amongst world religions, Christianity is the one which has sought most thoroughly to claim marriage as its own, going beyond blessing and assisting at the arrangements into which people are accustomed to enter, to assert its own right to control, regulate and define. We have seen how the religious service has Christian definitions built into it and may be explicitly used to assert them. These may or may not be directly relevant to the individuals being married; they are certainly not always even consciously registered by them. It was, however, as we saw in Chapter 1, the Church which formulated and propagated what became the distinctive European conception of marriage. Often against social practice and political interest, and with, it must be said, a varying propensity to compromise, it maintained a conception of the uniting of two essentially equal individual persons, a matter first and foremost for the two people concerned. Their welfare, spiritual, moral, emotional and material, was seen as the prime concern. In this the sexual relationship between them always loomed large. Everything else which might be entailed by marriage was contingent. Any change of group membership, any new relationships with other people or between those made affines by the marriage, even the birth of children and everything to which that may give rise, these were not here of the essence, nor were they what marriages should be made for. Their relevance would depend on circumstances: they might or might not occur, and they might or might not be desired by the people concerned. A wife was not properly to be acquired in order to produce heirs for her husband or new members to boost the family, the lineage or the tribe. In so far as procreation was a key purpose, in the Christian European tradition the conception was always grander: the couple together, as well as providing for their own mutual benefit, would provide for the proper continuance of humanity, humanity indeed in its highest Christian form.

The Scottish marriage services, arising from this tradition, set up a definition of a highly distinctive relationship which, it is asserted and reasserted whenever a marriage is performed, is what the two people marrying are entering into. Whatever else may be going on, marriages are a context in which this conception is presented and re-presented. Relationships conveniently labelled 'marriage' elsewhere in the world may share some aspects, differ in others, but what all those outside the Christian tradition differ in is this conception of the relationship. Rites and procedures outside it are different in a fundamental way in that they, whatever else they may be doing, do not relate to this conception.

The third ingredient is the popular understandings and practices. Even here a multiplicity of things are represented as going on: there is a transition for the individuals concerned; there are the formation of a married couple and the establishment of a new home; it is a crucial point in the development of the families of those centrally concerned; and it is a festival of marriage and the family.

For both bride and groom the idea that an important individual transition is taking place is represented and enforced in a series of single-sex and more or less involuntary, though not inevitable, events. In each there is a balance between what is fixed and what is open to choice and improvisation. The bride-to-be may be dressed up and taken out, and she may be taken on a hen night. She puts on and takes off the bride persona, expressed above all in the dress. She is veiled and unveiled as a part of this. The groom-to-be may suffer indignities at work and be taken on a stag night. At the reception he may again be attacked before he goes away with his new wife. Events for the woman tend more highly developed as customary procedures and therefore raise all the problems of interpretation of ritual; for the man more is left to improvisation. This means, first, that rather less tends to happen, and secondly, that the motivating ideas are relatively simple and transparent. In so far as actions go beyond a display, more or less exaggerated, of males having a good time together, those which appeal to potential participants combine destroying any chance of standing on one's dignity with some vague reference to sexual activity to come. Undressing, with special attention to removing the trousers, is what comes most readily to mind. The segregation by gender here, which shows signs of weakening but was still strong at the period studied, seemed to be maintained more by the requirement to make a contrast to the coupledom to come than from any real segregation from which those marrying might be emerging. The months or years leading up to a wedding may well indeed be the period in many people's entire lives of maximum cross-gender activity. None of these events make the formal change of status from single to married; this can be made, and sometimes is, without any of them. They do however mark it, for others at least, and they challenge the sense than many marriers have when it is all over that for themselves and their relationship with their partner nothing has really happened.

As for the formation of the married couple, this has come to be represented with all the ambiguity over equality and differentiation currently to be found in the society at large. It is foreshadowed in the engagement presents which already embody the idea of the couple as operators of a joint home. This idea then receives conclusive expression in the wedding presents, but these are identified particularly with the bride. In the show of presents they have their own celebration from which the groom, together with other men, is normally entirely excluded. On the wedding day, from the moment at which the couple first come together after the bride's arrival the two of them are firmly oriented right and left and the husband is always given formal precedence. Whenever they move together as a couple, whether in the procession or in the formally required dancing, the husband is always in the dominant position. But of the three most explicit statements of coupledom, two commonly assert equality and equivalence. In the service rings are most often exchanged and words to be spoken are for the most part carefully equivalent. The cake-cutting is also a carefully joint action; it is only relatively recently that it has acquired this character (Charsley 1988). In the making of speeches, on the other hand, the groom not only speaks for his wife but is expected to draw explicit attention to the fact. If he remembers to do so, he will be cheered for it. The couple relationship presented is therefore one in which both equivalence/equality and differentiation/precedence are displayed.

As regards families and their development, events are relevant to both domestic units and the wider patterns of familial relationships. The show of presents places the bride as a daughter within the context of her domestic family at the same time as, through the presents, it looks forward to the new domestic unit which she with her husband will be establishing. The wedding itself then, as has already been discussed, displays the immediate families of bride and groom as separate units and goes through a sequence of exchanges of partner amongst the parents or their substitutes. This displays the mixing entailed in the creation of the wider, joint family for the couple marrying. Going away marks the formal break between the old familial order and the new.

The last theme to consider as it appears in the succession of festivities is the aspect in which they have their most general significance: they become a festival of marriage and family. This is in a general sense true of everything which happens. All the events proclaim the importance of what is happening when two individuals are marrying one another; they deny, to the chagrin of some, that it is something private to the couple themselves or to be done on their own terms. The more events there are, the more people become involved and the more forceful this assertion of importance becomes. The Glasgow context studied here displays of course a striking proliferation of events. More particularly, wedding presents allow a wide range of people to associate themselves with any given marriage. The show of presents provides a way in which present-giving initiatives even by people who are not being invited to the wedding itself can be appropriately acknowledged. Of still wider relevance is the figure of the bride. A bride appropriately dressed and on her wedding day becomes the embodiment of a powerful symbol in the culture, a source of interest, attraction and often emotion even to people who do not know her at all. For the more limited circle who attend the service, Christian doctrines of marriage are reviewed, and many celebrants make a point of relating the making of a new marriage to the renewal of the marriages of others present. Throughout there is an emphasis on couples and on the family relationships created by marriage. When the reception retains its character and continues through to its customary end after the couple's departure, it is obvious that its character as a reunion rivals the significance it has as the celebration of a particular marriage. In all these ways each marriage provides the occasion for a festival, developed more or less elaborately over longer or shorter periods, a festival which celebrates and keeps alive sentiments and relationships which go way beyond the marrying couple themselves.

Change and its sources is a final topic which from a cross-cultural per-spective requires comment. As befits a market economy, marrying here is conspicuously serviced by specialists who make their living, at least partially, from their contributions to it. Such people provide an engine for change of a kind which is largely absent in classically anthropological con-texts. They provide expertise to people who are bound often to have had little previous experience of setting up such events, but at the same time they have a standing motive for innovation of a kind which will expand and add to the services or the goods they can supply. To the perhaps universal concern of some people to outdo others in the events they hold – the potlatch effect – is added a pressure to elaborate the basic prescription which even those, here certainly the majority, who wish to do no more than the right thing will feel themselves obliged to follow. Dressing and catering, transport, stationery and photography all therefore become conspicuously more elaborate and costly.

The financial implications are significant. By the time of the research it was clear that parental support would be needed for almost any young couple to have what would be regarded as a proper wedding. Even if a couple might be able to raise the substantial cost of this kind of wedding, for the majority it would be in competition with the requirements of buying houses and establishing homes. Such wedding customs, that is to say, pushed young people into increased and often renewed dependence on parents just at the point when their final independence was to be asserted. Where parents could afford it, and their children had no grave doubts about their being able to, this was not a situation which displeased either side. Where they could not, an at least partial opting out from the established patterns was inevitable. Whether at some point increasing relative poverty in some sections of the population would combine with the increasing elaboration of standard expectations to provoke the emergence of a more class-differentiated picture than was observed in the early 1980s remained to be seen.

Symbols and interpretation

Rites practised are or may be meaningful in many ways. The preceding sections of this chapter have reviewed a number of them. These are unproblematic to the extent that they are either ways in which actors intend what they do to have meaning or ways in which they have meaning for an observer in terms of some plainly external interest. Thus we have seen that actors rarely intend by what they do to make theirs a working-class wedding – that would be a matter of intended meanings – but that there are several features of the way weddings are conducted which the observer can identify as hallmarks of weddings conducted by people belonging to a particular section of the society. There is no way in which any account could exhaust the possible meanings of one or other of these kinds which someone or other may be attaching to weddings or any other important and complex set of customary procedures in any society, but a sense of their range and major varieties can be offered. This is what has been being attempted here.

A further kind of meaning poses a more difficult problem. Rites are a form which people may sometimes use to express their meanings, but do they also have some kind of analogous meaning of their own which their use expresses even if the performers have no understanding of it? Is there a kind of meaning which is intrinsic to a rite? Until recently it has been commonly assumed in anthropology that they do.

One school of thought, indeed, makes such meaningfulness the definining characteristic of rites and ritual generally: ritual is essentially communicative action and the handshake of greeting becomes the elementary form of rite (Leach 1954, pp. 10–14; Firth 1973, p. 301). As has been so clearly exemplified in the preceding chapters however, the action of rites is not often as simple and standardised or as regularly used with one slight but clear intention as the handshake. There is often a complex medium and no immediately apparent message. The idea of codes and encoding seems then to be called for. This is in any case a terminology which has a fashionable resonance with communication science. Rites are therefore often seen as having one true though complex meaning which is encoded in the actions and in the objects used, in something of the same way that individuals may encode messages in their everyday actions. A specialised interest of anthropology, with links into philosophy and communication science, becomes then decoding, its techniques and principles.

The roots of this idea are firmly established in the society studied; the extent to which it occurs and is given importance in any given society at any given time may be expected to be empirically variable (Sperber 1975, p. 50). For western society it has enormous historical salience, having been built into Christianity as the form of the basic rite on which Communion and the Mass were historically founded. Jesus Christ himself is considered to have originated an equation between bread and wine and his own body and blood. The rite constantly repeated through subsequent centuries not only uses this symbolic equation but it announces an intended meaning for it. Here we have seen a priest constructing a would-be rite, the lighting of the candle, on this same pattern, the symbolic objects and actions and the announced meaning. We have seen ministers declaring **the** meaning of the ring. We have seen ordinary people speculating on **the** meaning of taking girls out and of favours. We have also seen them declaring their bafflement as to what **the** meaning could possibly be. The idea of symbols is well known in the culture, that one thing or action may stand for another, and this is the basis both for encoding and for attempts to decode. Volumes are published professing to be dictionaries of symbols. Semiotics, the study of signs and how they relate to their referrents, has become a fashionable intellectual pursuit, with its own journals and a great fascination for many, anthropologists amongst them. Could there be any error here? What could be the source of unease?

It is that it takes one exceptional and limited form of rite – even if historically a highly significant one – and treats it as a model for all. It is not adequate to the task. Even in the case of the mass itself it is clear that much more is built around the original symbolic equation than can possibly be explained in terms of it, and few of the other rites we have considered have any comparable in-built assertion that symbols are involved or of the way in which they should be understood. Unlike the Christian prototype, rites typically appear without attributions of meaning or any idea as to their origin. There is commonly, on the contrary, a sense of not having been originated. It is when the idea of symbolic meaning is taken from such a very different and explicit context and assumed to be relevant to an indefinitely large range of diverse practices such as have been reviewed in preceding chapters that possibilities which are as exciting as they are unreal open up (Goody 1977, p. 34).

One reason why it is difficult to see that to impute meaning in this way is metaphysics is exactly those other kinds of meaningfulness which are indeed always potentially available. Assumptions and understandings, from the practical to the cosmological, are built into rites: unless they were not a product of people this could hardly be otherwise. Where circumstances and thinking change, people may be left practising rites, elements of which are quite mysterious to them. This is best thought of as lagging change rather than as the persistence of some original (Keesing 1987, p. 164). There are therefore always aspects of explorable meaningfulness, though often in part of kinds which, since in most circumstances they could be revealed only with the help of historical evidence, may not be available for those actually performing the rites concerned.

As with any metaphysical proposition, the assumption that otherwise mysterious features of ritual must have symbolic meaning cannot be disproved;[3] it can only be shown to be implausible and unnecessary. It is unnecessary because there are less problematic and more fruitful alternative ways of envisaging the matter. Once the idea of intrinsic symbolic meaning is called into question, the always suspiciously ingenious strategies of anthropologists to uncover it in the face of informants' apparent ignorance (classically Radcliffe-Brown 1922, pp. 234 foll.) and the manifest idiosyncracy of those few who do claim to know (Turner 1967, pp. 131–50) fall away.

Once this has happened the vision clears and there comes into view nothing more mysterious than patterns of action which are historical creations. This process of creation can be documented in specific cases. It has been hinted at here at numerous points and performed in some measure systematically for the religious forms. Elsewhere I carry out the exercise for the cake and its cutting (Charsley 1988 and forthcoming). These historically evolving forms present themselves to each successive generation as part of its heritage, the way its members find things being done. Sometimes indeed they find meanings already attached, in the form of interpretations being passed on in company with the rites themselves, and sometimes these meanings are expressed as symbolic equations. But more often they are not. The taken-for-granted character, particularly of rites which are not accompanied by interpretations, means that for most people most of the time no further explanation is called for. There may always be some however, the proto-anthropologists as well as those professionally qualified as such, and others in circumstances which generate a challenging frame of mind, who are lured by the possibilities of symbolic meaning (Fernandez 1965, pp. 908–11). Indeed even traditional interpretations may themselves be challenged, as happened with wedding rings. Ritual exegesis is then a sport with few rules, open to all with the talent and inclination to join in an esoteric pursuit.

As has been apparent in this work, rites in practice, which is to say as they are experienced rather than as they might be abstracted in an old-fashioned account of the customs of the Glaswegians or whoever, are always complex and variable. What is prescribed varies in the thoroughness and insistence with which it presents itself and intermingles in practice with matters of choice. Choice is itself sometimes circumscribed, sometimes very free. Even to establish realistic and thorough accounts is a major undertaking which can perhaps never be exhaustively achieved.[4] In such a context the range of objects and actions, and the characteristics of both, to which meaning might be attributed is invariably considerable. What to attend to is in principle a major problem; in practice whatever takes anyone's fancy in terms of their own interests and purposes is fair game.

Nothing more than a misleadingly simple example is practicable as illustration, but the point is easily made. What about wedding rings? They are round and continuous. This does not distinguish them from other rings, yet is a feature ministers not infrequently pose as symbolic: like the ring, the love of the couple marrying should have no end.[5] The fact that in this sense the ring has no beginning either – and is going nowhere – is of course here irrelevant. Other features are the finger on which it is worn, the material of which it is made, and the fact that it differs from most other rings in not having a stone. If any of these were matters of individual choice rather than of conformity, one could well ask why that finger, why gold, why no stone? In fact only the gold, perhaps the next least distinguishing feature of this ring after its roundness, was observed in this study having meaning attributed to it. This was in relation to an alleged purity of gold, again more than a little odd for a ring which is well known to be generally made, for practical reasons, of nine carat gold. Not since medieval times does the choice of a particular finger to carry the ring seem to have attracted any exegesis at all. It is simply an unquestioned practice carried on from one generation to the next.

It becomes implausible, therefore, to imagine meaning as intrinsic to rites as soon as one gets beyond schematic and simplified accounts to something closer to their complex reality. There are then far too many potentially meaningful elements and relationships, most of which are bound to be ignored. There are also extraordinarily few to which any of those concerned actually apply any interpretive thought. It is common to think of rites as something akin to carefully-composed Renaissance paintings, shaped by conscious symbolic thought which, with knowledge and understanding, can be deciphered. Though this is occasionally a good analogy, commonly a rite is more like one of Rorschach's ink blots. It offers, that is to say, a multiplicity of possible readings according to differences of attention, interest and inclination. It has the meanings that people give it, no more and no less. There is no intrinsic meaning to be discovered, though discovery is of course exactly what those attributing meaning usually think they are doing.

But, like any other analogy, this one holds only so far. Unlike the ink blot, a rite is not the creation of a particular moment. It is something shaped and reshaped through time. This happens largely in ways which are extraneous to any symbolic interpretation. We have seen here the importance of commercial interests. Individuals being forced to modify their performances in the light of circumstances, financial and otherwise, are a very general factor, as is the search for display and to impress, where available resources give scope for the pursuit of such ends. Misunderstanding and sheer chance affect performances too.

But as well as these factors, interpretation has its own contribution. An interpretation posed and turning out to have a wide appeal gives an extra salience to the feature picked out for interpretation. It will tend to bolster it against chance variation. The central symbolism of the mass may provide an example of this phenomenon, but it is difficult to illustrate anything specific to the marriage field, in part at least because of the paucity of any symbolic interpretation offered for its leading and persistent features. What is clear is that interpretation can also be a liability. An interpretation may apparently reveal a meaning which is unacceptable to those participating, and this may set in motion trends of change. The wedding ring offers a striking example of this in yet another aspect of its use. The earlier pattern of a single ring came to be widely seen as representing inequality in marriage. As equality here came in the period after the Second World War to be increasingly stressed, the single ring began to seem increasingly incongruous. Two rings, sometimes matching, became the more symbolically appropriate new norm. The significance of interpretation, patchy and essentially voluntary as it is, is not its ability to uncover a hidden truth but its role in the making, unmaking and remaking of rites through time.

Notes

Introduction

1 An account of the research is to be found in the Appendix. W. D. Edwards (1984) has recently made an interestingly parallel study in Japan. The role of commercially inspired innovation is strikingly greater there than in the Scottish context.

2 Leonard (1980), on Swansea marriers in the late 1960s, provides the closest British precedent for the present study though their scope and theoretical interests are rather different. It nevertheless contains a wealth of comparative material and much of the general pattern reported is strikingly similar. A history of many aspects of their common roots is presented in Gillis (1985). This is sub-titled 'British Marriages, 1600 to the Present' but any reference to Scotland is conspicuously rare.

3 Each piece of continuous quotation is referenced with an interview number. A list of these is to be found in the Appendix. This also provides notes on the circumstances and backgrounds of the people involved in them. Pseudonyms are used consistently throughout.

4 The study therefore makes extensive use of dialogue (Tedlock 1983, 1987) and is perhaps even 'experimental' (Marcus & Fischer 1986). It registers reflexivity in including its making within its frame (Watson 1987). It remains essentially 'realist', however, but without disguising the author's responsibility for the account constructed. The claim is only, as with every anthropological account properly understood, that this is the best the author is currently able to offer. He is qualified to offer an account by the various processes of research which have gone into it but there is no way that it can claim to be final and conclusive. That powerful anthropological writers have sometimes created impressions of omniscience and unchallengeable authority deserves notice (Clifford 1973; Geertz 1988) but neither this nor abstruse epistemological worries require a derailing of the established and successful anthropological enterprise (Spencer 1989).

5 Recent writers of more technical works who have been prepared to take the risk have sometimes arrived at positions similar to that underlying the present work. Barth (1987), though his empirical focus is very different, on cosmological variety in a small area of New Guinea, is one eminent example. See also Keesing 1987, p. 164.

Chapter 1: Contexts of Scottish marrying

1 Age of marriage was always strongly marked by social class: at the beginning of the 1970s there were more than five times the proportion of teenage marriages amongst Social Class IV as in Social Class I (Kendrick 1981, p. 37).

2 The main source for the account here is Clive's standard legal textbook (second edition, 1982). A similar but simplified account is provided by Nichols (1984). The reader who is interested in the history of Scottish marriage in greater detail and wider scope than is called for here should consult Smout (1981). He builds on a long line of interesting discussions, e.g. Edgar 1886, pp. 134–203; Andrews 1899, pp. 210–26; Hardy 1978; Boyd 1980.

3 The present tense is used here as the most natural for describing situations still current at the time of writing. This is the way the tense is used in this book; it is not intended as an ethnographic present, a usage which is often misleading and best avoided. The use of the present depends always, however, on knowledge and judgement, and the decision whether to throw accounts into historic mode with a past tense is sometimes a difficult one.

4 The principle adopted was more relaxed than the Committee recommended. They had wanted it to be compulsory for forms of marriage to make the monogamy and permanence of the relationship clear (Kilbrandon Committee 1969, p. 36). The 1977 Act is not explicit as to the point at which the marriage is to be considered accomplished. Clive (1982, pp. 47–9) discusses the matter learnedly and reaches the conclusion that the safest assumption is that it is once the formal consents have been given. This would be in conformity with Scottish common law reaching back to medieval times. Neither the pronouncement, if any – it will be seen that the current Scottish Catholic rite does not in fact have one – nor the completion of the schedule, though this is always legally required, are thought actually to make a marriage.

5 The Committee discussed residence qualifications such as were previously required. They concluded that there was no way they could be safely established even if desirable. People readily testified falsely, they thought, on behalf of would-be marriers, 'an example of the irresponsibility of otherwise worthy citizens who find themselves afloat on a sea of sentimentality' (Kilbrandon Committee 1969, p. 22).

6 Immigrants other than the Irish have also brought in their own religious organisations but these have, in Scotland, for the most part not been Christian: Jewish, Muslim, Sikh, Hindu, Buddhist and other organisations are all well established. These are outwith the scope of the present study.

7 Figures for 1982 are used here (Registrar General Scotland 1983: Q2.2). Proportions of religious marriages amongst city dwellers are likely to be slightly underestimated since city registry offices may, under current legislation, perform marriages for couples resident elsewhere. There are however complicating factors, such as the varying popularity of particular offices, and it would be difficult to make any kind of estimate of effects here. In general, with all its marginal complexities, figures for marriages give the best available indication of the geographical distribution of religious affiliations (Darragh 1979, p. 212).

8 Judged by marriages, one would have to conclude that the Church of Scotland was almost three times the size of the Catholic Church here, but it has been argued that the former's total is more affected than other Churches' by a high proportion of

marriages of people otherwise totally unconnected with it (Darragh 1979, p. 217).

9 Technically, what had previously been 'missions' only became parishes in 1946 (Gallagher 1987, p. 46).

10 The three major sources are the Rathen Manual, a book of liturgy originating in Scotland probably in the late fifteenth century, which includes a detailed order for marriage, Hay's lectures on the Church's doctrine and law on marriage, and Bishop John Hamilton's Cathecism of 1551. This last provides contemporary Scots language to flesh out Hay's Latin. See also Hardy 1978, pp. 567–9.

11 See Turner 1987, particularly p. 16. This distinctiveness has often been noted (Anderson 1980, p. 18) but its relationship to ideals rooted in the Christian tradition and rehearsed in liturgy has not been subjected to much discussion.

12 Brooke has recently summed up much of his own and others' earlier research in his *The Medieval Idea of Marriage* (1989). This is an enquiry which any anthropologist will recognise as close to the spirit of his own discipline, as well as a model which few have matched in the accessibility of its writing. Brundage (1987) has published an extensive compendium on sex and marriage in medieval Europe, from a legal standpoint in particular, the preoccupation with sex being one clear peculiarity of the western tradition of marriage (Turner 1987; Verdon 1988). On a smaller scale Martos (1981, pp. 397–452), as part of his history of sacraments, offers an important account, pointing to law and sacramental ideas as the twin roots of the peculiarity of Christian marriage. None of these focus on practices of marrying or liturgy which is the major concern here. In this more specialised field, Stevenson (1982) has combed the literature of Old World Christianity and provides a wide-ranging sourcebook, but above all, the work of Molin and Mutembe (1974) with its focus on France between the twelfth and the sixteenth centuries should be of peculiar interest to anthropologists. These two Catholic priests, one French, the other an African from Zaire, have examined the variety and progressive modification of Christian marriage ritual as it can be found in surviving liturgies. They display a strong sense of each liturgy as a distinctive cultural product.

13 The books were drawn up by a Scottish Liturgy Commission and vary in several respects from the forms adopted for England.

Chapter 2: Engagement

1 See Introduction, note 3.

2 Punctuation and its significance in such transcriptions as this are discussed in the Appendix.

3 'Girl' as a term used for adults came to symbolise for feminists varieties of denigration of female by male. Amongst people generally at the time of the study, however, both 'boy' and 'girl' were commonly used for couples marrying; the terms 'girlfriend' and 'boyfriend' might be used, if sometimes slightly uneasily, regardless of age; and women of all ages might use 'girl' for women of their own age or younger. While it could in a few circumstances carry some inegalitarian implication, far more often its most obvious implication was friendliness.

Chapter 3: Learning the lore

1 Registry office bookings were somewhat different. They included a higher proportion of second and subsequent weddings, which could not easily be separated out, and in other ways represented less of a cross-section of weddings as a whole. They were therefore more irregular and did not peak in the summer months popular for full-scale first weddings.

2 'Marry in May, rue for aye' is a presumably older form still occasionally heard.

3 Such offices are the responsibility of local authorities in Scotland. These dictate hours of work and, as an economy measure under pressure for public spending cuts, in 1983 the Glasgow evening session was ended.

4 The wedding-cake orders referred to above showed only 2 per cent destined for halls of this kind. This was certainly to exaggerate their rarity.

5 Dalmont, writing of wedding meals, seems to have been faced with the same phenomenon, namely the simple meal in the elaborate setting, though in her English case it is a middle-of-the-day event. She is able to invoke a contrast between the meal out and wedding catering done at home, a contrast which is not available in the field studied here since such home catering hardly occurs. She proposes 'two different ideal types, one where strange food in familiar surroundings marks the "special" occasion, the other where a "strange" location is familiarised by "proper" food, albeit of a celebratory kind' (1983, p. 147). The latter is said to be a working-class pattern, with the strange location a hotel and the food provided in it a 'proper, cooked dinner'; the former a middle-class pattern with the mother of the bride providing the special food herself at home. This allows Dalmont to assert that 'The wedding reception provided on commercial premises is, therefore, highly symbolic. It makes the wedding as [*sic*] an especially "sacred", "unusual", "non-normal" occasion, when the working-class woman **does not cook**. Because it is special, it reinforces the usual, profane, mundane meal provision which is the normal woman's usual task. Having a meal "out" is a rite of reversal commonly used to make important status passages' (*op. cit.*, p. 149).

Coming together for a wedding meal does of course have an easily attributed symbolic value; who is the host and how all the various participants relate to one another, and the complex schedule of actions to be performed may all be readily seen as meaningful. But, in a Britain in which eating out is a major and ever-increasing leisure activity, and where there is no practical possibility of brides or their families feeding and entertaining the numbers expected to attend weddings by their own efforts in the kitchen whether or not they themselves are accustomed to eating out regularly, Dalmont's kind of symbolic explanation of hotel meals as rites of reversal and the 'proper meal' nature of their menus is not even a possible construction.

6 The wedding cake is not discussed in the detail it merits here. I have examined it elsewhere already in some detail (Charsley 1987, 1988) and a further book on the subject is in press.

7 This issue had come up at the first visit. It was not a bone of contention:

Jan.　　　You have to promise to bring up the children as Catholics. I don't mind doing that. Because if you can get brought up as a Catholic ...,

but when they grow up they're going to be making decisions for themselves. I don't think you get any more brainwashed as a Catholic than
anywhere else. **You're** not very brainwashed.

Shuggie.   I'm not brainwashed at all. Most of my friends aren't particularly
             brainwashed. Everybody makes up their own mind in the end.

J.   If you're not brought up in religion, you haven't anything to reject.

S.   Yeah![T8]

8 There did exist also a much more elaborate and semi-official Catholic publication, *Your Wedding. A Guide to Your Catholic Marriage Ceremony with hints on
Wedding Arrangements.* This was said to have been published in annual editions
since about 1972, with advertising varying according to the diocese for which it was
intended. It was meant for free distribution by priests seeing intending marriers but,
despite being by far the most helpful and realistic account of Scottish marrying
practices in print, its use was at best patchy.

Chapter 4: Casting, dressing and participation

1 The kind of unease generated here might suggest that we have to do with
anomaly of the kind addressed in Douglas's theory of 'Purity and Danger' (1966).
This is not so, since a dress is understood as the immediate result of human choice,
deviant perhaps, rather than as part of a 'natural' order of things.

2 For the history of wedding clothing, see Lansdell (193) and Cunnington &
Lucas (1972). The former has a splendid collection of carefully annotated photographs, a number of them of Scottish relevance.

3 No other significance was attached to the colours of flowers. Indeed, that red
and white should not be mixed in any nursing or hospital context was the only
further idea encountered in the research. A young doctor said that the combination
symbolised death, a florist who also mentioned it thought the colours would be
seen as blood on bandages and would therefore be regarded as unsuitable. The
combination echoes the well-known Red Cross symbol.

4 James. You get more abuse actually in Scotland than you do anywhere else
             when you wear a kilt. I think people have a condescending attitude to
             you if you wear a kilt in this country. It's much more fun abroad. I used
             to wear it a lot in Italy, and in France.

SC.   It's not just that it's normal here?

J.   No, it's not normal. You get a sort of disdain. I think if you're going to a
             wedding or something it's acceptable, but as something to wear in the
             street ... . It's like everything Scottish, you know: it's great for
             foreigners, but everybody feels self-conscious about it [he laughs]. You
             know, they are great at playing at being Scots for foreigners, but once it
             gets back to being all Scots, everybody comes out self-conscious and
             really introverted.[T79]

Weddings are however a context in which many who would never think of it at other
times are interested in 'playing at being Scots', even without the stimulus of
foreigners, the English in particular, being present (Charsley 1986).

5 For a history of the creation of kilts and tartans see Trevor-Roper 1983.

6 The extent of the propaganda for this pattern is suggested by the publication at the time of the research of *Debrett's Etiquette and Modern Manners* as a cheap paperback. The name of Debrett is closely associated with the standard listing of the British peerage. The *Etiquette* provides for a wide market a prescription derived from the English professional and upper-middle-class wedding.

7 It is an elementary but interesting statistical fact that the average person belongs to a set of siblings larger than the average number of children in families. This in itself means that 'large' families will be encountered in research more frequently than might otherwise be expected (Langford 1982). In Glasgow this effect is accentuated by the strong representation of larger-than-average families in the Catholic population, particularly amongst older generations.

Chapter 5: Festivities before the Day

1 This is the same distinction Cheal found in his Hotel Chateau study in Winnipeg in 1981 (1988, pp. 131–6).

2 Cheal (1988, pp. 122–30) discusses the way money 'presentation', as a distinct practice of Ukrainian origin, had come in the 1960s and '70s in Winnipeg to predominate over the giving of objects in the manner familiar in Britain.

3 Cheal (1988, p. 131) suggests that objects not intended for daily use have advantages as symbolic gifts. This was not apparent to participants in the present study.

4 This was for an engagement but attitudes and principles are much the same.

5 Care has to be taken in any direct comparison of the figures to notice that donors are largely couples, whereas attenders are counted individually.

All these were standard first weddings, with church services followed by receptions of the usual form. All couples were of normal marrying age though couple D were in their mid rather than their early twenties. All had living parents and all had a bought home of some kind to go to. In other ways the weddings and their social contexts differed considerably. A and C were Church of Scotland weddings, B and D Catholic, but both A and D were mixed marriages, the woman marrying out in A, the man in D. A was unambiguously working class; B fell into the upwardly mobile borderlands of the working and middle classes; C was sharply interclass, D firmly middle. These and related factors affected each case in particular ways: in two, for example, people who might have expected to have been invited were ignored, and in two, people who were invited boycotted it. Such occurrences have to be regarded as normal, though it is as equally normal to keep them out of sight as far as possible.

Of the categories, 'family and kin' speaks largely for itself, though its tricky boundary, particularly as affecting cousins, was discussed in the previous chapter. For the eight individuals in these marriages, the numbers of family and kin giving presents ranged from three to twenty-six. The couple's associates include friends – frequently going back to schooldays and including workmates, perhaps employers, and godparents if these are not kin. If either or both members were not in employment or had jobs which did not provide them with workmates, the potential numbers in this category are cut considerably. Whilst women do not necessarily have more than men, the two large collections here were quite disproportionately attached to the bride. Some tendency towards this kind of imbalance seemed common, though the data to establish differences on any statistical basis are not available. 'Parents' associates' are again friends, colleagues, employers, workmates, but also normally neighbours and even former neighbours, fellow members of churches or other organisations who take an interest in one anothers' families but fall short of being describable as friends. People in this category may well not have any personal knowledge of the couple themselves. The residual category accounts for others who may be thought still more remotely connected to the event, people who are rarely guests but who wish to associate themselves with it by giving a present. They are friends' mothers, grandmothers' friends, sisters' workmates and the like. They seem again to occur more frequently on the bride's side. (A^{T87}, B^{T26}, C^{T18}, D^{T13})

6 It attracts popular etymologies. Rattling pennies in bottles was one encountered, bottling the beer for the wedding another. Commonest is the idea that it must refer to some equivalent of the stag night at which the contents of bottles would be poured into the bride (cf. *Scottish National Dictionary*, II (1941), X (1976)). None of these appear likely either historically or in relation to the contemporary event. Partridge (1984) offers a set of related terms, 'bottle', 'bottling', 'bottler', as showmen's language for the collection of money from an audience in response to a street performance. The bottle is the takings. This at least relates clearly to contemporary practice, even if it explains little.

7 The candle, confirmed by others from the past, was also reported in contemporary use, together with the baby doll, by one participant.[T8]

8 'No' was almost certainly the implied answer; it would certainly have been the correct one. The question was in any case put the wrong way round: it is being kissed by the men rather than necessarily kissing them. The practice may well be older than going into pubs but it probably does not date even as far back as the Second World War.

9 It provides, more likely, an example of the way practices of courtship and marriage have often been taken up into the play of children.

10 Westwood's account (1984, pp. 112–19) of comparable practices in an English hosiery factory is relevant here. She contends that, despite an official awareness of dangers, 'the ritual was too important and too deeply entrenched in shopfloor culture for it to be outlawed'. She offers no account of its history in the factory in question and it must be suspected that this judgement may rest on little more than the functionalist illusion that what is is has to be. In the Glasgow context it was apparent that developments of this kind always depend on the tolerance of those in charge and this may be withdrawn. Cycles might therefore occur in particular establishments. From simple beginnings, local customs might grow until an elaborate and time-consuming event had been created, one which had even become an ordeal for the girl or for the boy concerned. When things are felt to be going too far or accidents occur, management withdraws its tacit support and such 'customs' collapse or are suppressed.

11 It provides a surprising echo of one of the earliest accounts of marriage celebrations in Scotland (Burt 1759, p. 262). The occasion here was a Penny Wedding in the early part of the eighteenth century.

12 She asserts a symbolic interpretation in terms of the predicament of women in marriage. Her claim that it was 'abundantly clear that marriage was associated with bondage and the binding of a woman to a man – the notion of capture and plunder

lingers on in the ritual' – reads uneasily in the Scottish context. If the binding is, as in Glasgow, first of husbands-to-be and only then emulated by women, the proper frame for interpretation looks a great deal less than 'abundantly clear'.

13 Westwood's English account (1984, pp. 120–26) suggests something both more commercially established and fiercer in its rivalry of male excess than would often have been found in Glasgow. Even the impression given by Leonard's account would seem a little exaggerated in the Glasgow context, and her identification of the hen party as a Gluckmanesque ritual of rebellion (Leonard 1980, p. 152; Gluckman 1963) unrealistic. In Glasgow as in Westwood's Needletown (*op. cit.*, p. 106), parties of women out together were not unfamiliar, even without the pretext of a hen night.

Chapter 6: Wedding Day 1: the ceremony

1 The procedures in civil marriages were briefly considered in Chapter 1; they will be disregarded here. Where first marriages are concerned, the general patterns followed do not diverge greatly from those discussed in the two following chapters.

2 The man on whose arm the bride comes down the aisle at the start of the service is said to be 'giving her away', but there is no formal recognition of 'giving away' in Church of Scotland services.

3 'Symbols of all that you are going to share together' was another version.

4 This is completed with some version of the famous Biblical pronouncement: 'Those whom God hath joined together, let no person separate.' By one minister this was rendered: 'Mr and Mrs ... , God bless you! God has joined you together. Don't ever let anyone keep you apart!'

5 The bride here was herself an occasional organist for weddings in the church. She could therefore, somewhat unusually, compare how her own had gone with a number of others. She commented interestingly on the difference their own Christian identity may have made. The minister, she thought,

> varies the way she says it but it's basically the same for everybody. She's usually more pointed, because most of the people who get married in the church have got nothing to do with the church anyway, and she very pointedly says things about, you know, coming to the church and such ... you should't just come to get married. [...] People come and say 'Can we get married?' and she doesn't know them and she'll not see them once they're married. And she ..., she doesn't brush over anything – she's not that type of person – but everything goes sort of quicker. She spends more time on it if she knows you. She's just a wee bit different. She knows it means something to you.[T36]

6 In the light of the kind of day the bride in particular had so far experienced, to become clearer in the following chapter, the unlikeliness of this assertion struck the observer at the time.

7 The presentation of a Bible 'used at your own wedding' which some ministers like to make to the couple at this point would not have fitted with the procedure here.

8 This could in some ministers' hands be taken a good deal further. The possibilities are suggested by the introduction which began:

So we're here to join you two together as husband and wife. [...] Don't worry: you're with people who hope and pray you'll have a great deal of happiness, not just today but in the future too. You've got the flat up in Oban Drive – there's just that wee bit of ceiling repair to attend to ... .

9 She thought that they had agreed with the priest in advance that there was to be no 'gold and silver'. The priest had apparently forgotten this and insisted on the groom finding something to hand over. The best man found a 50p coin. The bride, when it came to her turn, somewhat heatedly repeated the words on her own and gave the same coin back to the groom.[N51, T50]

10 A rubric also allows a sprinkling with holy water, though this was never actually observed in the course of the research.

11 Recorded music or no music at all are possible, but some music, live, is to be expected for all but the 'quietest' wedding. The organist reported to have played the theme music from *Z Cars*, a popular police series on television, for the entry of the bride, and 'When the Saints Come Marching In' for the procession out may or may not have been mythical.

12 SC.   Do you think it is a remarkable new age in the Church which actually allows people to be inventing new rituals?

Priest.   I don't think it's inventing new rituals. It's making a greater and wider use of what has been part of the Church, you know, through the ages.

Chapter 7: Wedding Day 2: framing the cermony

1 Being required, a question mark is placed over their interpretation as intentional action and an extra frame of meaning in terms of conformity/failure to conform is placed around them. The possibility that practices have meaning or purpose independent of the meaning of those who perform them may appear, just as the source of the requirement is more often than not conceptualised in quasi-personal terms.

2 The photographer eventually booked for her wedding, a part-timer, in the event confused time and place and arrived only after everyone else had already reached the reception. Hers became, therefore, unplanned, one of the few full celebrations without a photographer to direct sections of it. For the observer the experience highlighted the extent to which couples themselves and even the rest of the bridal party are kept separate from the guests until after the meal by the operations of the photographer.

3 Civil weddings were not fundamentally different. Though there was never any question of photographs being taken within the Registry Office, for the rest of the celebrations a photographer might be employed in the usual way. At the Glasgow Office a studio had been established. Exclusive use of this was let on the basis of an annual tender, but one firm which won it in the early 1980s found that less than 20 per cent of weddings booked for photography, even at specially reduced prices, and that such bookings did not lead into full-scale orders.

4 The expansion of wedding photography progressed faster and further in the United States (King 1986. p. 93); in the 1970s there were Americans lecturing in Britain on the latest styles and possibilities.

5 For an interesting account of the fight in the north of England to retain the garter against the forces of respectability see Gillis 1985, pp. 147–55. The fight was lost by the 1830s.

6 Videos were relatively new at the time of the research and were still looking for a viable form. They raise interesting issues but must, for lack of space, be ignored here.

7 Holy (1983) carries out such a 'dredging' in relation to Berti space and critically assesses its validity. This is highly instructive, though his conclusion, endorsed by the present study, is perhaps more radical than the case he actually argues: 'A formal analysis of symbolic classification which conceptualises its object as collective representations, with the implication that they are shared to the same extent, is unable to come to grips with the coexistence of different notions among the actors and with the ensuing flexibility and variability of their thought' (p. 286).

Chapter 8: Wedding Day 3: the reception

1 Mrs G. We haven't had a silver wedding and don't intend to have one anyway when it comes along. So that is perhaps the other occasion.
SC.   Won't the children do something about it?
Mrs G.   I doubt it. They know our feelings.[T40]

2 Since the great majority of celebrants were men, they will for convenience be given the masculine pronoun in the rest of this chapter.

3 One instance in which the guests moved down the line in the reverse direction, from bridesmaids along to bride and groom, was also noted on a wedding video in circumstances which did not give scope for any further enquiry. Such a pattern disregarded the standard rationale which provides a special place for the bride's parents as hosts and suggested an alternative view of the line as a succession of people of increasing importance leading up to bride and groom at the end. The bride on this occasion had no father present and this may well have been relevant too. One other occasion on which bride and groom were given priority was observed, the bride's parents on that occasion being elderly and self-effacing. On another occasion with no line-up as such, guests greeted only the bride and groom as they went in to take their seats at table.

4 In the form of a toast to nothing in particular – 'Cheers!' – the same action is used simply to initiate collective drinking. It then marks what would otherwise be no more than individual consumption of alcohol as a joint or group activity.

5 Cake cutting is not further discussed here since it has been taken up extensively and in considerable detail elsewhere (Charsley 1987; 1988; forthcoming).

6 By those not, like this best man, new to the wedding scene, this episode was still generally known as 'reading the telegrams'. In fact by this time the only brief, telegraphed messages in the former style were being received from overseas. At most weddings there were therefore few or none. The resulting gap in proceedings had been filled by a reading of greetings cards, usually the hand-written messages accompanying them and occasionally even with printed rhymes too. Each recital would be clapped, as had previously been telegrams from those unable to attend. Cards might however be far more numerous and were often being sent by people actually attending. This latter fact occasioned no concern, but the practical problem of reading

and applauding perhaps fifty or sixty cards did. Strategies were often adopted, generally at the last minute, to ease the situation. The guests might be requested not to applaud, only the names might be read or groom and best man might spend part of the meal going through the set and selecting out a small number for reading. One possible criterion then was whether the sender was or was not present.

7 Music and dances have been discussed in Chapter 3 above.

8 She had originally fancied a fashionable black taffeta outfit which she had seen. Her mother immediately ruled it out because of its colour, and, to Tracy's surprise, her husband-to-be echoed the rejection.

9 For the earlier stages of their history in England, see Gillis (1985, pp. 57, 61). There they never became identified with the decorations for the wedding cake – themselves of Scottish origin – and died out after the First World War. Some further discussion of their Scottish form and origins is to be found in Charsley 1987.

10 This was very obviously the mother's re-creation of the conversation rather than a report of what was actually said.

11 Since he is not wearing an individuating outfit he may occasionally change in the course of the evening, once the first waltz has been safely completed. One groom changed into the kilt which he had been in two minds about wearing for the wedding itself, another into a white dinner suit. He donned this in company with the other men of the wedding party. Much to the surprise of the rest of the company, they then entered as a chorus line and performed a dance which they had rehearsed beforehand.[T101] The groom will then change again to leave. Brides who feel really uncomfortable in their dress may occasionally also shed it early, but this will be in favour of their going-away outfit. One who did felt it necessary to apologise 'profusely' to the one or two late-arriving evening guests who missed seeing her in the dress.

12 This is a Scottish construction: 'chapped the door' would be more usual.

13 She had also organised her sister/bridesmaid into dealing entirely with the favours and had managed to break away from being the passive focus of the wedding to the extent of taking her own photographs at it.

Chapter 9: Familiar rites and anthropological interpretation

1 Average gross weekly earnings in Britain in 1982, i.e. before deduction of tax etc., were £135.90 for men and £90.00 for women.

2 Efforts at cross-cultural comparison of marriage have a history going back at least as far as de Gaya (1681). They reached what for long had to be regarded as their culmination in Westermarck's final three-volume edition of *The History of Human Marriage* (1922), but the enterprise has never been altogether abandoned. Goody in particular has been surmounting the caution engendered by functionalist social anthropology with comparative studies of ever-widening scope (Goody 1990).

3 'Symbolic' has become such a key term in anthropology that to restrict its use in this way has not recently been common. An alternative response has been to retain the term, seeking some other way of defining it but denying that symbols 'mean'; rather they 'evoke' (Sperber 1975). This may permit the re-creation of elaborate analyses of multivocality in evocation to replace such analyses of meanings (Strecker 1988, pp. 203–26), but this can only be to suggest culturally grounded possibilities. What is

actually evoked and for whom, whether indeed anything is at all, is bound to be empirically variable (Fernandez 1982).

4 Turner (1967, pp. 151–279) gives an impressive demonstration of the magnitude of the task of accounting even for a single performance. Bloch's various accounts of Merina marriage rites are also instructive in this respect (1971; 1978; 1980; cf. Keenan 1975).

5 Ethnographic examples of this kind call into question the Ethiopian response of Sperber (1975) and Strecker (1988) to the problem of defining symbols with no apparent meaning. This study suggests that no general theory will tell you what aspects people will actually 'focalise', let alone register as 'displaced' and therefore 'evocative'.

Appendix

The project was formulated after some pilot interviewing in Glasgow in 1981, was funded by the Social Science Research Council as it was then, and started in the summer of 1982. Fieldwork was carried out by two people. The author – 'SC' when he appears in conversations quoted – was a middle-aged Englishman living with wife and young family in Glasgow and teaching for the previous fifteen years at the University. The other was Diane McGoldrick – 'DM' in conversations – a Sociology graduate of Glasgow College in her early thirties, born, brought up, married and living in Clydebank immediately to the west of the Glasgow city boundary. Each sought out people from whom they could learn, with priority to those in the process of getting themselves married.

The intention was to recruit such people to the study on a snowball principle, each contact leading to others. An informative range of cases would then be selected to follow up. This would mean meetings up to and beyond the wedding itself, attending weddings and other events wherever possible, and bringing in family, friends and the wedding 'professionals' with whom couples had dealings. Each of the researchers would in this way build up a caseload which they would be managing through the year of the project. The principle turned out to be sound, but wishful thinking had entered into the expectation that it could be thoroughly developed within the planned one-year timescale. An acute sense of privacy repeatedly held back recruitment even in what appeared to be the most favourable of circumstances and usually aborted or at best severely hindered alternative strategies for recruiting participants. Progress in acquiring caseloads was therefore slower than had been allowed for, and the methodical procedures envisaged were reduced to a much less orderly seizing of opportunities.

In the event, forty marriages were discussed with their principals but the extent to which each was developed as a case varied greatly. Weddings were attended in whole or in part as the opportunity offered, and recordings and videos were used when they could be made available. These, like wedding photographs, were usually discussed with the principals. Discussions were also held with ministers, priests, registrars and representatives of the various suppliers and performers in the wedding industry, generally people involved with couples already in the study. A few older people were approached chiefly for their ability to talk about the past but, in general, change was a topic to be discussed with all except the very young. Documentation was collected wherever possible. In the end 116 long discussions were recorded and transcribed by the researchers themselves and over a hundred sets of notes on other discussions, on events attended and on other kinds of evidence were compiled.

All this material was read and regularly discussed by the researchers so that the issues arising could feed back into subsequent discussions with other participants. Much that was studied lacked for the researchers the usual anthropological stimulus of being unfamiliar, and they themselves lacked in differing degree the obvious quality of outsiders for whom explanation was clearly in order. Particularly in the early days, DM, who was by far the more completely at home in Glasgow, studying a society and a culture to which she herself unambiguously belonged, felt an acute difficulty in enquiring from others about matters with which she ought as a competent adult to be herself familiar. The difficulty eased however as experience built up. It became clear that individuals' own knowledge and experience are so distinctive and differentiated as to be always valid subjects of enquiry. Both researchers had to struggle throughout, however, to know what needed asking about matters which were too familiar to be immediately problematic. The wedding cake was only the most spectacular example here: it took several months of coming across cakes in a research capacity to overcome a socialisation in which they were simply a part of the expectable furniture of life. Only then did we register that such cakes and action in relation to them formed exactly the kind of ritual complex which would immediately strike the exotic anthropologist as interesting and problematic.

James and Margaret – pseudonyms as are all the names except for those of the researchers – were the couple with whom the strategy as originally conceived was most fully developed. Four long sessions were held with them at intervals over the eight months before their wedding, the wedding itself was attended and another session was held with them three weeks afterwards. In addition there were meetings with their parents and other family members. Such was the interest of their own presentation of their experience that the author persuaded them to take part further in writing an ethnography based upon it. To this end a series of chapters drawn from the transcripts of previous conversations were drafted, and these were discussed by Margaret, James and the author in eight further sessions over the spring and summer of 1984. These sessions were again recorded and provided amplification, correction and comment upon the original record. The work produced was completed with an introduction by James and Margaret themselves and a set of contextualising and comparative notes by the present author. After much effort over a period of eighteen months it had to be accepted that the result would not be published. It was too 'academic' for general publishers and, for the avowedly academic, it was too 'popular'. The present book, using Margaret and James as anchors rather than focusing on them, makes use of the earlier efforts in a scheme which is both more traditional and more explicitly anthropological than was originally intended.

A comment on transcription is required. The first object has been to catch the vigour of spoken language, more spontaneous but less tidy than written forms and not always ideal for conveying meaning clearly and economically. Punctuation has to do a double job here, to indicate how things were said as well as assisting the reader in making sense of them, if possible without more of a struggle than a hearer at the time would have experienced. Compromises are inevitable. As much continuity of conversation as constraints of space allow is provided, so that the flow and context of ideas is as far as possible made available. '...' indicates a breaking off in the original, '[...]' an editorially imposed break within the flow of a conversation, and breaks between distinct passages in a single conversation and between separate conversations are indicated by a superscript [T] or [N] number. These refer to original transcripts (T) or fieldnotes (N), the relevant ones of which are listed below for reference. Anonymity for the 'professionals' involved is more difficult and it has been decided neither to name nor offer any further identification of them.

Though a few non-standard forms have had to be introduced to represent words of the Scots English used by some participants, it was early decided not to try to represent variation which is merely phonetic. Little of value can be recorded without going the full distance to phonetic transcription, and anyone's language can be made to look peculiar by the use of eccentric spelling. While Glasgow accents are complexly valued by Glaswegians, who often use a variety of registers for different purposes and effects, for outsiders non-standard spellings create a false sense of distance, as well as, for everyone, impeding ease of reading.

Transcript and fieldnote numbers referred to in the text

T1	Twenty-year-old ex factory worker, just before her marriage in 1981 (from the pilot study).
T6	Aileen and Drew, would-be teachers in their early 20s. Two discussions a fortnight after their wedding.
T8	Jan and Shuggie, nursery nurse and clerical assistant, both 24. Four discussions from six months before their wedding till after it (T41, 57, 71, N38).
T9	Jane, a clerkess in her early 20s, marrying Donald, a boutique manager three years older. Discussion three weeks before the wedding. Robert is her elder brother, a hairdresser.
T13	Barbara and Donald, a medical research assistant of 24 marrying a lawyer of 27. Four discussions from three months before the wedding till after it (T42, 54, N23, 40).
T15	Grace and Bert, a clerkess of 24 marrying an electrician of 29. They had recently put off a planned wedding.
T17	Carol and Angus, a hospital scientific officer marrying a sales rep., both in their mid 20s. Two discussions, three weeks before the wedding and afterwards (N9, T36).
T18	Pat and Richard, a sales rep. marrying an architectural assistant, both in their early 20s. Three discussions from three months before the wedding till after (T53, N49).
T19	Donna and Brian, a clerkess marrying a graduate engineer, both in their early 20s. Discussion a month after the wedding.
T20	Catriona and Mark, bank clerks of 19 and 21. Three discussions with Catriona alone, with her mother, and with her mother alone before and after the wedding (T40, 43).
T25	June, a shop assistant, engaged to unemployed Robbie, both 20. They had bought a flat and were hoping to marry in a year's time. One discussion and meetings also in connection with Tracy and Gordon's

wedding (see T28).

T26 Margaret and James, students in their early 20s, their fathers a retired headmaster and a trade union official respectively. Twelve discussions with them and also with parents, relatives, and friends (T59, 69, 91, 94, 106, 108–16, N73, 98).

T28 Tracy (20), unemployed, marrying Gordon (27), a bus driver. Three discussions from four months before the wedding to after it and meeting at hen night (T64, 65, N28, 30).

T30 Moira and Ted, a bank clerk marrying a chef, both 24. Discussion with Moira two months before the wedding, and this with her mother immediately afterwards (T10).

T36 Carol and Angus: see T17.

T37 Aileen and Ben, a clerkess of 21 marrying a project engineer of 30. Two discussions a month before and after the wedding (T58, N44)

T38 Cathy and Roy, a shop assistant marrying a pipe fitter, both in their early 20s. Discussion 2–3 months before the wedding and telephone calls (N25).

T40 Mrs Gilligan, Catriona's mother: see T20. Sarah is her elder daughter, already married.

T41 Jan and Shuggie: see T8.

T42 Barbara: see T13.

T43 Catriona and her mother: see T20.

T44 Lisa and Jim, a clerical assistant in the DHSS marrying an apprentice box maker, both 20. Discussion seven months before the wedding (N72).

T46 Jean, a teacher, herself married for about two years and involved with her cousin Moira's wedding (T30).

T48 Mr Hillis, a retired craftsman and entertainer, who lived around the Gorbals until the 1950s when he was rehoused in one of the large peripheral schemes of the period. Discussion with him and his wife in December 1982.

T50 Margaret and Lorenzo, a display designer marrying a trainee teacher, both in their early twenties. Discussion with him before the wedding and with her afterwards, as well as observation at the ceremony (N51).

T52 Marie, a computer operator, married to James, the brother of Tracy (T28). Discussion six weeks after her own wedding.

T53 Pat and Richard: see T18.

T58 Aileen and Ben: see T37.

T59 Margaret and James: see T26.

T60 Mrs Dobson, brought up in the East End, a bus conductress in her youth and for long resident in one of the peripheral schemes of the east, now retired. Discussion in February 1983.

T61 Laura and June, friends, counter staff at DHSS and Inland Revenue, both in their early 20s, living in a large peripheral scheme and with expectations of marriage within the year. Discussion with them and June's mother. Ambrose is June's cousin.

T62 Mary and Anthony, a senior sales assistant (24) marrying a wedding shop manager (28). Two discussions, a week before the wedding and afterwards, and several lengthy telephone calls (T80, N31, 34, 50).

T64	Tracy and Gordon: see T28.
T65	Tracy and Gordon: see T28.
T67	Catherine and Alan, a hairdresser (24) marrying a heating engineer's mate (21). Three discussions from five months before the wedding – this one was with Catherine and her younger sister – to after it (T81, 104, N80).
T69	Margaret's parents: see T26.
T71	Jan and Shuggie: see T8.
T74	Mrs Maguire, brought up in central Glasgow, married in the East End in the 1920s. Discussion in March 1983.
T76	Jean and Murdo, an inventory analyst marrying a typewriter engineer, in their early and mid twenties. Three discussions from eleven months before the wedding, mainly with Jean (T21, T97, N90).
T79	James: see T26.
T80	Mary and Anthony: see T62.
T87	Sandra and Ronald, a shop assistant marrying a labourer, both in their early 20s. Discussion just before the wedding (T87, N69).
T91	Margaret and James: see T26.
T92	Iris and Charles, accountant and further education teacher, the parents of Ailie marrying Gerry. Discussions with the family and the couple from ten months before the wedding (T12, 63, N77).
T94	Margaret and James: see T26.
T101	Lorna and Colin, teachers in their mid 20s, married the year before. Discussion with them and with Lorna's parents based on detailed wedding videos (T102, 105)
T105	Lorna and Colin: see T101.
T106	James's family: see T26.
T108	Margaret and James: see T26.
T109	Margaret's brother and sister-in-law: see T26.
T110–3	Margaret and James: see T26.
T115	Pam and Jack, friends of Margaret's family: see T26.
T116	Margaret and James: see T26.
N4	Secretary in her early 20s married to a welder. Discussion four months after the wedding.
N6	Would-be teacher, currently shop-assistant living in a large peripheral scheme, who had broken off her engagement after three years.
N9	Carol and Angus: see T17.
N28	Tracy and Gordon: see T28.
N30	Tracy and Gordon: see T28.
N38	Jan and Shuggie: see T8.
N51	Margaret and Lorenzo: see T50.
N73	Margaret and James: see T26.
N76	Sandra and Ronald: see T87.
N77	Ailie and Gerry: see T92.
N98	Margaret and James: see T26.

References

Anderson, M. (1980), *Approaches to the History of the Western Family 1500–1914*, Macmillan, London.

Andrews, W. (ed.) (1899), *Bygone Church Life in Scotland*, Andrews, London.

Asad, T. (1983), 'Anthropological conceptions of religion: reflections on Geertz', *Man*, XVIII, pp. 237–59.

Aspinwall, B. (1982), 'The formation of the Catholic community in the West of Scotland', *Innes Review*, XXXIII, pp. 44–57.

Barth, F. (1987), *Cosmologies in the Making. A Generative Approach to Cultural Variation in Inner New Guinea*, Cambridge University Press, Cambridge.

Bloch, M. (1971), *Placing the Dead*, Seminar Press, London.

Bloch, M. (1974), 'Symbols, song, dance and features of articulation', *European Journal of Sociology*, XV, pp. 55–87.

Bloch, M. (1978), 'Marriage among equals: an analysis of the marriage ceremony of the Merina of Madagascar', *Man*, XIII, pp. 21–33.

Bloch, M. (1980), 'Ritual symbolism and the nonrepresentation of society', in M. L. Foster, and S. H. Brandes (eds.), *Symbol as Sense*, Academic Press, New York.

Boyd, K. M. (1980), *Scottish Church Attitudes to Sex, Marriage and the Family, 1850–1914*, Donald, Edinburgh.

Brooke, C. (1989), *The Medieval Idea of Marriage*, Oxford University Press, Oxford.

Brundage, J. A. (1987), *Law, Sex, and Christian Society in Medieval Europe*, Chicago University Press, Chicago.

Burt, E. (1759), *Letters from a Gentleman in the North of Scotland*, 2nd ed., 2 vols., London.

Catholic Directory for Scotland 1988, Burns, Glasgow.

Charsley, S. R. (1986), ' "Glasgow's Miles Better": the symbolism of community and identity in the city', in A. P. Cohen (ed.), *Symbolising Boundaries: Identity and Diversity in British Cultures*, Manchester University Press, Manchester.

Charsley, S. R. (1987), 'Interpretation and custom: the case of the wedding cake', *Man*, XXII, pp. 93–110.

Charsley, S. R. (1988), 'The wedding cake: history and meanings', *Folklore*, IC, pp. 232–41.

Charsley, S. R. (forthcoming), *Wedding Cakes and Cultural History*, Routledge, London.

Cheal, D. (1987), ' "Showing you love them": gift-giving and the dialectic of intimacy', *Sociological Review*, XXXV, pp. 150–69.

Cheal, D. (1988), *The Gift Economy*, Routledge, London.

Church Service Society (1901), *The Book of Common Order of the Church of Scotland, Commonly known as John Knox's Liturgy*, Blackwood, Edinburgh.

Clifford, J. (1983), 'On ethnographic authority', *Representations*, I, pp. 118–46.

Clive, E. M. (1980), 'Marriage: an unnecesary legal concept?', in J. M. Eekelar, and S. N. Katz (eds.), *Marriage and Cohabitation in Contemporary Societies*, Butterworths, Toronto.

Clive, E. M. (1982), *The Law of Husband and Wife in Scotland*, 2nd ed., Green, Edinburgh.

Cooper, J. (1904), Introduction and notes to *The Book of Common Prayer ... for the Use of the Church of Scotland (Laud's Liturgy, 1637)*, Blackwood, Edinburgh.

Cowan, I. B. (1982), *The Scottish Reformation. Church and Society in the Sixteenth Century*, Weidenfeld, London.

Cunnington, P., and Lucas, C. (1972), *Costumes for Births, Marriages and Deaths*, Black, London.

Dalmont, S. (1983), 'Lobster, chicken, cake and tears: deciphering wedding meals', in A. Murcott (ed.), *The Sociology of Food and Eating*, Gower, Aldershot, pp. 141–51.

Darragh, J. (1979), 'The Catholic population of Scotland, 1878–1977', in D. McRoberts (ed.), *Modern Scottish Catholicism 1878–1978*, Burns, Glasgow, pp. 211–47.

Debrett (1981), *Debrett's Etiquette and Modern Manners*, Debrett's Peerage, London.

Derraugh, P. and W. (1983), *Wedding Etiquette*, Foulsham, London.

Douglas, M. (1966), *Purity and Danger*, Routledge, London.

Edgar, A. (1886), *Old Church Life in Scotland*, Second Series, Gardner, Paisley.

Edwards, W. D. (1984), 'Ritual in the Commercial World: Japanese Society through its Weddings', Unpublished Ph.D., Cornell University.

Fernandez, J. W. (1965), 'Symbolic consensus in a Fang reformative cult', *American Anthropologist*, LXVII, pp. 902–29.

Fernandez, J. W. (1982), 'The dark at the botton of the stairs: the inchoate in symbolic inquiry and some strategies for coping with it', in J. W. Fernandez *et al.*, *On Symbols in Anthropology*, Undena Publications, Malibu.

Firth, R.W. (1973), *Symbols Public and Private*, Allen & Unwin, London.

Freedman, J. (1977), 'Joking, affinity and the exchange of ritual services among the Kiga of Northern Rwanda: an essay on joking relationships theory', *Man*, XII, pp. 154–65 (with subsequent corrrespondence, *Man*, XIII, pp. 130–3).

Frith, S. (1987), 'Why do songs have words?', in *Lost in Music*, Sociological Review Monograph XXXIV, Routledge, London.

Galbraith, J. (1984), 'The Middle Ages', in D. Forrester and D. Murray (eds.), *Studies in the History of Worship in Scotland*, Clark, Edinburgh, pp. 17–32.

Gallagher, T. (1987), *Glasgow, the Uneasy Peace. Religious Tension in Modern Scotland*, Manchester University Press, Manchester.

Gaya, L. de (1681), *Cérémonies Nuptiales de Toutes les Nations*, Paris.

Geertz, C. (1988), *Works and Lives*, Polity Press, Oxford.

Gillis, J. R. (1985), *For Better, For Worse. British Marriages, 1600 to the Present,* Oxford University Press, London.

Gluckman, M. (1963), 'Rituals of rebellion in South-East Africa', in his *Order and Rebellion in Tribal Africa,* Cohen & West, London, pp. 17–32.

Goody, J. (1977), 'Against "ritual": loosely structured thoughts on a loosely defined topic', in S. F. Moore and B. G. Myerhoff (eds.), *Secular Ritual,* Van Gorcum, Assen.

Goody, J. (1990), *The Oriental, the Ancient and the Primitive. Systems of Marriage and the Family in the Pre-industrial Societies of Eurasia,* Cambridge University Press, Cambridge.

Hamilton, J. (1882), *The Catechism set forth by Archbishop Hamilton ... 1551,* Paterson, Edinburgh.

Handley, J. E. (1964), *The Irish in Scotland,* Burns, Glasgow.

Hardy, J. (1978), 'The Attitude of Church and State in Scotland to Sex and Marriage, 1560–1707', Unpubl. M.Phil. Thesis, Edinburgh University.

Hay, W. (1967), *Lectures on Marriage,* (ed. and trans. J. C. Barry), Stair Society Publications, XXIV, Edinburgh.

Helmholz, R. H. (1978), *Marriage Litigation in Medieval England,* Cambridge University Press, Cambridge.

Herring, S. (1973), 'Dissent in Scotland', Appendix IV, in P. L. Sissons, *The Social Significance of Church Membership in the Burgh of Falkirk,* Church of Scotland, Edinburgh.

Hertz, R. (1909), 'La préeminence de la main droite', *Revue Philosophique,* LXVIII, pp. 553–80.

Highet, J. (1960), *The Scottish Churches,* Skeffington, London.

Holy, L. (1983), 'Symbolic and non-symbolic aspects of Berti space', *Man,* XVIII, pp. 269–88.

Hyde, L. (1983), *The Gift. Imagination and the Erotic Life of Property,* Random House, New York.

Jules-Rosette, B. (1975), 'Song and spirit: the use of songs in the management of ritual contexts', *Africa,* VL, pp. 150–66.

Karp, I. (1987), 'Laughter at marriage: subversion in performance', in D. Parkin & D. Nyamwaya (eds.), *Transformations of African Marriage,* Manchester University Press, Manchester, for IAI.

Kay, B. (1980), *Odyssey,* Polygon Books, Edinburgh.

Keenan, E. (1975), 'A sliding scale of obligatoriness: the polystructure of Malagasy oratory', in M. Bloch (ed.), *Political Language and Oratory in Traditional Society,* Academic Press, London.

Keesing, R. M. (1972), 'Simple models of complexity: the lure of kinship', in P. Reining (ed.), *Kinship Studies in the Morgan Centennial Year,* Anthropological Society of Washington, Washington.

Keesing, R. M. (1987), 'Anthropology as interpretive quest', *Current Anthropology,* XXVIII, pp. 161–76.

Kendrick, S. *et al.* (1981), *Demography,* Social Structure of Modern Scotland Project, Working Paper 1, University of Edinburgh, Edinburgh.

Kilbrandon Committee (1969), *The Marriage Law of Scotland,* Cmd. 4011, Scottish Home and Health Department, Edinburgh.

King, G. (1986), *Say 'Cheese'! The Snapshot as Art and Social History*, Collins, London.

Langford, C. M. (1982), 'Family size from the child's point of view', *Journal of Biosocial Science*, XIV, pp. 319–27.

Lansdell, A. (1983), *Wedding Fashions 1860–1980*, History in Camera, Shire, Princes Risborough.

Leach, E. R. (1954), *Political Systems of Highland Burma*, Athlone Press, London.

Leach, E. R. (1961), 'Polyandry, inheritance and the definition of marriage', in his *Rethinking Anthropology*, Athlone Press, London, pp. 105–13.

Leishman, T. (ed.) (1901), *The Westminster Directory*, Blackwood, Edinburgh.

Leonard, D. (1980), *Sex and Generation*, Tavistock, London.

Lewis, G. A. (1980), *Day of Shining Red: an Essay on Understanding Ritual*, Cambridge University Press, Cambridge.

Macdonald, R. (1979), 'The Catholic Gaidhealtachd', in D. McRoberts (ed.), *Modern Scottish Catholicism 1878–1978*, Burns, Glasgow, pp. 56–72.

McGregor, D. (ed.) (1905), *The Rathen Manual*, Transactions of the Aberdeen Ecclesiological Society, IV (Special Issue), Aberdeen.

McIntyre, S. (1977), *Single and Pregnant*, Croom Helm, London.

McRoberts, D. (1979), 'The restoration of the Scottish Catholic hierarchy in 1878', in his *Modern Scottish Catholicism 1878–1978*, Burns, Glasgow, pp. 3–29.

Malinowski, B. (1922), *Argonauts of the Western Pacific*, Routledge, London.

Marcus, G., and Fischer, M. (eds.) (1986), *Anthropology as Cultural Critique*, Chicago University Press, Chicago.

Martos, J. (1981), *Doors to the Sacred*, SCM Press, London.

Mauss, M. (1923–4), 'Essai sur le don', *L'Année Sociologique*. (English trans. I. Cunnison, *The Gift*, Cohen & West, London, 1966.)

Merriam, A. P. (1964), *The Anthropology of Music*, Northwestern University Press, Evanston.

Molin, J.-B., and Mutembe, P. (1974), *Le Rituel du Mariage en France du XIIe au XVIe Siècle*, Théologie Historique, XXVI, Beauchesne, Paris.

Murray, D. (1984), 'Disruption to Union', in D. Forrester and D. Murray (eds.), *Studies in the History of Worship in Scotland*, Clark, Edinburgh, pp. 79–95.

Needham, R. (1973), *Right and Left: Essays on Dual Symbolic Classification*, University of Chicago Press, Chicago.

Napier, J. (1879), *Folk Lore in the West of Scotland*, Gardner, Paisley.

Nichols, D. I. (1984), *Living Together*, Scottish Association of Citizens' Advice Bureaux, Edinburgh.

Opie, I. and P. (1969), *Children's Games in Street and Playground*, Oxford University Press, Oxford.

Ottenberg, S. (1989), 'The dancing bride: art and indigenous psychology in Limba weddings', *Man*, XXIV, pp. 57–78.

Panton, K. J. (1973), 'The Church in the community: a study of patterns of religious adherence in a Scottish burgh', *Sociological Yearbook of Religion in Britain*, VI, pp. 183–206.

Partridge, E. (1984), *A Dictionary of Slang and Unconventional English*, 8th ed., Routledge, London.

Quinn, J. (1979), 'Ecumenism and Scottish Catholics', in D. McRoberts (ed.), *Modern*

Scottish Catholicism 1878–1978, Burns, Glasgow, pp. 204–10.

Radcliffe-Brown, A. R. (1922), *The Andaman Islanders*, Cambridge University Press, Cambridge.

Radcliffe-Brown, A. R. (1952), 'On joking relationships', in his *Structure and Function in Primitive Society*, Cohen & West, London, pp. 90–104.

Registrar General Scotland (1983), *Annual Report*, HMSO, Edinburgh.

Rivière, P. G. (1971), 'Marriage: a reassessment', in R. Needham (ed.), *Rethinking Kinship and Marriage*, ASA Monograph 11, Tavistock, London, pp. 57–74.

Robertson, D. R. (1966), 'The Relationship between Church and Social Class in Scotland', Unpublished Ph.D. thesis, Edinburgh University.

Rorie, D. (1934), 'Chamber-pots filled with salt as marriage gifts', *Folklore*, VL, pp. 162–3.

Sampley, J. P. (1971), *And the Two Shall Become One Flesh*, Society for New Testament Studies, XVI, Cambridge University Press, Cambridge.

Sarsby, J. (1983), *Romantic Love and Society*, Penguin Books, Harmondsworth.

Schneider, D. M. (1984), *A Critique of the Study of Kinship*, University of Michigan Press.

Scottish Law Commission (1980), *Consultative Memorandum on The Law of Incest in Scotland*, Edinburgh.

Scottish National Dictionary (1931–76), (II 1941; X 1976), Edinburgh.

Sissons, P. L. (1973), *The Social Significance of Church Membership in the Burgh of Falkirk*, Church of Scotland, Edinburgh.

Smout, T. C. (1981), 'Scottish marriage, regular and irregular, 1500–1940', in R. B. Outhwaite (ed.), *Marriage and Society*, Europa, London.

Spencer, J. (1989), 'Anthropology as a kind of writing', *Man*, XXIV, 145–64.

Sperber, D. (1975), *Rethinking Symbolism*, Cambridge University Press, Cambridge.

Sprott, G. W. (1882), *Worship and Offices of the Church of Scotland*, Blackwood, Edinburgh.

Stevenson, K. I. (1982), *Nuptial Blessing: a Study of Christian Marriage Rites*, Alcuin Club, SPCK, London.

Strathern, M. (1981), *Kinship at the Core: an Anthropology of Elmdon, Essex*, Cambridge University Press, Cambridge.

Strecker, I. (1988), *The Social Practice of Symbolization*, Athlone Press, London.

Tedlock, D. (1983), *The Spoken Word and the Work of Interpretation*, University of Pennsylvania Press, Philadelphia.

Tedlock, D. (1987), 'Questions concerning dialogical anthropology', *Journal of Anthropological Research*, XLIII, pp. 325–44.

Trevor-Roper, H. (1983), 'The invention of tradition: the Highland tradition of Scotland', in E. Hobsbawm and T. Ranger (eds.), *The Invention of Tradition*, Cambridge University Press, Cambridge, pp. 15–41.

Turner, J. G. (1987), *One Flesh. Paradisal Marriage and Sexual Relations in the Age of Milton*, Clarendon Press, Oxford.

Turner, V. W. (1967), *The Forest of Symbols*, Cornell University Press, Ithaca.

Van Gennep, A. (1909), *Les Rites de Passage*, Nourry, Paris.

Verdon, M. (1988) 'Virgins and Widows: European kinship and early Christianity', *Man*, XXIII, pp. 488–505.

Walker, W. M. (1972), 'Irish immigrants in Scotland: their priests, politics and parochial life', *Historical Journal*, XV, pp. 649–67.

Watson, G. (1987), 'Make me reflexive – but not yet', *Journal of Anthropological Research*, XLIII, pp. 29–41.

Westermarck, F. (1921), *The History of Human Marriage*, 5th ed., 3 vols., Macmillan, London.

Westwood, S. (1984), *All Day Every Day*, Pluto Press, London.

Index

anthropology at home, 1–2, 156, 213
assault on bridegrooms, 108–10, 174–5, 187
Auld Lang Syne, 177

baby doll, 102, 106–8
band, 37, 43, 55–6, 167, 169–71, 177–8, 187
band leader, 167, 177, 186
banns, 10
baptism, 121, 124, 135–6, 138
best maid, 74–5
best man, 74–8, 85, 110, 120, 129–30, 142, 162–5, 167
birthday, 32, 91
blessing, 110–24, 130
Book of Common Order, 24–5, 116, 122
Book of Common Prayer, 22, 24
bottling, 101–8
bouquet, 63, 75, 156, 172; *see also* flowers
brainwashing, Catholic, 203 n. 7
bride, 66–75, 89, 97–8, 100–1, 110, 129, 134, 140–2, 144, 146–7, 151–2, 156, 167, 170, 172–3, 180–2, 194, 210
  dressing up and taking out, *see* bottling
  pregnant, 68, 108, 110
bridegroom, 142, 146–7, 156, 161, 167, 173
  clothes for, 74–7
bride's father, 44, 47, 53, 69, 88, 141, 146, 151, 160, 164, 171, 182
bride's list, 90–3
bride's mother, 46, 66, 68–9, 78–80, 89, 96–101, 104, 141, 144, 154–5, 173

bridesmaid, 73–5, 97, 106, 140–1, 163, 165, 167, 173
Brooke, C., 202 n. 11

cake
  engagement, 35, 37
  silver wedding, 40
  wedding, 43, 54, 70, 156–7, 170, 172, 203 n. 6
candle, 101, 108, 135–8
cars, wedding, 44, 64–5, 141, 143–4, 148, 170
caterers, 51–2, 88
Catholic *v.* Protestant, 18, 189
celebrant, 11–12, 47, 86, 88, 142, 144–6, 155, 159–65, 188
ceremony
  civil, 11, 139, 170
  religious, 11–12; *see also* wedding service
chamber pot, 101, 107–8
champagne, 51–3, 68, 144, 159
Cheal, D., 205 n. 1–3
children, 27–8, 73–5, 85, 117, 122–3, 147–8, 185, 203 n. 7
Christianity, 20, 121, 136–7, 160–61, 191, 196, 207 n. 5
Church
  of England, 14, 22, 135
  Free, 13, 132
  Free Presbyterian, 13
  Reformed Presbyterian, 13
  of Scotland, 11, 13, 15–16
  Scottish Catholic, 13–14, 16–18
  Scottish Episcopal, 14, 17
  United Free, 13

Churches
  Anglican, 14, 120
  British Council of, 19
  Catholic, 17–19, 22, 136
  co-operation between, 18–19, 132
  opposition between, 17
  Reformed, 13–14, 17
  Scottish, 13–26
church halls, 50
class, social, 8, 15–17, 25, 29–31, 49, 52,
    57, 63–4, 73, 77, 88, 105, 108, 148,
    169–70, 185–6, 195, 201 n. 1, 203
    n. 5, 205 n. 5
clothes for weddings, 66–80, 204 n. 2,
    210 n. 9 & 11
community, 116, 121–2
confetti, 141, 147, 176
couple, 40, 42, 85–8, 96, 143, 147, 151,
    156, 192–3
cousins, 85–6, 184–5
cross-cultural comparison, 2–3, 210 n. 2
culture, family, 41–2
cutting the cake, 144, 155–7, 170

Dalmont, S., 203 n. 5
dances, Scottish country, 55, 168
dancing, 36, 55, 113, 166–8, 170–3,
    175, 177, 210 n. 11
debt, the marital, 20–1
dialogue, 200 n. 4
diamonds, 32, 34
disco, 37, 55–6, 169, 171–2
distinctions, invidious, 186–7
divorce, 7–9, 13, 27, 88
dress
  formal, 76–7, 80
  Highland, 76–7; *see also* clothes for
    weddings
drinking, 50, 52–4, 61, 97–8, 109–14,
    140–1, 157, 159, 167–9, 172, 178,
    209 n. 4
drunkenness, 109–11, 113–14, 169, 187

Engaged Encounter, 137
engagement, 29–42, 88
  celebration of, 35–7, 180; *see also*
    presents
English influence, 23–5, 49, 53, 61–3,
    77, 90, 111, 205 n. 6
equality, marital, 8–9, 20, 152, 166, 171,
    191–3, 199
ethnographic present, 201 n. 3

etiquette books, 61, 90, 165, 204 n. 8,
    205 n. 4
evening reception, 50, 86, 95, 172–3

families, large, 81–5, 89, 160, 205 n. 7
family, 9, 28, 35–7, 41–2, 53, 68–9, 75,
    80–5, 87, 94–7, 100, 117, 149,
    182–5, 193, 205 n. 5
  relationships, changing, 37, 39–41
father-in-law, 165–6
favours, 54, 172–3
feast, European, 158
feminist issues, 41–2, 109, 128, 153,
    166, 171, 202 n. 3, 203 n. 5, 208 n. 9
fertility, 106, 147
flowergirl, 73, 75
flowers, artificial and natural, 63–5, 73,
    75–7, 141, 163, 167, 172
food, 51–2, 158, 203 n. 5
football, 109, 161
formal/formality, 76–7, 80, 117, 157–9,
    163
friends, 81, 83–5, 89, 96, 116, 161, 166,
    205 n. 5

games, children's, 102–3
garter, 112, 144, 171, 209 n. 5
gender segregation and interaction,
    41–2, 96, 98–9, 101–14, 175, 192
gift, 90–1, 94, 99, 131–2
gift-exchange, 38, 90–101, 118, 158
girl, 66, 202 n. 3
giving away, 23, 141–2, 146, 151–2,
    164, 207 n. 2
Glasgow, 2, 13–16, 18, 48–51, 62, 65,
    92, 96, 105, 147, 189, 214
going away, 173–6, 187, 193
greeting, 131, 155–6, 162
Gretna, 12, 30, 44
groom, *see* bridegroom
guest list, 80–6
guests, 48–9, 51, 146, 148, 155–9, 161,
    168–70, 173–4

habit and repute, 12
hairdressing, 73, 140–1
hall, the, 43, 49–51
hat, 78–9, 102
Hay, William, 20–1
headdress, 73
heather, 77, 172
hen night, 111–14

holds, 151–3
Holy, L., 209 n. 7
home, 28, 122
  leaving, 28, 141, 162, 173, 178, 193
honeymoon, 49
horseshoe, 144
hotel manager, 47, 49–50, 155, 157–8
hotels, 49–51, 176
humour, 117–18, 120–1, 129, 144,
  159–63, 165–6, 176–7
husband, 147, 150, 165, 173–4
hymns, 62, 98, 116, 122–3, 126, 128,
  130, 133–4

identity, Scottish, 14, 24, 61, 105,
  185–6, 204 n. 4
immigration, Catholic, 13–14
innovation, cultural and ritual, 67–8,
  107–8, 110, 135, 171; *see also* interpretation and innovation; liturgy,
  experiment and innovation
interpretation, 6, 68, 100, 106–8, 119,
  136, 148–53, 195–9, 206 n. 12
  and innovation, 198–9
invitations, 62–3, 80–88
Irish, 13, 58–9, 159–60
  immigration, 13–14

James, *see* Maclaren
jewellers, 32, 34
joking relationship, 166
Judaism, 20

Kilbrandon Committee, 11–12, 201 n. 4
  & 5
kilt, 75–6, 185, 205 n. 5, 210 n. 11
  wearing, 204 n. 4
kin/kinship, 95, 185; *see also* family
kissing, 56, 101, 103–4, 106, 108–9,
  121, 130–31, 146, 156, 206 n. 8
Knox, John, 13, 23–4

legislation, 7–13
Leonard, D., 200 n. 2, 207 n. 13
line-up, 155–6, 209
liturgy, 20–25
  Anglican, 22–5
  Catholic, 22, 25–6, 124–35
  Church of Scotland, 23–5
  experiment and innovation, 20, 22–5,
    115, 131–3, 135–8, 202 n. 12, 208
    n. 12

history of Scottish, 22–6
  text and performance, 115–16, 120–5,
    128–31, 133–5
living together, 12, 27–8, 30, 32, 139–40
love, 27–9, 56, 116–18, 120–2, 126–9,
  160
luck, 102, 104–6, 144

Maclaren, Margaret and James, 3, 31–7,
  39–44, 66, 69–71, 78, 81–5, 114,
  126–9, 131–2, 134–8, 140–2, 152,
  159–63, 165–8, 172–3, 177–8, 208
  n. 2, 213, 215
make-up, 73, 140
Margaret, *see* Maclaren
marriage, 5, 100, 193–4
  age of, 7, 10, 21, 201 n. 1, 205 n. 5
  Catholic, 18–19
  children and, 27–8
  Christian, 19–26, 28, 60, 116–17
  civil, 11
  conception of, 9, 12–13, 20–2, 27, 34,
    42, 99, 116, 189–92
  consummation, 21
  decision for, 27
  equality in, 34
  inter-Church, 18–19
  irregular, 12
  law, 7–13, 201 n. 2, 4 & 5
  place for celebration, 24
  pre-Christian and non-Christian, 20
  procedures required, 10–13
  prohibitions, 9–10
  pronouncement, 23, 25, 120, 201 n. 4
  reasons for, 27–9
  religious, 11
  as sacrament, 20, 126
  see also debt, the marital; mixed
    marriage
marriages, civil, 201 n. 7
  numbers of, 7, 201 n. 7
married life, difficulties of, 121, 124,
  126–7
matron of honour, 74
meal, 49–52, 157–9, 180–1, 203 n. 5
  proper sit-down, 157–9
  seating, 86–8
methods of research, 3, 212–13
middle class, *see* class, social
minister, Church of Scotland, 57, 59–62,
  115–24, 133, 188
missions, Irish, 13

mixed marriage, 18–19, 58–9, 125,
    132–3, 205 n. 5
mixing, 36, 43, 86–8, 147, 149, 168,
    183–5
mother of the bride, *see* bride's mother
music, 61–2, 133–5, 146–7, 168–9, 171,
    208 n. 11

newspaper announcements, 31
noise-making, 101–2, 104
nuptial mass, 22, 49, 59, 124–35

offertory procession, 59, 130–2
Orange Lodge, 18
order of service, 62, 124

parents, 28, 69, 81–2, 88, 121, 156, 167,
    177, 205 n. 5
Penny Wedding, 207
performance, 124
photographer, 44, 47, 76, 141–5, 147,
    155, 169, 208 n. 2 & 3
photographs, 78, 204 n. 2
photography, 142–5, 147, 167, 170–1,
    204, 209 n. 4, 210 n. 13
pipers, 186
potty, 102–4, 106–8
prayer, 118–19, 121–3, 125–8
Prenuptial Inquiry, 58–9
presents
    engagement, 30–1, 36–9, 92
    enthusiasm for giving, 38
    money, 38–9, 91, 93–6, 100, 102,
        104–5, 108
    wedding, 38–9, 45, 84, 90–101, 112,
        158, 205 n. 5
    see also gift-exchange; show of
        presents
priest, Catholic, 57–9, 125–33, 135–8,
    159–63, 171
privacy, 212
procession, 62, 122, 131–2, 136, 142,
    144, 146–7, 150
procreation, 22, 117
proposal of marriage, 31
Protestant *v.* Catholic, 18
pub (public house), 30, 41, 50, 80, 104,
    106, 110–14, 148, 170
publishers, 213

queue, 155

Rathen Manual, 22, 202 n. 10

reading the telegrams, *see* telegrams
reception, 47, 85, 154–73, 177, 203 n. 5
    drinking, 50, 52–4, 61
    menus, 49–52
    music for, 55–6
    numbers attending, 49–50, 95
    table plan, 86
    venue, 43, 46–7, 49–51
reciprocation, 158; *see also* gift-
    exchange
reflexivity, 200 n. 4
registrar, 10–12, 44, 48–9, 56, 60; *see
    also* marriage, civil
religion, 5, 181, 203 n. 7
reproduction, 21
rice, 101
right hand, 119, 150
right/left, 142, 146–7, 150–51
ring
    engagement, 30–37
    symbolism, 33–4, 120
    wedding, 23, 25, 56, 120, 128, 130,
        198–9
rings, exchange of, 33–4, 120, 124, 128,
    130
rites, 179–81, 195–9
    of passage, 5, 23, 35–7, 113, 139–40,
        192–3
ritual, 5–6, 89, 106–8, 121, 125, 130–3,
    136–7, 139, 145, 150, 156–7, 167,
    174, 181, 206–8
    innovation in, 107–8, 110
rituals of rebellion, 207
rubrics, 130–1

sacrament, 20, 126, 202
salt, 101, 106, 108
schools and religion, 17–18, 59
Scots language, 21–2, 202
scramble, 61, 101–2, 142, 147–8
sentimentality, 201 n. 5
sex, 21, 27–8, 117, 176–7, 192, 202 n.
    12
show of presents, 41, 96–101, 103
sides, 43, 76, 81, 86, 147, 149, 183–4
sign of peace, 130–1, 134
signing the register, 124, 142–4
silver wedding, 40–1, 209
sin, 21, 136
singing, 36, 40, 55–6, 62, 98, 102–3,
    113–14, 116, 120, 122–4, 126, 128,
    130, 133–5, 168–71, 173, 177

speech, forms of, 4, 210 n. 12, 213–14
speeches, 75–6, 159–66
Sperber, D., 210 n. 3, 211 n. 5
stag night, 109–14, 171, 175
stationery, 63, 188
Strecker, I., 210 n. 3, 211 n. 5
structural oppositions, 150
surname, Scottish practice, 12
symbolism, 33–5, 56, 66, 72, 78, 87, 90,
    96, 106–7, 120, 128, 131, 135–8,
    150–1, 182–3, 196–9, 203 n. 5, 204
    n. 3, 205 n. 3, 206 n. 12, 207 n. 13,
    210 n. 3

taking the bride out, *see* bottling
tartan, 76, 205 n. 5
telegrams, 162, 164
thanking, 118–19, 158, 161, 163–4
three cheers, 178
toast, 49–50, 52–3, 157–8, 160, 163,
    165, 209 n. 4
top table, 86–8
transcription, 213–14
transport, 141, 178; *see also* cars

unemployment, 98, 111
upper class, Anglo-Scottish, 49, 185–6;
    see also class, social
usher, 76, 110

Van Gennep, A., 35
veil, 67, 73, 110, 121, 142, 147
video, 141, 209 n. 6
vows, 56, 116–17, 119–20, 122–4,
    128–9

wedding, 181
    Catholic, 49, 57–9, 61–2
    Church of Scotland, 57, 59–62, 132
    civil, 48, 56, 203 n. 1 & 3, 208 n. 3
    dates for, 43, 46–9, 57
    family slights and reconciliation,
        82–6, 184, 205 n. 5
    free drinks, 43, 53
    hall, 50–1

May, 48
participation and escalation, 44–7
paying, 44–7, 53, 65, 69, 74, 81, 98,
    182
quiet, 45, 66
religious, 56–62
silver, 40, 209 n. 1
times of, 43, 48–9, 141
who organises, 46, 80, 89
working-class, 186, 195
wedding dress, 44, 66–73, 109–10, 173,
    210 n. 11
    hiring, 72–3
    keeping from groom, 71
    secondhand, 72
    shops, 69–72
wedding industry, 44–56, 62–5, 68–73,
    76, 88–90, 140–5, 148, 155, 157–8,
    167, 188, 204 n. 8
    cultural innovation and the, 194, 200
        n. 1
wedding list, 90–93
wedding night, 176
wedding service, 56–62, 115–38, 146
    Church of Scotland, 60–1, 115–24,
        129, 134–5
    minister's control over, 24, 60–1
    music for, 61–2
    personalising, 59–60, 123–4, 126–9,
        133, 137, 171
    readings for, 121–3, 171
    rehearsal, 140
    Scottish Catholic, 124–38
wedding . . ., *for further combinations
    see second term, e.g.* wedding cake,
    see cake
Westminster Directory, 23–4
Westwood, S., 206 n. 10, 206 n. 12, 207
    n. 13
white, 54, 64–8, 77, 141, 147, 170, 176,
    204 n. 3, 210 n. 11
wife, 150, 162, 173–4
witnesses, 74
words and actions, 181
working class, *see* class, social
workplace, 100, 103, 108, 206 n. 10